The Meanings of Home in Elizabeth Gaskell's Fiction

CAROLYN LAMBERT

Victorian Secrets 2013

Published by Victorian Secrets Limited
32 Hanover Terrace
Brighton BN2 9SN

www.victoriansecrets.co.uk

The Meanings of Home in Elizabeth Gaskell's Fiction
First published 2013

Carolyn Lambert has asserted her right under the Copyright, Designs and Patents Act 1988 to be identified as the author of this work.

Composition and design by Catherine Pope
Cover image © iStockPhoto/Akabei

A catalogue record for this book is available from the British Library.

ISBN 978-1-906469-47-4

CONTENTS

ACKNOWLEDGEMENTS

Elizabeth Gaskell would have enjoyed the research journey I undertook for this book, combining, as it did, food, drink, laughter, conversation and elements of fairytale with, of course, serious scholarship.

The journey started in my 'home library' at the University of Sussex, where Helen Webb provided the luxury of individual tuition into the wonders of internet searching and the virtual reality of any number of nineteenth century periodicals and documents. The British Library was a constant source of information and an entertaining day spent poring over the Catalogue of the Great Exhibition of 1851 could be rounded off with a trip round the current exhibition at the Library on a wide variety of topics. An unannounced visit to Harris Manchester College library in Oxford, found a warm welcome from the Librarian Sue Killoran who provided tea, cake, and the first Gaskell letter I held in my hand – not all together of course! The archive proved to be a rich source of dissenting and Unitarian material and Sue was indefatigable in her support and help.

Gaining access to Dr Williams's library in Bloomsbury was a bit like breaking into Sleeping Beauty's castle. Once past the prickly bureaucratic barricades however, the Victorian Gothic splendour of the building, now undergoing renovation, was suitably atmospheric. The floor to ceiling bookcases of the Reading Room with its creaking floorboards provided an appropriate setting for reading William's sermons, overlooked by the marble busts of Dissenting Divines.

Several trips to Manchester were perhaps the highlight of my research journey. Janet Allen, Chair of the Manchester Historic Buildings Trust, was supremely generous with her time, support and information and provided my first introduction to the Portico Library as well as a conducted tour of every nook and cranny of the house in Plymouth Grove. The Portico

Library offered a joyous combination of tea, books and friendly staff - unlike Elizabeth, I had access to all the current periodicals! The new reading room at the John Rylands library is a worthy addition to the older building and the staff were unfailingly helpful.

This book is based on my doctoral thesis undertaken at the University of Sussex. Professors Jenny Bourne Taylor and Lindsay Smith – my 'more than' supervisors – were truly wonderful. It was a privilege to be supervised by them and with their help I managed to turn a loose and baggy monster into something more appropriately tailored for the occasion.

I was not left afloat in the post-doctoral sea for long. My publisher, Catherine Pope, combined an eagle editorial eye with an irresistibly dry wit and has seen both me and the book safely to shore. Thank you, also, to Carolyn Oulton for her perceptive comments on the MS, and to Tanya Izzard for preparing the index.

And finally my own family, who have endured more 'Gaskell moments' than anyone has a right to expect! My husband Roger patiently proof read everything I produced and managed not to cackle too much at the howling grammatical errors that I somehow missed – his composure throughout, has been, like William's, remarkable.

ABOUT THE AUTHOR

Carolyn Lambert recently finished her PhD at the University of Sussex and now teaches at the University of Brighton. Before pursuing an academic career, Carolyn worked for many years in local government and was Chief Executive of a regeneration project in East Sussex. Her current projects involve Fanny Trollope and knitting socks.

INTRODUCTION

LINGERING 'ON THE BORDERLAND': THE MEANINGS OF HOME IN ELIZABETH GASKELL'S FICTION

Elizabeth Gaskell's experience of home was always that of an outsider, lingering on the borderland.[1] She was never totally excluded, but, equally, never fully belonged. Her mother's death in 1811, when Gaskell was thirteen months old, meant that she was fostered with her mother's sister, her Aunt Hannah Lumb, whose own experience of home was disrupted. Lumb discovered that her husband was insane and she left him a few months after their marriage. Her adult daughter, Marianne, whom she brought up as a single parent, died on 31 March 1812, soon after Lumb had taken in Gaskell.[2] There is no doubt that Aunt Lumb provided a secure and loving home for her niece, and she was welcomed into the extensive circle of her Unitarian relations, but it is hard to believe that the difficulties and sadness experienced by her aunt did not have an impact upon the effectively orphaned Elizabeth. Some evidence of this might be gathered from the fact that Gaskell named her first surviving child Marianne, after her dead cousin.

Gaskell's father was absent from her early life.[3] He remained in sporadic contact with her, but he was a restless character who frequently changed jobs and location, launching himself with enthusiasm into each new project, but often struggling financially.[4] He re-married in 1814, and although Gaskell visited her father from time to time, her relationship with her step-mother and half-brother and sister was uneasy and distant. She did however form a close bond with her older brother John Stevenson, who disappeared either at sea or in India some time in the winter of 1828, and his loss was followed, a year later, by the death of her father who had been left devastated by his son's unexplained disappearance.

Marriage to William in 1832 and a move from her aunt's home in Knutsford, Cheshire, to Manchester gave Gaskell the opportunity to create her own home and family, but the fault lines of death and loss continued to run beneath the apparently conventional surface of her life. Her first child was stillborn, and she was to lose two further children, including her beloved son, Willie, leaving her with a powerful residual anxiety about her remaining four daughters. She lingered on the borderland, too, of life as a minister's wife. While she dutifully taught her servants and Sunday School class in her home, and undertook much charitable work, she chafed against the restrictions of domestic life and the expectations placed on her by others.

She was sensitive about her status as a Unitarian since Unitarians attracted great opprobrium both for their association with revolutionary views and for their religious doctrines. The Unitarian faith was illegal until the passing of the Trinity Act in 1813, and to be born and bred a Unitarian, like Gaskell, was to be familiar with controversy, social ostracism, and protest. William was highly regarded by his colleagues in Manchester, but even a visit to the Bishop, although humorously described in a letter to Tottie Fox of 26 April 1850, reveals her expectation of criticism and her sense of exclusion. The subject of Unitarianism, as she explains to Tottie, was like a bombshell going off among the 'cursing Evangelicals' at the Bishop's reception.[5]

Gaskell was never entirely comfortable either living in Manchester. Her ambivalence is reflected in her description of the city in 'Libbie Marsh's Three Eras' (1847), the first of Gaskell's stories to be set in 'ugly, smoky Manchester, dear, busy, earnest, noble-working Manchester.'[6] She was continually torn between her duty to her husband and family, and her own yearning for a more rural environment. Her secret purchase of a large house in Hampshire for William's retirement is astonishing in the degree of planning required as well as the practical difficulties she encountered.[7] It is also an illustration of the gulf between her enforced residence in the urbanised north and her preference for life in the south.

Although Gaskell found a stable home with her Aunt Lumb, and had a secure place among a wide circle of relatives with whom she continued to correspond and stay throughout her life, the disturbance, separations and losses of her early years are contained in her fictional representations of homes and in her varied and recurrent exploration of this theme. Gaskell's fictional homes are made up of a number of components. The home must provide a physical place of safety and a concomitant psychologically safe space; it is the forum in which key relationships are negotiated; and finally, the domestic interior provides a showcase for self-expression and creativity. Each of these components can of course be aligned with the nineteenth-century cultural construct of the home as a domestic sanctuary offering protection from the strains and stresses of the external world, an enclosed and private space which operated as a microcosm of an ideal society. Gaskell's fictional homes, however, often challenge this paradigm and present a concept of home which is unstable, fluid and unconventional. Her concept of home is multi-faceted, complex, and nuanced, encapsulating issues of class, gender, power, and the need for psychological security and stability, within the physical structure of a building. I explore this further in the chapters which follow, but I continue here with a fuller definition of each of these aspects of the meaning of home.

The idea of the home as a physical place of shelter and safety is intimately linked to issues of class, wealth and power which are well illustrated by Gaskell's own homes in Manchester. Gaskell moved to 14 Dover Street in the Ardwick district of Manchester in 1832 after her marriage to William. Alexis de Tocqueville's contemporary description of the city sets out some of the geographical features which contributed to the appalling living conditions so graphically described by many campaigners:[8]

> Two streams (the Medlock and the Irk) wind through the uneven ground and after a thousand bends, flow into the river. Three canals made by man unite their tranquil lazy waters at the same point. On this watery land [...] are scattered palaces and hovels. Everything in the exterior appearance of the city attests the individual powers of man; nothing the directing power of society.[9]

It is difficult to imagine a more striking contrast to the small market town of Knutsford where Gaskell grew up. De Tocqueville describes the six storey factories towering like skyscrapers on top of the hills with the 'wretched dwellings of the poor [...] scattered haphazard around them.' It is an alienating landscape in which the homes of the poor are anthropomorphised as beggars, surrounding the 'huge palaces of industry and [clasping] them in their hideous folds'.[10] De Tocqueville's graphic description illustrates the interdependency of social and human geography: the location of the factories was determined by the need for water for power, and to transport raw materials and finished goods, but the low-lying marshy ground and the effluvia of soot pumped out from the factory chimneys affected the health of rich and poor alike.

Irish migrants fleeing the potato famine formed sizeable proportions of the population in Manchester and Liverpool. In 1851, for example, Irish immigrants comprised one seventh of the population of Manchester. A large settlement of Irish lived in cellars built on low swampy ground, liable to flooding, beneath the Oxford Road near Gaskell's first home in Manchester. Their situation was desperate. They lived in extreme poverty and it was not unusual for them to die in the street on arrival.[11]

Manchester, like other cities, developed as a series of concentric circles. When Gaskell arrived in 1832, the centre of the city was inhabited by shopkeepers and the labouring classes who worked in the nearby cotton factories.[12] Merchants, superior servants and the most respectable part of the working population lived outside the city centre, although still within walking or riding distance.[13] Gaskell's three Manchester homes reflect the development of the city and the pattern of settlement of the middle classes, as, with each successive move, she edged further from the urban centre towards her rural ideal. In 1842, she moved from Dover Street near the Oxford Road, to a house in Upper Rumford Street, still in Ardwick, but slightly larger than her previous home and with views over the fields. Kay-Shuttleworth, writing about the Ardwick and Ancoats area in 1832 describes it as almost exclusively inhabited by poor labourers with less than half the streets being paved and nearly three quarters containing 'heaps of refuse, deep ruts, stagnant pools, ordure etc'.[14] Clearly there were more pleasant parts of this area since Gaskell describes her home at Dover Street as being very countrified for Manchester, very cheerful and comfortable.[15] Even so, as W. Henry Brown points out, in 1842:

The town authorities spent £5,000 a year on cleansing the streets – those of the first class were cleaned once a week; the second class every fortnight; and the third class once a month, while the courts and alleys were disregarded altogether. [...] Two thousand families, near where Mrs. Gaskell lived in ministerial comfort, were found to have a weekly income of 1s.2½ d. per person.[16]

Plymouth Grove, to which the Gaskell family moved in 1850, was set in some 1,500 square yards of grounds in Victoria Park on the outskirts of Manchester, yet was only about one and a half miles from the city centre. Despite these pleasant surroundings, Gaskell was very well aware of the dank, unhealthy cellars of the poorest, sunk from sight below street level, but within a short walk of her own large detached villa. A house in Plymouth Grove appeared to offer a safe physical space for the Gaskell family, but like other middle-class homes, it was constantly threatened by contagion and contamination from the homes of the poor pressing against its protective walls.

There is, therefore, a close interrelationship between the idea of a home as a safe physical space and the psychological need for safety, and Gaskell was highly attuned to this. It is the walls of a home that give a building its solidity and structure, but this protective façade is broken by the insertion of windows and doors. These are liminal features representing the porous boundary between private and public, personal and shared space. They are both a threat, in that they allow the safety of the home to be invaded, and an opportunity, since they enable the occupants to make contact with the wider world outside. In Chapter 1, I discuss how the physical configuration of Gaskell's house at Plymouth Grove affected her need for privacy, and impacted upon on her psychological well-being, and I examine the ways in which these concerns are reflected in her fiction. The physical environment of the home was also unable to prevent the intrusion of death, a key destabilising event in Gaskell's life, and a key theme in her fiction. I focus on the death of her son Willie, aged nine months, from scarlet fever, and the disappearance of her brother John, and the ways in which these events are recreated and reworked in her fictional homes.

The underlying fragility of Gaskell's concept of home, balanced on the borderland between the reality of bricks and mortar, and the internalised emotional and spiritual needs of the individual, finds perhaps its most complex and nuanced expression in her fictional representations of the homeless. Homelessness for Gaskell is better defined as a psychological, social, and emotional separation, rather than the literal lack of a physically enclosing space, and I suggest that this is rooted in her own experience of home where she was always fostered rather than belonging, by birthright, to a family.

It is within the home that character and personality begin to be formed and children are educated. Gaskell's Unitarian faith emphasised the integral links between the moral and spiritual ambience of the home and the education and development of the individual. This is well illustrated in the diary which Gaskell began in 1835 when her daughters Marianne and Meta were babies. In the first entry, made when Marianne was six months old, Gaskell acknowledges her moral responsibility as a mother to shape and mould Marianne's character, encouraging positive associations in order to promote good behaviour and self discipline. She links this to her spiritual duty to provide a lifelong foundation for her daughter by acting on principles which 'can be carried on through the whole of her education'.[17] Each section of the diary ends with a prayer.

The diary is an intimate document, not intended for publication, but written as a memento for Marianne in the event of Gaskell's death. The thread of uncertainty which runs throughout the entries is not simply the anxiety of a new mother, but is also an indirect expression of the loss of Gaskell's own mother. The chain of associations which should have enabled Gaskell to call on her mother for advice and support with Marianne's upbringing has been broken. It is no coincidence that the opening paragraph of the diary is an assertion of the bond between mother and daughter: Gaskell wishes to give her daughter the memorial that she herself never had until thirty-eight years after her mother's death when she wrote to George Hope in 1849, thanking him for his

> kindness in sending me my dear mother's letters, the only relics of
> her that I have, and of more value to me than I can express, for I
> have so often longed for some little thing that had once been hers
> or touched by her.[18]

She continues in this letter to describe the craving she has for her lost mother and the fact that she has been brought up 'away from all those who knew my parents'.[19] This is a strange assertion, given that her Aunt Lumb was her mother's sister, and that she continued to visit her father until his death. Her brother John would also certainly have had some clear memories of his mother as he was thirteen when she died. The statement in Gaskell's letter may indicate something about the way in which her extended family relationships worked. The Unitarian faith encouraged rational, unemotional behaviour which might suppress discussion of painful events. Gaskell certainly complained to her sister-in-law, Anne Robson, in 1841, that William would never allow her to talk to him about her anxieties which would have been a relief to her.[20] The diary can therefore be considered as an early example of the way in which Gaskell used her writing as a self-reflexive tool to explore the wounds in her psyche created by her disrupted experience of home and family relationships.

Gaskell explored the complexity of relationships within a domestic setting in some unusual ways. In Chapter 2, I concentrate on her exploration of masculinity. Gaskell was acutely aware of the complex of traits and emotions that make up character and personality, her own included, as she described in her letter of April 1850 to Tottie Fox:

> One of my mes is, I do believe, a true Christian – (only people call her a socialist and communist), another of my mes is a wife and mother, and highly delighted at the delight of everyone else in the house, […]that's my 'social' self I suppose. Then again I've another self with a full taste for beauty and convenience whh is pleased on its own account. How am I to reconcile all these warring members?[21]

Gaskell was a sensual woman who was as attracted to men as they were to her.[22] She was intrigued by the ways in which gender affected behaviour and her exploration of sexuality in her novels is both subtle and complex. The Unitarian faith acknowledged the need for both men and women to receive a similar, well-rounded education. This would enable women to fulfill their critical role in the home to bring up well-balanced, self-disciplined and integrated families, in accordance with associationist psychology.[23] Her spiritual training therefore made Gaskell both naturally cautious of categories which confine gender too closely, and lead to an imbalance of personality, and tolerant of the wide range of behaviour within which individuals express and develop themselves. Gender allocation in her writing is never simple, and she is unusual among her contemporaries in exploring issues of gender through a range of narrative techniques which challenge and re-interpret sexually allocated roles in contemporary life.

An important feature of a stable home life for Gaskell included servants, and the servants in her fiction are often loyal, long-term employees in a quasi-family relationship with their employers, just as Gaskell's own servants were. Julie Nash argues that both Gaskell and Maria Edgeworth used servants to explore the tensions created by social change and conflicting values, particularly those caused by the concept of separate spheres and rigid cultural and social hierarchies.[24] This is a convincing argument, since by foregrounding servants who have a long and stable relationship with their employers Gaskell is able to provide the reassurance of a well-ordered society governed by a benevolent ruling class, and to explore social change from a 'safe' viewpoint. Servants, after all, are there to protect and serve their employers and to see them safely through change and turbulence. Servants therefore have a crucial narrative purpose in that they enable Gaskell to broaden and deepen the range and scope of her thematic explorations of change, often expressed metaphorically in her fiction by situations of physical or emotional danger. In Chapter 3, I focus on the role and portrayal of servants in Gaskell's shorter fiction, since it is here that she often explores and tests controversial ideas and themes including illegitimacy, class conflict, power, and sexual behaviour.

The final aspect of Gaskell's fictional homes which I examine is the way in which domestic interiors are the site of self-expression and creativity. During Gaskell's lifetime, homes were gendered spaces filled with cultural and social signifiers which could precisely denote their occupants' class, wealth and moral values.[25] James Martineau, the charismatic Unitarian reformer well known to Gaskell, asserts that:

> where in the presiding genius of a home, taste and sympathy unite (and in their genuine forms they cannot be separated) – the intelligent feeling for moral beauty and the deep heart of domestic love,

– with what ease, what mastery, what graceful disposition, do the seeming trivialities of existence fall into order, and drop a blessing as they take their place![26]

In this comment, he neatly encapsulates both the intimacy of the private domestic setting and the extraordinary efforts made by families to create an idealised environment that could be decoded by external visitors in order to measure the 'taste', 'sympathy', and spiritual status of the family. Thad Logan, in her detailed examination of the Victorian parlour, argues that within these domestic settings, tensions between binary opposites (male and female, public and private, individuals and society) were symbolically negotiated.[27] Cluttered, highly decorative interiors were therefore a reflection of wider social and cultural debates. Domestic artefacts, fixtures and fittings, together with the rituals that were enacted within the home, served as visual statements of opinions which could not be verbalised, or as a mute code to interpret the complex hierarchy of ideological and social relationships. Gaskell used her precise descriptions of domestic interiors to fulfil a distinct narrative purpose in that they offer a codified way to explore themes and situations which could not be discussed openly and explicitly.

Gaskell's fiction is notable for its intense concentration on domestic detail, on the minutiae of day-to-day living. An anonymous obituarist writing in the *Christian Freeman* four years after her death commented that:

Her writings, it is well known, are marked as almost perfect delineations of domestic life; accuracy o[f] detail, with pathos of description and fondness for the heroism that can be found in every social lot.[28]

The critical history of Gaskell has been deeply affected by this reductive view of her as a charming, but essentially conventional and unchallenging writer, despite the fact that in her lifetime she was highly regarded and acknowledged as an important influence on other major writers including Charles Dickens, Alfred, Lord Tennyson, and George Eliot. The lack of an authoritative biography and access to published letters increased both the difficulty of a balanced scholarly assessment of Gaskell's writing, and the temptation to confuse fact with fiction.[29] The centenary of Gaskell's death in 1965 stimulated the production of some important criticism, including the publication of the first collected edition of her letters.[30] The emergence of feminist criticism in the 1970s also had a significant impact on Gaskell scholarship, as did the establishment of the Gaskell Society in 1985 with its stated aim of promoting and encouraging the study and appreciation of her work and life. More recently, another important area has been the biographical focus on Gaskell, including Uglow's literary biography on which I have drawn. The appearance of the Pickering Masters edition of *The Works of Elizabeth Gaskell*, which I use in this book, enables scholars to have access to a comprehensive annotated edition of Gaskell's writing, both fiction and non-fiction.

It is this challenging, questioning writer, too long masked by the fluidity of her prose and the apparent conventionality of her private life that I seek to uncover in my analysis of the meanings of home in Gaskell's fiction. I have used all of Gaskell's writing, letters, journalism and fiction, since I argue, with David Masson, that 'She wrote, as the birds sing, because she liked to write.'[31] In each form, she worked on and perfected her craft, and although she described her fictional writing as her 'real writing', I suggest that it is through letters, which also play an important part in her fiction, that insight can be gained into the creative process.[32] Gaskell herself recognised the importance of letters as a source for assessing and shaping the life and work of her friend, Charlotte Brontë, and I use her own letters to illuminate her manipulation of narrative themes, her language and her social purpose.[33]

This approach however is not without its difficulties. Care must be taken when fiction is interpreted in the context of personal and other documents. As Rosemarie Bodenheimer notes, letters and novels are both acts of self-representation which differ markedly in tone, style, structure and the relationship which the writer establishes with the reader.[34] I acknowledge Bodenheimer's reservations about the potentially distorting effect of using excerpts from letters to comment on fiction, by privileging the fictional writing above other primary and secondary sources. Gaskell remodelled her life experiences in her writing, particularly traumatic events such as the loss of her brother and her son, as a way of exploring and resolving personal pain, and consideration of this can add to our understanding of her narrative approach and use of language. I take a cross-cutting approach to Gaskell's work in that the themes explored in each of the chapters are considered across a range of her writing. This method of analysis is supported by feminist critics who argue for a holistic approach to Gaskell's writing that embraces its inherent contradictions as part of the development of the novel form and the nineteenth-century recognition of the moral role of novelists in society.[35] This approach more readily identifies Gaskell's development as a novelist, the consistency of the presentation of home as a fundamental theme in her work and thought, and the coherence of her artistry across a range of writing.

Letters and their use in Gaskell's fiction

A number of critics have noted that the academic study of letter writing has lagged behind that of autobiography and diaries. Yet letters often have great significance in Gaskell's fiction, as they did in the personal lives of her and her contemporaries, since they formed a fundamental part of cultural, personal, and social discourse.[36] Letters freely entered and left the home in the nineteenth century, effortlessly breaching the boundaries and conventions that protected domestic space. A reliable, regular, and comprehensive postal service meant that letters could be conveyed efficiently and economically without fear of interception.[37] Letters however had an ambiguous status, since as well as being personal correspondence between two people, they were also public property in that they were read and shared between a circle of friends and acquaintances, and were therefore, liminal objects, as Bodenheimer notes, 'on the boundary of public and private discourse'.[38]

The fluid cultural nature of letters sometimes resulted in delicate social negotiations. For example, in August 1838, Gaskell tells her sister-in-law, another Elizabeth Gaskell, that her husband looked at her last letter and told her that it was "'slip-shod'" – and seemed to wish me not to send it'.[39] She circumvents his censorship by replying to Elizabeth while William is away. She tells her that she was given her letter by her brother-in-law Sam and that she read him selected extracts as she confesses that 'I am more open with Sam than I dare to be with William.'[40] Gaskell ends her letter by offering to let Elizabeth read William's letters to her. This is a potent illustration of the way in which even intimate letters were shared, not just to pass on news, but to further develop and deepen existing relationships, or even to subvert them.

The ubiquity of the letter, and the ease with which it could be dispatched and received, together with its fluid private/public status, meant that it could present a threat to the security of the home and to social relationships. Ellis Chadwick records a story she was told by the daughter of Gaskell's friend Mary Howitt about the fate of some of her mother's letters, including some from Gaskell, which combines the Victorian fear of dishonest servants with the kind of elegant economy worthy of *Cranford*. Mary Howitt's pageboy:

> surreptitiously disposed of piles of letters [...] which had been deposited in an old chest, selling them as waste-paper to a cheese-monger. The tradesman freely used the manuscripts to wrap up his Dorset butter and double Glos'ter, until, perceiving the signature of Charles Dickens [...] he very honestly restored the residue to the lady to whom they were addressed.[41]

Gaskell was acutely aware of the fact that private letters were often, in reality, public property, and was very careful to differentiate between those letters which could be shared and those which were private.[42] She writes to her other sister-in-law Anne Robson, in December 1841, unburdening herself of fears about her health, and asking her to look after her children if anything should happen to her. She makes it clear to Anne that this letter is to be regarded as private.[43] She constantly warned her daughter Marianne in particular to burn her letters, and tells her publisher, George Smith,

> when I write a letter beginning with a star like this on its front [draw-ing of a star], you may treasure up my letter; otherwise please burn them, & don't send them to the terrible warehouse where the 20000 letters a year are kept. It is like a nightmare to think of it.[44]

After her death, her daughter Meta burnt most of her letters and many pri-vate papers. Catherine Winkworth, who, with her sisters, was a pupil of Wil-liam's and became a lifelong friend of the Gaskells, was an important cor-respondent whose letters to Gaskell have also been destroyed.[45] Her sister Susanna is perhaps even more extreme than Gaskell in the dire warning she issues in the dedication to her sister's memorial:

To my nephews and nieces

> I now present this Volume to you under the strict condition that you will keep it to yourself, and not lend or show it to any friend, however intimate; that is, not till after my death, and then only with the consent of your Parents, should they survive. I depend upon your honour to observe this condition.[46]

The horror of her thoughts and feelings becoming public property does not however prevent Gaskell's letters from being a joyous outpouring, often amounting to a stream of consciousness, any more than her realisation that the subject of her novels would provoke controversy prevented her from writing about the truth as she perceived it. As Angus Easson argues, she is not writing letters, as did many earlier writers such as Pope and Lamb, with a view to their later publication.[47] The immediacy and detail contained in her letters reinforces the ubiquity of the form as a means of communication, as well as illustrating the everyday pressures on Gaskell which meant she had to snatch any possible moment to write. She explains to her two eldest daughters that she is writing while eating her dinner so her letter may not be very legible, and in August 1860, cheerfully admits to them 'Its after dinner & I am drunk.'[48]

Coral Lansbury observes that Gaskell's facility for writing letters, particularly to close friends, included the posing and answering of questions, in effect modelling a conversation she wanted to have with her correspondent.[49] As Bruce Redford notes in his critical analysis of eighteenth-century letter writing, contemporary conduct books dictated that letters should be written substitutes for conversation, a convention which extended into the nineteenth century and led to the development of performative techniques through which the writer could engage the absent listener.[50] It was in letters therefore that Gaskell began to think through the issues which appear in her fiction and other writing. They are therefore an important source from which an understanding of her creative process can be derived and analysed.

Letters are also the source of autographs which, Pamela Corpron Parker argues, were used by Gaskell to create a performance of another kind. Her autograph collection is 'an epistolary dossier of her literary credentials' which demonstrates Gaskell's personal perception of her standing within Victorian literary, social and cultural circles.[51] Any collection is carefully chosen and arranged to express something about its owner. Susanna Winkworth, for example, explicitly acknowledges this in her introduction to her sister's memorial which is composed of extracts from her letters and journals. She describes the method she used to select and arrange her material, explaining that while keeping Catherine as the central figure, she has inserted letters from other members of the family 'which help to connect the thread of events'.[52] Although Gaskell gave away and exchanged many of her autographs, Corpron Parker notes that those she chose to keep were carefully selected and arranged, 'giving precedence to those that testified to her significant contributions to British literary history'.[53]

In common with many of her contemporaries, Gaskell loved reading letters as an entertainment. 'Don't you like reading letters?' she asks John Forster in a letter of 17 May 1854. 'I do, so much.'[54] She sends him letters of Charlotte Brontë's which she has been reading as well as '2 clever letters' from Madame Mohl, Gaskell's close Parisian friend whose salons placed her at the centre of French social, political and cultural life.[55] Letters were read aloud. Gaskell writes to Catherine Winkworth from Lea Hurst, the Nightingales' home, to tell her that she has been listening to Florence Nightingale's family reading aloud her letters from Egypt. These letters were obviously written with a view to private publication, and Gaskell tells Catherine that she has been told she will have access to a copy 'only "not to circulate – not to be talked about"'.[56] Gaskell of course, as she was probably intended to, immediately says she plans to send a copy to a friend to read after her confinement. Letters in this context become a means of conferring status, of creating a public persona, and are far removed in purpose and content from Gaskell's gossipy, informal, and often acerbic outpourings. Letters locate their writer in a particular social and historical context and, within families, give a sense of continuity and security. This is particularly poignant when the writers are long dead.

In her fiction, Gaskell uses letters as powerful objects that threaten the security of her characters, act as catalysts for fundamental change or sometimes perform both functions. For example, letters have a critical narrative purpose in two very different works of fiction which were written concurrently. *Ruth* was published in January 1853 and *Cranford* appeared in irregularly spaced instalments in *Household Words* from 13 December 1851 to 21 May 1853. At the end of the second volume of *Ruth*, Ruth is staying at the seaside with the family for whom she works as a governess, leaving behind her son Leonard, whose birth she has kept secret from his father. A chance remark reveals her secret, and Ruth is convinced that his father will take away her child. Gaskell voices Ruth's internal torment in a passage which is both psychologically consistent within the context of the novel and a reworking of her own grief at the loss of her son Willie, a wound she tells her friend Annie Shaen in a letter of 24 April 1848, that will never heal on earth and which changed her profoundly.[57] The passage is a complex layering of the workings of the conscious and unconscious mind and moves backwards and forwards in time:

> In her dreams she saw Leonard borne away into some dim land, to which she could not follow. Sometimes he sat in a swiftly-moving carriage, at his father's side, and smiled on her as he passed by, as if going to some promised pleasure. At another time, he was struggling to return to her; stretching out his little arms, and crying to her for the help she could not give.[58]

Ruth's unconscious mind reworks in her dream the loss of Leonard as his death – his journey into a land where she cannot follow. His departure in a carriage at his father's side is an ironic inversion of her own seduction, in which she was powerless to prevent herself being swept away, not back to Milham as she asked, but to London, and life as Bellingham's mistress.[59] Leonard's efforts to return to her in her dream can be seen both as Gaskell's memory of her own son's death, and as Ruth's rejection of life as Bellingham's mistress, a position which has meant her own social death, and her struggles to return to society. Ruth considers writing to Benson to ask for his help, but is paralysed by thoughts of the complex and destructive consequences that her letter would unleash. Instead, she receives a letter from Miss Benson, including a few lines from Leonard. Like so many of Gaskell's own letters, Miss Benson 'always wrote letters in the manner of a diary' and this letter is no exception, being full of descriptions of domestic activities and a minutely detailed account of a meeting between Leonard and his father.[60] Miss Benson, unaware of the relationship, is unable to account for the interest Donne shows in the boy, and the letter therefore becomes the site of a complex interaction between the omniscient reader, who knows the truth, Ruth's anxiety and impotence, and the irony of Miss Benson's revelations. Mr Donne's gift to Leonard of his watch and chain symbolises his claiming the boy as his own. Like Squire Hamley's watch, it is passed down the generations, and the implied threat contained in his comment, faithfully reported by Miss Benson, 'I allow no one to interfere with what I choose to do with my own'[61] is lost neither on Ruth nor the reader.

Ruth then receives a short, unsigned note from Mr Donne summoning her to a meeting, and it is this note which sets in train the final actions of the narrative. The fact that it is unsigned, and therefore unattributable should it fall into the wrong hands, is symptomatic of Donne's moral cowardice, and his anxiety to protect his public position as a parliamentary candidate from any suspicion of scandal. The impersonal post box number to which the reply has to be sent emphasizes Ruth's exclusion from society and her isolation. The note is a curious mixture of cloying emotion – 'my fond heart entreats' – and threat: 'your boy's welfare depends on your acceding to this request.'[62] Ruth is given no choice as to the time and place of the interview. She is as powerless now as when she became an orphan. The note finally crystallises Ruth's resolve: 'she would know all, the best, the worst. No cowardly dread of herself, or of others, should make her neglect aught that came to her in her child's name.'[63] She picks up her pen and replies. The act of replying underlines one of the key narrative themes of the novel, the redemptive power of maternal love, of which Ruth's reply becomes a physical symbol.

'Old Letters' is the title of a complete episode in *Cranford*, indicating the thematic importance of correspondence in what Tim Dolin describes as an 'exploration of stories and their collection in a world without beginning, middles, and ends.'[64] Ellis Chadwick claims that in gathering materials for *Cranford*, Gaskell had access to many old family letters which she used in her stories.[65] The reading of Miss Matty's collection of letters is set in the context of Cranford's 'elegant economy'.[66] Like Gaskell herself, Miss Matty is aware of the 'desirableness of looking over all the old family letters, and destroying such as ought not to be allowed to fall into the hands of strangers;'[67] The packet of letters smells of Tonquin beans, evocative of the eighteenth century and snuff.[68] As Jeanette Eve notes, Gaskell often associates scent and flowers with the passing of time.[69] Yet the opening and reading of the letters is far from being a nostalgic trip into the past, but instead, like the objects in Lady Ludlow's bureau, opens up memory for re-evaluation and the possibility of a happier future.

The letters offer an interesting insight and contrast to the portrait of Miss Matty's parents and family life discussed in more detail in Chapter 2.[70] They are an oblique commentary on the marriage which turned the Rector from a young man 'full of eager, passionate ardour;' to the angry, rigid father who is unable to help and support his son.[71] Equally, the 'pretty and delicate-looking' mother is more concerned with the acquisition of a Paduasoy (thick, corded silk), than with the Rector's expressions of love. The letters trace the emotional development of Miss Matty's mother and the way in which 'girlish vanity was being weeded out of her heart by love for her baby'.[72] The reading of the letters enables Miss Matty to grieve for her dead parents, for her family who were so violently separated and for herself and the loss of her opportunity to marry Mr Holbrook. By sharing her grief with Mary and consigning the letters to the fire, she is simultaneously handing on her memories and putting them to rest. These old letters are followed by the receipt of two very different ones announcing the collapse of Miss Matty's bank, and the loss of all her money. This crisis motivates Mary to write to Peter and seek his help, and is the only point in the novel at which she steps out of her role as a detached, amused observer and bystander to take positive action. The description of the letter she sends to Peter is redolent with associations:

> It was gone from me like life – never to be recalled. It would get tossed about on the sea, and stained with sea-waves perhaps; and be carried among palm-trees, and scented with all tropical fragrance; - the little piece of paper, but an hour ago so familiar and commonplace, had set out on its race to the strange wild countries beyond the Ganges![73]

The letter, in this short passage, may be read as a metaphor for the loss of Gaskell's brother, John Stevenson, who also can never be recalled to life. It is tossed and carried on its journey, as powerless as the sailor in his ship, and acquires stains and scents that record its journey. The route travelled by the letter is the same as that travelled by John. The letter is an exotic object which draws to itself signs and tokens of the Empire, a world far beyond the narrow confines of Cranford. The letter's journey mirrors the narrative tapestry of *Cranford* which is composed of a warp and weft that creates both tension and inner strength. The episodic nature of the stories alternates between centripetal and centrifugal forces, drawing inwards to individual drawing rooms in a small English town, and pulling outwards to the wider world symbolised by Signor Brunoni and his travels. The symbolic importance of the Great Exhibition, which drew together collections of items from all over the Empire under the dome of the Crystal Palace, seems to find an unlikely echo in this most comforting and familiar of Gaskell's novels.

Letters in 'My Lady Ludlow' (1858), and *Wives and Daughters* (1866), are used to precipitate a narrative crisis. The letter which Margaret Dawson receives from Lady Ludlow offering her a home changes her life, and the appearance of the letter with its seal and heavy yellow paper is suitably impressive for such a seminal moment – indeed, Margaret Dawson 'sees' the letter in her mind's eye, years later as she recalls its arrival.[74] The physical appearance of the letter provides a great deal of information about the writer and the etiquette associated with letter writing. The coat of arms seal indicates Lady Ludlow's aristocratic position, and it is lozenge shaped, rather than being on a shield, to show that she is a widow.[75] The delicate Italian writing suggests femininity, and anticipates the later scene discussed in more detail in Chapter 4 in which Lady Ludlow recalls her Grand Tour of Italy. The wide margin indicates someone who is used to wealth and can afford to be generous in their use of expensive resources, an ironic comment on Lady Ludlow's actual circumstances which are constrained, although she is generous with what she has. The letter is read aloud and used to instruct Margaret's younger siblings in the virtues and reputation of their dead father. The memory of Margaret's father is contained and passed on in this letter, just as the memory of Lady Ludlow is later recalled and passed on in Margaret's recollection of the same

letter. The second letter of significance in 'My Lady Ludlow' is the one concealed in the bunch of flowers, 'written so as to look like a fragment'. This is
intercepted by the boy Pierre who uses it to betray Virginie. The appearance
of the letter, 'all blurred with moisture',[76] anticipates the tragic ending of the
tale within a tale. Like the torn Valentine in *Mary Barton* used to wad the gun
with which John Barton murders Harry Carson, this scrap of paper is associated with both love and death: what is written down can kill you.

Letters in *Wives and Daughters* are used as the means to conduct relationships. Mrs Kirkpatrick receives regular letters from the London Kirkpatricks
which she uses to elevate her own status and social standing, although her
relationship with them is of a superficial nature. Cynthia's relationship with
her mother is conducted almost entirely through the medium of letters, and
in this epistolary space, what is not addressed is as revealing as what is actually written, as she tells Molly:

> you must have seen some of mamma's letters, though; don't you
> know how she always seems to leave out just the important point of
> every fact? In this case she descanted largely on the enjoyment she
> was having, and the kindness she was receiving, and her wish that I
> could have been with her, and her gladness that I too was going to
> have some pleasure, but the only thing that would have been of real
> use to me she left out, and that was where she was going to be next.[77]

The tone of Cynthia's speech reveals her bitterness at the way her mother
has treated her and her feelings of abandonment are clear. Mrs Kirkpatrick's
letters are like her conversation. They skate lightly over the surface and evade
any discussion of issues of importance. Letters are an ideal medium for her
in the opportunities they provide for evasion, and Mrs Kirkpatrick's letters to
her daughter are a complete contrast to the outpourings of advice and support sent by Gaskell to her own daughter, Marianne, when she was away at
school. Mrs Kirkpatrick's masterly use of the epistolary space leaves Cynthia
unprotected and enables Mr Preston, the Cumnors' land agent, to fulfil the
emotional and practical needs her mother fails to meet.

The letters also illustrate the complexity of the relationship between
mother and daughter indicated by their names, Hyacinth and Cynthia. Gaskell
was notorious for forgetting the names of her characters, so these unusual

choices are significant. In the Victorian language of flowers, Hyacinth means rashness or sorrow and is a flower dedicated to Apollo. Apollo was one of the most complex and powerful of the gods of classical mythology ruling over music, poetry, healing and ill health, oracles and prophecy, light and knowledge. He was also the god of the sun, and twin brother to Artemis, goddess of the moon. Artemis was born on Mount Cynthus, hence Cynthia was another of her names. The names of mother and daughter therefore indicate their similarity and dissimilarity. They are inextricably entwined, twin souls, yet their relationship is often dissonant and jarring, and like the sun and the moon, they are rarely seen together.

Mrs Kirkpatrick's abandonment of Cynthia is exploited by Mr Preston, and the story of their relationship with its themes of sexual desire, money, and power, played out in a series of letters, recalls the seduction of Clarissa by Lovelace, and echoes some of the main narrative themes that Gaskell had previously explored in *Mary Barton* and *Ruth*, both of which deal with the sexual threats to which unprotected young women are exposed. Mary Donaldson, who writes often to Cynthia 'singing the praises of Mr. Preston as enthusiastically as if she had been bribed to do it,' [78] recalls Sally Leadbitter who physically tried to force Mary Barton to meet with Harry Carson. The constant threats which Mr Preston makes to Cynthia, although not physical like those in *Mary Barton*, are nonetheless devastating in terms of her reputation and potential to make a successful marriage which will secure her position financially and socially. His physical appearance recalls Monsieur de la Tourelle in 'The Grey Woman' whose outward effeminate beauty is a masquerade. Mr Preston 'is cruel in his very soul – tigerish with his beautiful striped skin and relentless heart.'[79]

Cynthia attempts to disentangle herself from the relationship by writing to Preston, but her letter is intercepted by Madame Lefevre the head of the school she attends. Madame Lefevre's intervention, in loco parentis, is ironic and also too late, and Cynthia's situation is further complicated by her informal engagement to Roger Hamley. Mrs Kirkpatrick's neglect of her daughter has exposed herself, as well as Cynthia, to Preston's revenge. Cynthia's letters, written when she was not yet sixteen, are, she laments, 'like a mine under my feet, which may blow up any day: and down will come father and mother and all.'[80] Her ironic reference to the line in the lullaby, 'Down will come baby, cradle and all', emphasises her youth and vulnerability, as well as the domestic catastrophe which would be the result of the exposure of her relationship with Preston.

In this extremity, it becomes Molly's responsibility to rescue her step-sister, and, by implication, the whole family from scandal. Her encounter with Preston is a key moment in the narrative, and shows Molly to be capable of acting both bravely, and with a new degree of maturity. Gaskell uses the weather and the landscape to set the emotional tone: 'It was a cloudy bluster-ing day, and the noise of the blowing wind among the nearly leafless branches of the great trees filled her ears, as she passed through the park-gates and entered the avenue.'[81] The bluster and noise filling Molly's ears are like the bluster of Preston's threats which she must overcome. The avenue she walks down to her meeting is straight, apart from one bend, where Molly chooses to wait for the encounter. The bend symbolises Molly's dilemma. It is the corner into which she has been forced. It conceals her from view, and there-fore from society, since her task is to protect her family, but it also represents a turning point in her own emotional life, the point at which she takes on a greater degree of responsibility. It is also indicative of the bends and twists with which both Cynthia and her mother negotiate their flexible moral lives. The meeting has been arranged through a note:

> In her simplicity she had believed that Cynthia had named that it was she, Molly Gibson, who would meet Mr. Preston [...] but Cynthia had been too worldly-wise for that, and had decoyed him thither by a vaguely worded note, which, while avoiding actual falsehood, had led him to believe that she herself would give him the meeting.[82]

The dialogue between Molly and Preston is a duel, during which Molly consistently attempts to defuse the danger posed by the letters. The situation begins to spiral out of her control, with Preston threatening to involve the Hamleys as well as Molly's own family. Molly finally counters with her own threat to expose Preston to the Cumnors, putting not only his livelihood but his pretensions to gentlemanliness at risk. However, although she succeeds in returning the letters to Cynthia, she is tainted by them. She is seen talking to Preston and becomes the subject of gossip.

Letters then are small, portable but potent objects, which can easily overcome the physical barriers of the home and affect the lives of those within. Letters can destabilise relationships by changing perceptions. This can be positive where they reveal unexplored or misunderstood aspects of the correspondent, or negative where letters reveal what the correspondent would wish to keep hidden. Letters are also objects which are sent out from the home into the wider world where they are equally powerful; indeed, the examples discussed show how letters are literally a matter of life or death. I conclude this introduction by considering a small example, drawn from Gaskell's first published novel, which describes the invasion into the home of an equally small but potent object that also provides a cogent illustration of the richness and complexity with which Gaskell uses a domestic setting in her fiction.

Mary Barton (1848) contains several highly detailed descriptions of domestic interiors, some aspects of which are considered further in Chapter 4. Here, I explore the comic incident of the scorpion which Job Legh acquires to add to his collection of insects. Chapter 5 of the novel in which this drama occurs opens with an extended passage of authorial intervention:

> There is a class of men in Manchester, unknown even to many of the inhabitants, and whose existence will probably be doubted by many, who yet may claim kindred with all the noble names that science recognises.[83]

Gaskell here is fulfilling her intention stated in the Preface to *Mary Barton*, to give utterance to the 'dumb people', the working classes of Manchester.[84] In the opening paragraphs of this chapter, she makes some large claims, aligning the working class botanists and entomologists with their aristocratic and more famous counterparts. The apparently effortless prose mirrors the opening sequence of the novel in which Gaskell's description of a pastoral Whitsunday walk through Green Heys Fields contains hidden allusions to Chartist claims for the land as 'the people's farm.'[85] In her exposition of the activities of the many working-class botanists and entomologists who are 'scattered all over the manufacturing districts of Lancashire', Gaskell asserts the common bonds that hold society together and, by demonstrating this commonality, offers a counterview to the fear of the working classes, a fear intensified by the Chartist riots.[86] The passage moves from the internal to the external, from the factory where copies of Newton's *Principia* lie open on the loom, to the fields within a day's walk of home where the workers go to gather their specimens. The veracity of the claims being made is given authority by the intrusion of the authorial voice:

> If you will refer to the preface to Sir J. E. Smith's *Life* (I have it not by me, or I would copy you the exact passage), you will find that he names a little circumstance corroborative of what I have said.[87]

Now that Gaskell has 'placed' Job Legh as a man to be respected, part of a community of knowledgeable working class scientists, she draws the reader into his home. This looks 'not unlike a wizard's dwelling' with wooden frames of impaled insects instead of pictures on the walls, cabalistic books on the table, and a case of mysterious instruments.[88] The reader's expectations are further destabilized by Job's treatment of his grand-daughter. He caresses her 'as a mother caresses her first-born; stroking her with tenderness, and almost altering his voice as he spoke to her'.[89] Both gender and class roles are confounded here: a working-class man appears to have almost mystical powers and knowledge, and in addition, has assumed the role and characteristics of a mother. Even Mary is confused by her surroundings. These are nothing like the interior of her own home, and she is further battered by the technical terms that Job rattles off 'like hail on a skylight'.[90] Margaret comes to the rescue with the comic tale of the scorpion, now a prized part of Job's collection, which nonetheless illustrates some of the main themes of the novel.

The purchase of the scorpion from a sailor in Liverpool is an early allusion to the critical role that the sailor Will Wilson plays in securing Jem's release after Mary's desperate journey to the docks to find him. Working-class naturalists, unlike their aristocratic counterparts, cannot travel to other countries, as Roger Hamley does in *Wives and Daughters,* to collect their specimens. They have to rely on sailors importing 'some queer thing or another from the hot countries they go to'.[91] The mutual reliance of individuals upon each other is an important narrative theme throughout Gaskell's fiction and reflects her Unitarian faith in the power of the individual and the importance of a cohesive society.

The geography of *Mary Barton* moves constantly from the domestic and intimate homes of the working classes to the public arena of the factories and streets, from the fields surrounding Manchester to the regional manufacturing districts of Lancashire, and from the port of Liverpool to distant parts of the Empire. This repeated narrowing and broadening of narrative settings reinforces Gaskell's primary message about the importance of society, eloquently outlined by William Gaskell in 'The Duties of the Individual to Society: A Sermon on Occasion of the Death of Sir John Potter M.P. Preached at Cross Street Chapel, Manchester, October 31ˢᵗ, 1858':

> We are every one parts of the community, and bound to do something for its welfare. [...] the world beyond, whenever we come into contact with it, has a full right to our service, for it is the world of our fellow-beings; and our best instincts and feelings require that we should acknowledge them as brethren and treat them as such under all varieties of circumstance and condition.[92]

This lesson is comically acted out in Job Legh's parlour when the scorpion, a creature from another country, is brought back to life by the warmth of the fire. Gaskell uses the nature of fire in its dual aspect here, both as a ubiquitous contemporary symbol for domestic security and stability, and as a dangerous elemental force. The scorpion, an intruder into the home from the outside world, is a highly poisonous creature that disrupts the domestic routine of Margaret's ironing. It is finally contained and rendered harmless, (domesticated), by being boiled in the kettle, and is then added to Job's collection. What Mike Hepworth describes as 'deviant nature' has been disciplined, and integrated into the social and moral world of the novel.[93]

This short episode from Gaskell's first published novel, illustrates in miniature the themes addressed in more detail in subsequent chapters. Job Legh has provided a safe space for the orphan Margaret, whose parents died when she was a baby, and their relationship, and the close bond between them, is the emotional reflection of the safe walls that surround them. Yet the outside world is allowed to enter in the form of the scorpion, an exotic addition to

Job's collection of insects, which he uses to educate not only himself, but his granddaughter and anyone else who enters his home. Finally, Job's collection of insects, together with the books and instruments strewn about the room, are an expression of his personality – his home is a safe place within which his creativity and true interests can be displayed.

1 - HOME SWEET HOME

Home for Elizabeth and William was the place where they both lived and worked. Gaskell began her writing career in 14 Dover Street, the house in Manchester she moved to on her marriage to William. She lived in Dover Street from 1832 to 1842 and produced 'Sketches Among the Poor' (1837), written jointly with William, 'Clopton Hall' (1838), and 'Notes on Cheshire Customs' (1839). While living in Dover Street, she also gave birth to a stillborn daughter, her daughters Marianne and Meta, a son who died while a baby, and her daughter Flossie. In 1842, the family moved to 121 Upper Rumford Street where Gaskell wrote 'Life in Manchester: Libbie Marsh's Three Eras' (1847), 'The Sexton's Hero' (1847), 'Emerson's Lectures' (1847), 'Christmas Storms and Sunshine' (1848), *Mary Barton*, (1848), 'Hand and Heart' (1849), and 'The Last Generation in England' (1849). She also gave birth to her son Willie and her daughter Julia. By far the greater part of her writing career therefore was spent at the house in Plymouth Grove to which the Gaskells moved in 1850.

Little information now exists about their first two homes, since they were located in areas of Manchester which have long since been redeveloped. However, *Figure 1* shows a section of an 1851 Ordnance Survey map of Manchester from which it is possible to make some assessment of the Gaskells' accommodation in Dover Street and Upper Rumford Street.[1] Dover Street contains a row of eight terraced houses with small front gardens. An alleyway runs along the rear of the properties giving shared access to the pump for water and the back gardens. The map scale is 5 inches to 1 mile (1:1056) which equates to approximately 1 square inch to an acre. It is likely therefore that the Dover Street house was modest in size and would not have offered Gaskell much privacy for writing. The family moved to what seems to have been the second of the two semi-detached houses in Upper Rumford

Street, described by Gaskell in a letter to Tottie Fox dated 29 May 1849:

> our home is a mile and a half from the very middle of Manchester;
> the last house countrywards of an interminably long street, the other
> end of which touches the town, while we look into fields from some
> of our windows; not very pretty or rural fields it must be owned, but
> in which the children can see cows milked and hay made in summer
> time.[2]

The house shown on the map is clearly considerably larger than the one in Dover Street, but it was the move to Plymouth Grove which was a huge change in scale. The house, the location of which is shown in the section of an 1851 map of Manchester in *Figure 2,* was large, grand and expensive, and only William and Meta, Gaskell's second, most artistic daughter, were unconstrained in their delight.[3] Gaskell herself was deeply uncomfortable at moving to such a luxurious home when, less than a mile away, families were living in the utmost squalor. She uses a letter to Tottie Fox to explore her inner conflict, the quarrel among her divided selves, in which she identifies an intimate connection between her physical surroundings and her psychological well-being.[4] She fully appreciates the beauty of the house but is concerned about its affordability as well as the morality of spending so much on a home for herself and her family. Her solution is to make the house as much of a pleasure to others as possible, a solution which also meant sacrificing her own time and energy, fitting in her writing whenever and wherever she could. The house was run at times like a hotel, with a constant stream of visitors, destabilising domestic routine and demanding all of Gaskell's attention. The physical layout of the house could not protect her, and she never lost her awareness of the fragility of the concept of home and the family it contained. Disappearance and death formed part of her experience of home, painful memories which could only be exorcised through writing, and which had to take second place to making her home as pleasurable as possible to as many people as possible.

It seems probable that one of the reasons William was so delighted to move to Plymouth Grove was because he had a study, a self-contained and single purpose sanctuary situated next to the front door, for easy access by students and parishioners, but allowing an equally swift departure to his commitments in the outside world.[5] *Figure 3* shows the internal layout of the house with William's study immediately to the right off the entrance hall.[6] William had bookshelves built to his own design, probably to accommodate reports such as those of the Domestic Missionary Society, and spent so many hours closeted away that Gaskell complained she never knew what made him so busy, and that his family only saw him at mealtimes.[7] Gaskell, by contrast, wrote in the dining room at Plymouth Grove, in the heart of the house, with all three doors constantly open to servants, family and friends.[8] Elizabeth Haldane and Mrs Ellis Chadwick claim that the interior of Plymouth Grove, built by a rich and eccentric old bachelor, was both unique and ingenious in its layout, with one room leading into another.[9] Recent research however, carried out as part of the restoration of the Plymouth Grove house, indicates that both the Gaskells' house and those on several of the adjoining plots were in fact built as a speculative development, probably between 1838 and 1840, as middle-class families increasingly moved out of Manchester and into the suburbs. The houses share several common architectural features.[10]

The dining room was considered to be a masculine space and this extended to the decoration of such rooms in dark, masculine colours.[11] The current restoration of Plymouth Grove has however revealed that the walls of the dining room were pale green, with a warm cream cornice and ceiling, and mid-oak joinery. The table at which Gaskell wrote was situated at the end of the room under a large central window, with two adjoining windows at the side, and a door into the conservatory. The dining room was the most public room in the house and multi-purpose. It was from here that women organised the running of the house, did their accounts and wrote their letters, so Gaskell's choice of space in which to write was not unusual for the period. The dining room at Plymouth Grove is directly over the kitchen, so may have been both noisy with the sound of food preparation and redolent of the smell of cooking, although the current renovation of the house has revealed a layer of sawdust between the floorboards of the dining room and the ceiling of the kitchen, a common form of insulation in the nineteenth century. Gaskell escaped whenever she could to more congenial surroundings in order to work without interruption. Annette Brown Hopkins also records

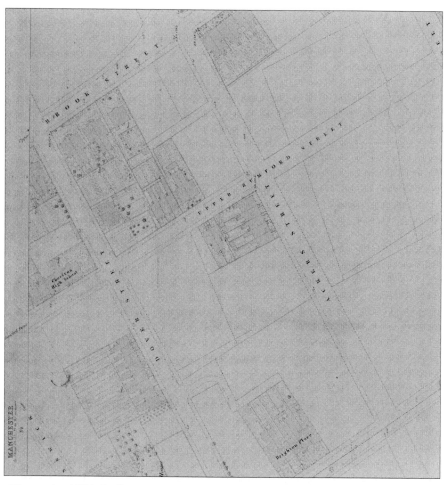

Figure 1 - 1851 Ordnance Survey map of Manchester, showing Dover Street
and Upper Rumford Street (courtesy of The John Rylands Library, The
University of Manchester)

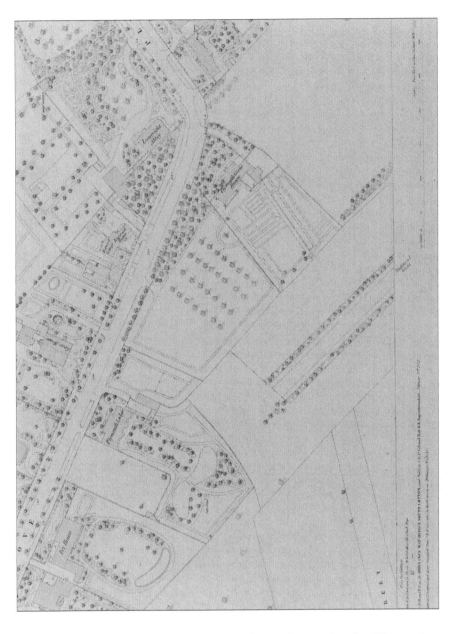

Figure 2 - 1851 Ordnance Survey map of Manchester showing Plymouth
Grove (courtesy of The John Rylands Library, The University of Manchester)

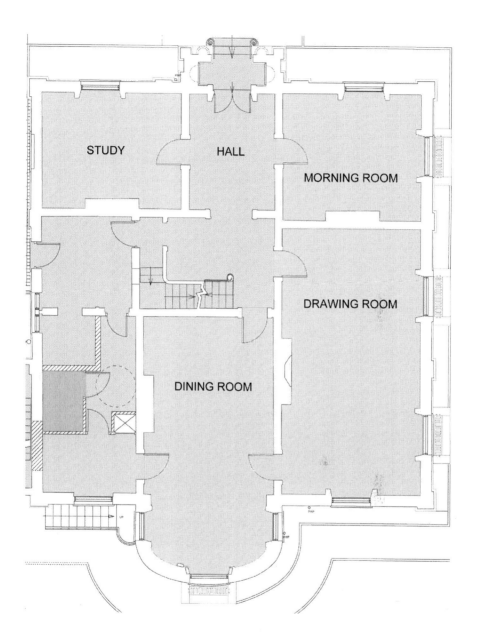

Figure 3 - Floorplan of Plymouth Grove (kindly provided by Bernard Taylor Partnership, Architects)

a comment of Marianne, Gaskell's eldest daughter, that her mother was a poor sleeper and did a great deal of her writing in her bedroom, early in the morning, when she could have peace and privacy.[12]

The evidence uncovered by the restoration work is intriguing as it seems to challenge some assumptions about how the Gaskells lived and worked in the house. Although William's study was a space dedicated to his personal use, he was not entirely divorced from the activity going on in the rest of the house. Gaskell describes, for example, how Julia's shrieks of delight at the arrival of a parcel from George Smith drew him out of his study to see what all the fuss was about.[13] The girls used the morning room opposite William's study as a day nursery – Julia and Florence engraved their names on a pane of glass in the window – and William is known to have breakfasted there. The dining room in which Gaskell wrote was light and pleasant, and she would have been protected from interruptions from visitors by the double doors which shut off the public area of the entrance hall from the private areas behind. Visitors would presumably have been shown into the morning room while a servant checked to see if the Gaskells were available. It is also easy to assume that Gaskell wrote with the doors of the dining room open, whereas it is just as possible that they were closed or even ajar, to indicate that she should not be interrupted.

Gaskell's description of the layout of Hanbury Hall in 'My Lady Ludlow' (1858) with its interlocking rooms, most of which have two doors, and some three or four, may be a fictional representation of Plymouth Grove. Lady Ludlow is always accessible to manage either the business of the estate or the running of the house. Gaskell rather wistfully comments: 'I suppose great people do not require what we smaller people value so much, – I mean privacy.'[14] Yet for all her apparent accessibility, Lady Ludlow is fiercely resistant to change, and the doors in Hanbury Hall are a physical manifestation of her intransigence. They allow her to control her household, with her housekeeper and butler always within calling distance. Her chosen route into the garden takes her through the servants' quarters, so that she can constantly monitor what is happening and keep the hierarchical structure of her internally ordered society perfectly preserved and running smoothly. The savage Hanbury wolfhounds, extinct everywhere else, which are rumoured to have eaten a child, are another symbol of her fierce resistance to change. They guard the main, public entrance to the house where only the most powerful are allowed to enter, and a footman guards the terrace door which is used by all other visitors. Symbolically and actually, both are guarding Lady Ludlow's status and authority. The combination of the hounds, the impenetrability of Hanbury Hall, and the footman, have echoes of the fairy tales from which Gaskell drew so much inspiration.

Like Sleeping Beauty, however, Lady Ludlow must be awakened to the real world, and Mr Gray is the unlikely hero who breaks the spell by coming in through the grand main entrance, past the fearsome hounds. His appearance is followed by a noisy altercation in the ante-chamber and the precipitate entrance of Harry Gregson, 'a lithe, wiry lad, with a thick head of hair, standing out in every direction, as if stirred by some electrical current'.[15] The reference to electricity brings the shock of the modern right into Lady Ludlow's own room which lies at the heart of Hanbury Hall. This, together with the additional revelation that Mr Horner has taught Harry to read and write, profoundly disturbs Lady Ludlow. Both Harry and Mr. Gray have effortlessly breached the protective barriers of Hanbury Hall and set in motion fundamental change. Mr Gray's reception by the hounds who normally respect only those who are born a Hanbury, makes it clear that he has a right to insist on change and a more equal and educated society. As Edgar Wright notes, the irony of the narrative rests in the fact that it is Lady Ludlow, rather than Harry Gregson, who is educated by the course of events to a new understanding of rights and duties.[16]

In *Mary Barton* (1848), open and closed doors symbolise deteriorating economic and social conditions as John Barton slides into drug addiction, George Wilson dies, and the workers turn to Chartism and trade unionism. In good times, doors are always open for easy communication with friends and neighbours. After Wilson's death, home is no longer a safe or friendly place and the front door of the house is firmly closed. The disembodied hand and arm which appear round the half open door of John Barton's house conceal the identity of those who are beckoning him away from the security of home, and away, ultimately, from the community and society in which he was once a respected figure. The image, which is the more threatening because of its anonymity, is suggestive of similar images on trade union banners and indicates the middle-class fear of the invasive and destructive power of the emerging unions and the Chartist uprisings.

Mary too, is in danger even inside her home. She has closed the house door, a sign that visitors are not welcome, and kept the candle unlit so that it will look as if no-one is at home. Sally Leadbitter nevertheless forces her way in to persuade Mary to come with her to meet Harry Carson. She physically prevents Mary from barring the door against Harry who has threatened to 'break the door open but he'd see you.'[17] John Barton, who should be Mary's protector, is away from home leaving her to struggle physically with Sally while Harry's threatening footsteps are heard pacing up and down outside the house. The front door of a house was a protective barrier which sealed off the sanctuary of home from the infection of the streets. Esther, for example, is shut out of the domestic space of the home because she is infected with consumption as well as corrupted morally by her status as a prostitute.[18] There is a double irony at work in Sally's invasion of Mary's home. It is Sally, Mary's friend, who is acting as procurer for Harry and not Esther, the prostitute who tries to protect her niece. Sally's forced entry into Mary's home is like that of the domestic visitors, who consistently invaded the private space of working families without respecting a door as a barrier.[19] Sally's intentions are far from benign. It is only after Esther's visit and warning that Mary is able to fasten the door and put up the shutters to protect herself.

Elsewhere in Gaskell's fiction, it is notable how women, in times of crisis, retreat to a secure room in the house where they can lock themselves in. This is often associated with the need to keep a secret of some kind. For example, Miss Matty in *Cranford* (1853) insists that the door is locked to prevent anyone coming into the room while she is telling Mary the story of Peter's expulsion from home. Margaret Hale in *North and South* (1855) similarly locks herself into her father's study after she has been interviewed by the police inspector. She is overcome by the strain of having to keep the secret of her brother's presence in the home, and needs a safe space in which to deal with her emotional turmoil. Although her father is away, his study still offers her protection. Gaskell also uses Margaret's choice of sanctuary to reinforce the fact that she has taken on a patriarchal role within the family, and is therefore entitled to a masculine refuge. In contrast, her mother does not have the privilege of a lockable door, but has to use a candlelighter in the keyhole to signify that she is asleep. Mary Kuhlman further notes that after Boucher's suicide, Margaret pays an uninvited visit to his home and locks the door behind her, 'taking control over the house and situation by right of her personal competence and superior social class.'[20] This is some time after the riot at the mill where Margaret's entrance through the front door onto the step to protect Thornton is a dramatic transition from domestic to public life, from the female to the male environment.[21] Helen in 'The Half-Brothers' (1856), Bridget in 'The Poor Clare' (1856) and Sylvia (*Sylvia's Lovers*, 1863) all lock themselves in their rooms at times of emotional crisis: Helen, when she receives a life-changing proposal of marriage, Bridget, to brood over her lost daughter, and Sylvia, when Philip tells her about Kinraid's philanderings.

Doors are also barriers which can be used to comment on gendered space and restrictions placed on women. Alexandra Warwick notes, for example, the Gothic nature of the Brontë's domestic space: 'The novels are full of images of doors and windows, with women inside prevented from leaving and the same women outside, barred from entering.'[22] Although none of Gaskell's characters is physically locked into rooms like Rochester's wife, doors and windows are used to symbolise their entrapment. As soon as Mrs Mason has left the workroom in *Ruth* (1853), for example, Ruth 'sprang to the large old window, and pressed against it as a bird presses against the bars of its cage'.[23] The verbs suggest her active desperation, her instinctive longing to be free. The imagery of closed doors and windows persists throughout the novel, with doors representing Ruth's exclusion from society, and windows, the wider natural world with which she has an instinctive affinity. In this context, doors and windows are indicative of moral values. The closed door of Bellingham's sickroom, for example, represents the narrow morality of conventional society, whereas the view from the window on the landing outside shows the natural landscape with its sense of timeless, more accepting values.

    Angus Easson, in his detailed analysis of the use of domestic and public space in *Ruth* and the ways in which this reflects the themes of the novel, notes how domestic settings are critical to Ruth's emotional and spiritual development. This begins with her first meeting with Benson outside in the natural environment rather than inside in the shared public/private space of the local inn.[24] Other critics have noted how *Ruth* is both a novel written in the Romantic, pastoral tradition and a critique of that same genre. Holly Pike for example, argues that Ruth has been left to grow wild, like the untended tree she sees out of the window of the workroom, and that she does not therefore recognise and accept the boundaries set for her, symbolised by the window.[25] Hilary Schor argues that Gaskell used the Romantic inheritance to comment on female silencing.[26] Rosemarie Bodenheimer notes that *Ruth* is a novel in the pastoral tradition in which the natural world creates 'an alternative interior realm that protects its subject from the conventional language of social judgement.'[27] She notes further that Gaskell's use of the pastoral tradition disappears from *Ruth* when Bellingham vanishes from her life, although her development is still recorded by references to flowers and gardens. The consensus of these interpretations is that the story of Ruth's emotional development is told through her response to the natural environment, setting her seduction apart from conventional social norms and facilitating Gaskell's desire to evoke empathy for this disregarded, discarded young girl.

Margaret Hale is another heroine whose character is rooted in the pastoral tradition, although Victoria Williams also argues convincingly for the use of fairytale motifs in the novel, including descriptions of the rural idyll of Helstone where Margaret is free to roam the heathland and forest at will.[28] However, on her final walk on the evening of her departure from Helstone, after the house has been stripped of its familiar furnishings, the external landscape too becomes full of threats. Easson discusses the way in which Gaskell uses colour in this passage so that the gathering dusk blurs familiar objects, adding to the atmosphere of change and disruption.[29] The singing of the robin which Margaret hears is traditionally believed to signify death, and this passage marks the death of Margaret's childhood. The crack of a fallen branch sends her running towards the safety of home: 'she was afraid, she knew not why. She heard Charlotte shutting the windows, and fastening up for the night, unconscious that any one had gone out into the garden,'[30] She is shut out of her home and cannot return until she has completed her journey into adulthood. The concept of home as a secure sanctuary is conspicuously undermined by this episode, but it has always been an unstable concept for Margaret, located jointly between London and Helstone. Margaret's idealised view of Helstone as a home which provides an assured sense of place is undermined by the disruptions and demands of modern society which make constant change inevitable.[31]

Privacy in the Victorian home was always contested, and indeed, the external urban environment in which Gaskell lived was also hugely congested. Until the 1840s, the merchant, manufacturer, or professional man who needed to be within reach of his business, had to be able to ride or drive there in a reasonable time.[32] Plymouth Grove is set in some 1,500 square yards of grounds in Victoria Park on the outskirts of Manchester yet is only about one and a half miles from the city centre. Manchester had no need of a cab stand until 1839.[33] Yet within these constrained geographical confines, the population exploded. It grew by 40.4% in the decade 1811-1821 and by a further 60% between 1831 and 1851, at which point it stabilised.[34] The middle classes responded to this pressure by retreating to the suburbs and a more private residential style. Outdoor life ceased to be social and disappeared from view behind the garden hedge or yard wall.[35] Inside the home, clear boundaries began to be established to denote the various functions taking place within specified spaces, yet at the same time, the interior of the middle-class home was never private, but was instead a site of encounter, of private and public interaction and a space which outsiders and strangers could enter.[36]

In many Victorian homes, with their large families and numbers of servants, it must have been very difficult to find private space. Gaskell complains constantly about interruptions to her work from visitors and enforced concentration on the domestic management of the house.[37] Holidays were not always a respite as they were often spent with the extended family.[38] Like many Victorian men, William resorted to going on holiday on his own or with male friends.[39] Gaskell alternated between complaining that he would not take a holiday, explaining that he did not feel that they should both be away from home together because of the children, and worrying about his lack of replies to her letters.[40] She established a pattern very quickly after the publication of each novel of either leaving home or becoming ill.[41] Several of her female characters such as Mary Barton, Margaret Hale and Ruth experience episodes of crisis and renewal which parallel the pattern of Gaskell's writing life.[42] Home was far from being a safe haven.

Death and the home

Death in Victorian times almost always occurred within the home and further contributed to the instability and insecurity of family life. It also provided another link between the sacred and the secular, reinforcing the spiritual meaning of home. As Mike Hepworth notes, home was 'a secluded place to struggle with those realities such as illness and death which succeeded in breaching the walls'.[43] James Martineau, the charismatic Unitarian preacher and friend of the Gaskells, is explicit about the ubiquity with which death affected Victorian homes and the fragility of family ties:

> Members of the same home cannot dwell together, without either the memory or the expectation of some mutual and mortal farewell. Families are for ever forming, for ever breaking up; and every stroke of the pendulum carries the parting agony through fifty homes.[44]

The domesticity and intimacy of a Victorian death is starkly illustrated by a series of articles in *Cassell's Household Guide*, where advice on registering a death is sandwiched between articles on making a pincushion, and the manufacture of boots and shoes.[45] Further articles point out the necessity of holding a funeral as soon as possible after the death as 'in many cases – especially in the summer – the corpse is retained too long and thus becomes injurious to the health of those living in the house.'[46] Samuel Bamford, for example, Gaskell's model for John Barton, kept the body of his daughter Ann at home for so long that the authorities had to intervene.[47]

Death, and its aftermath, was also divided by the allocation of gendered roles and separate spaces. Female relatives should not attend the funeral since 'being unable to restrain their emotions, they interrupt and destroy the solemnity of the ceremony with their sobs, and even by fainting.'[48] William Shaen, writing to Catherine Winkworth about Gaskell's death in 1865, noted that this separation of genders was to be adhered to at her funeral: 'No one will be asked to attend except Mr. Gaskell's brothers, Charles Crompton and

Thurstan.'[49] Margaret Hale in *North and South* points out that this advice is also related to class:

> Women of our class don't go, [to funerals] because they have no power over their emotions, and yet are ashamed of showing them. Poor women go, and don't care if they are seen over-whelmed with grief.[50]

It is a measure of Margaret's newly acquired status within her family, and her acceptance of the lessons she has learned by associating with the Higgins family, that both she and Dixon are allowed to attend Mrs Hale's funeral.

The robust advice in *Cassell's Household Guide* for mourners to separate and return home as soon as the funeral is over, avoids prolonging grief with any kind of wake and also indicates the cultural need to deal with the fragility of life and frequent death by compartmentalising and containing emotion. Additional advice not to provide the undertaker's men with alcohol suggests a level of repressed emotion transferred onto those who have to carry out the final tasks associated with putting the body to rest.[51] Like Shakespeare's clowns, drunken undertakers provide an acceptable form of relief from overpowering emotion which weeping women from a similar social and cultural background would expose too overtly. As the century progressed, death gradually became more detached from the home, and the ever-helpful Cassell's Guide informed readers that

> some of the cemetery companies have places set apart where, without paying any extra fees, the coffin containing the corpse may be privately conveyed, and kept in safety until the time appointed for the funeral.[52]

In her wide-ranging study of the literary representation of death in the nineteenth century, Mary Elizabeth Hotz examines the social and cultural reasons behind this state appropriation of dead bodies.[53] She argues convincingly that Edwin Chadwick, Commissioner for the Board of Health from 1848 to 1852, sought to sanitise death by bureaucratising it. At the heart of this preoccupation, she suggests, are Chadwick's views on the importance of the home as a cultural site which had to be protected from physical and spiritual disease. The home is the centre of a network of sewer and water supplies which protect the physical health of the inhabitants, and this is threatened by the practice of keeping corpses at home before burial:

> In Manchester and in several northern districts, it appears that by custom the corpse seldom remains unburied more than three or four days, but during that time it remains in the crowded rooms of the living of the labouring classes. Every day's retention of the corpse is to be considered an aggravation of the evil; but the evidence is to be borne in mind that the miasma from the dead is more dangerous immediately after death, or during the first and second day, than towards the end of the week. [...] decomposition often proceeds with excessive rapidity in the crowded rooms, which have then commonly larger fires than usual.[54]

Chadwick extrapolates from this physical threat of infection the possibility of emotional and spiritual infection, leading to complete moral degeneration:

> the body is never absent from their sight – eating, drinking, or sleeping, it is still by their side, mixed up with all the ordinary functions of daily life, till it becomes as familiar to them as when it lived and moved in the family circle. [It is] not seldom the hiding-place for the beer-bottle or the gin if any visitor arrives inopportunely. [...] who does not see that when the respect for the dead [...] is gone, the whole mass of social sympathies must be weakened – perhaps blighted and destroyed?[55]

Hotz argues that in nineteenth-century England, 'economic value was related to bodily well-being, but – ironically – articulated in terms of bodily illness, death, and apparent death.'[56] By insisting on the removal of the body from the home on health grounds therefore, Chadwick was both protecting the national economy and attempting to establish control over the working classes under the guise of health reforms. Hotz notes some important subtexts to Chadwick's report. One is the link to the Chartist struggles in Sheffield where the Anglican church forbade meetings in churchyards, and the other is the 'undercurrent of fear that widows, overcome with grief [...] would be forced to abandon the home and work outdoors as prostitutes.'[57] Thus, she suggests, burial reform was intimately connected to the fear of social unrest and the need to control and manage the excesses of the working classes in order to ensure the smooth running of the national economy by men and the domestic economy by women. Reform therefore necessitated the building of parallel homes in which to keep corpses before burial, watched over not by grieving families, but by cemetery inspectors and medical officers.

In her extensive examination of death in the Victorian family, Pat Jalland examines the cultural rituals which middle- and upper-class Victorians developed to manage the trauma associated with death, especially when dealing with terminal illness and the death of children.[58] Jalland notes how the Evangelical revival and Romanticism allowed the Victorians to give full expression to their grief, either by keeping diaries of a terminally ill person's progress towards death, talking and writing freely about their sorrow as well as their joy and their love, or by exhibiting what might now be considered excessive displays of emotion. Evangelicalism set out a prescriptive model for a 'good' death. This was ideally a family event that took place within the home. Deathbed scenes in novels helped to disseminate this model from Evangelical tracts to a wider public and increased the melodrama and emotional temperature. After death, cultural signifiers of status (mourning and half mourning), and prescribed social behaviour further helped to control and manage fear and anxiety until the bereaved could once more be included in society.

The Unitarian attitude to death was, however, noticeably different. Unitarians did not believe in the doctrine of atonement or everlasting punishment but sought perfectability in this life. Jalland examined the personal records of three Unitarian families and found that the deaths of family members, when described at all, 'were economical, factual and surprisingly unemotional.'[59] William Gaskell, for example, describes the death of Sir John Potter as 'disturbed by no distressing fears,' a phrase he repeats at the address on the interment when he states that 'in the spirit of confiding trust, he sank so calmly and peacefully to his last sleep.'[60] Even when he describes the early and painful death of John Ashton Nicholls, William is insistent that the pain associated with death is that of a new birth and that 'He who has never suffered has not attained to any thing like true moral elevation and maturity of character.'[61] His message is one of hope in which death is part of a spiritual education, and he is careful to point out that Nicholls 'remained, in the midst of acute and wearying pain, calm, patient, and resigned to the last.'[62] Martineau discusses the blending of earthly and heavenly families, stating that:

> since the grave can bury no affections now, but only the mortal and familiar shape of their object, death has changed its whole aspect and relation to us; and we may regard it, not with passionate hate, but with quiet reverence.[63]

Gaskell's experience of death

Gaskell's first conscious experience of the death of a close family member was that of her aunt and foster mother. Hannah Lumb suffered a stroke, accompanied by a severe and continuing headache, and was eased into death by Gaskell's uncle, the doctor Peter Holland, who prescribed 'an anodyne draught which sent her into a most gentle & easy sleep'.[64] At the time of Aunt Lumb's death, Gaskell was at home in Manchester awaiting the birth of her second daughter while Aunt Lumb looked after her eldest daughter, Marianne, in Knutsford. Her death therefore became the focus of a number of conflicting emotions, as Uglow notes: guilt that looking after Marianne may have precipitated the fatal stroke, happiness associated with the birth of a new baby, and concern about managing Marianne's confusion and anxiety.[65] This is reflected in Gaskell's account of her final illness which focuses on Aunt Lumb's physical suffering and the best way to alleviate it, admiration for her continuing concern for others even when she is in acute pain and concern about how to fulfil her desire to see Marianne again.[66] This is far removed from the good Christian death described in the tracts but does reflect Unitarian practicality and deep concern for the individual.

The death of Gaskell's son Willie was a different matter. Jalland notes the incidence of infant mortality which remained consistently high throughout the nineteenth century, despite improvements in public health, diet, and sanitation.[67] Infant mortality was particularly high in Manchester, especially in the central districts.[68] This was due mainly to infectious diseases such as diarrhoea, pneumonia, bronchitis, measles, and whooping cough. The mortality rate for scarlet fever, from which Willie Gaskell died in 1845, aged nine months, doubled between 1840 and 1870 after which it diminished, with infants under twelve months suffering the highest mortality rate.[69] The

Victorians had a constant fear of contagion, particularly in the city. The bumping and jostling Margaret Hale experiences in the streets of Milton is symbolic of the porous boundaries between rich and poor and the ways in which disease and contamination moved through the streets, carried on the clothes and breath of men, women, and children.[70] The built environment had a detrimental effect on the health of all who lived there. Disease in the overcrowded, poorly ventilated properties and cellars, lacking any form of piped water, was rampant and spread quickly. Gaskell's alarm on hearing in 1854 that scarlet fever was within fifty yards of her home in Plymouth Grove is therefore entirely understandable, as is her reaction in immediately sending the girls to Poulton where there was no known case of the disease at such speed that they went 'clothes-less, for all their clothes were at the wash'.[71] Willie died in the arms of his nurse, Fergusson, in the boarding house in Wales to which the Gaskells had retreated to escape the disease which was rife in Manchester.[72] Gaskell was overwhelmed: 'I don't believe even Heaven itself can obliterate the memory of that agony.'[73]

Deathbeds were private affairs, usually limited to a relatively small number of members of the immediate family. Children who had been diagnosed with scarlet fever were isolated, even from their parents, in an attempt to prevent the disease from spreading, so Gaskell's account of Willie's death in the arms of his nurse is therefore not unusual.[74] The death of children was regarded as a particular spiritual challenge. The churches recognised this by producing consolation literature explaining the meaning of such deaths in Christian terms and showing mourners how their faith could console them. No doubt William, in his work as a minister, had much experience of consoling grieving parents and his suggestion that Gaskell write a novel as a way of dealing with her own grief may have been a variation on this literary tradition where the act of writing itself provided a form of therapy. Certainly, both parents remained constantly anxious about their surviving children and this may explain in part William's reluctance to leave home to go on holiday, particularly when the children were young.[75]

Death in Gaskell's fiction

Maria Edgeworth was not alone among contemporary critics of *Mary Barton* to complain about the many deathbed scenes in the novel – 'There are about a dozen too many deaths' – and death remained a constant theme in Gaskell's fiction, but always a theme with a purpose.[76] In *Wives and Daughters* (1866) for example, the death of the first Mrs Gibson has a narrative purpose in that it moves the plot forward and makes Mr Gibson's remarriage and the resultant consequences for the interlocking circles of families portrayed in the novel inevitable. In *North and South* (1855), the deaths of Margaret's parents mark critical points in the development of her character and her journey to maturity. Deaths which occurred in the past haunt both 'The Old Nurse's Story' (1852) and 'A Dark Night's Work' (1863) and contribute to the atmospheric effect in both of these Gothic short stories. Many of these characters are dispatched briskly and their death happens 'off-stage'. Gaskell is primarily concerned with the living: her Unitarian beliefs encouraged practical charity and, as the narrator in *Mary Barton* remarks when Mary learns that her father has murdered Harry Carson, 'some kind of action (bodily or mentally) in times of distress, is a most infinite blessing'.[77] Hotz convincingly argues that Gaskell's treatment of death in her fiction, including, for example, her account of working-class death and burial in *Mary Barton,* seeks to reaffirm the centrality of the corpse within the domestic environment as a reaction against the burial reforms which sought to isolate it from its social and political contexts.[78] This interpretation can be aligned with the Unitarian belief in the importance of the individual in society and the contribution each individual makes to the well-being of the community. Certainly, in the early part of the century, 'the successful death very much depended upon the presence and agency of the living'.[79]

Ellis Chadwick offers an interesting insight into Gaskell's own death which took place dramatically and unexpectedly in her newly acquired house in Hampshire. She claims that: 'A death masque of the face was taken soon after Mrs. Gaskell died, and for a long time it hung in the drawing-room at Plymouth Grove.'[80] This sentence is deleted from the revised edition of her book which appeared in 1913. Her mention of the death masque however, suggests the intimate way in which death invaded the home and was integrated into family relationships, and the removal of the sentence may indicate that this exposed too private a moment in the life of the family.

I focus now on Gaskell's treatment of the death of children and young men, recurring figures that haunted Gaskell because of her own life experiences. Gaskell depicts the death of five children in her fiction: the twins in *Mary Barton* (1848), Nanny in 'Lizzie Leigh' (1850), Sophie's brother, Walter, in 'Mr Harrison's Confessions' (1851) and Owen Griffiths's baby in 'The Doom of the Griffiths' (1858). When Mary Barton enters the Wilson's house, one twin is already dead, the other dying from fever, probably typhus. The twins have always been fragile and in need of special care and the intensity of Mrs Wilson's love for her children is such that Alice fears she is 'wishing him':

> There's none can die in the arms of those who are wishing them sore to stay on earth. The soul o' them as holds them won't let the dying soul go free; so it has a hard struggle for the quiet of death. We mun get him away fra' his mother, or he'll have a hard death, poor lile fellow.[81]

Mrs. Wilson is persuaded to relinquish her son to Alice and he dies peacefully. Gaskell's treatment of this scene is interesting, given the close association of the writing of this novel with the death of her own son. There are clear echoes of Willie's death in the actions of the mother relinquishing her child to another in whose arms he dies. Yet there is a detachment in the scene which we see through the eyes of Mary Barton. There is pathos and distress, and grief is clearly expressed, but there is no melodrama and there is a reference to an old superstition rather than to any form of Christian comfort. Jem is heartbroken at the death of his brothers, but 'felt a strange leap of joy in his heart' when Mary comforts him and a moment of intense emotion melts into sensuality:

> He did not speak, as though fearing to destroy by sound or motion the happiness of that moment, when her soft hand's touch thrilled through his frame, and her silvery voice was whispering tenderness in his ear. Yes! It might be very wrong: he could almost hate himself for it; with death and woe so surrounding him, it yet was happiness,

was bliss, to be so spoken to by Mary.[82]

There is a curious disjunction of language and tone between this passage and the description of the twins' death and its aftermath. The rituals surrounding the death are rooted in practical domestic action like those described earlier in the novel after the death of Mary's mother. The narrator and the reader are emotionally detached from the event – the sobs of the bereaved mother are heard occasionally, but she is in another room. Jem's entry into the house and his overpowering distress at hearing the news of his brothers' deaths enables Gaskell to move the romantic narrative forward, but it is an uneasy transition. Touch is important throughout the novel as a way of releasing emotion or to assist the narrative flow. Mary's hand on Jem's arm is associated with his sexual desire for her and his confession of his feelings. Jem's seizure of Mary's hand is unwelcome and is an ironic version of the physical threats made by Harry Carson, but it forces Mary to re-evaluate her relationship with both Jem and Harry.[83]

'Lizzie Leigh' (1850) opens with the death of Lizzie's father after she has disappeared in Manchester, pregnant and disgraced. His death is the catalyst which frees and motivates his wife to find her daughter, despite opposition from her eldest son. As Emily Jane Morris notes, the narrative of 'Lizzie Leigh' is a powerful argument for practical action by women to assist the re-demption and recuperation of fallen women.[84] Gaskell believed passionately in practical action rather than the giving of money as a response to those in need and felt equally strongly about the importance of not judging others.[85] The death of Lizzie's child also enables Gaskell to re-model the conventional narrative in that, as Morris notes, she dies while in the care of Susan Palmer, the model of feminine purity.[86] Rather than being the punitive outcome de-manded by society therefore, Nanny's death provides the means for Lizzie's spiritual redemption and for her reunion with her mother. Deborah Denen-holz Morse further explores the bonding between Lizzie, the fallen woman, and Susan, the angel in the house.[87]

Lizzie, the shadow in the street, follows Susan and the doctor into the house where her child lies dead. In the passage which follows, Gaskell eco-nomically describes Susan's transition from terror at the wild eyed prostitute to an empathetic acceptance and care for the bereaved mother. The narrative describes a complex exchange of roles and challenges conventional assumptions about maternal responsibilities. It is Susan who has left the child, not her mother. Susan takes on a quasi-maternal role towards Lizzie: 'Susan took out some of her own clothes, and softly undressed the stiff, powerless, form.'[88] This description of Lizzie, prostrate with grief, suggests that she is a corpse and Susan is carrying out the traditional function of women who wash and dress the body prior to burial. This rite of passage enables Lizzie to make the transition from prostitute to bereaved mother. She takes on the signifying garments of a mother and, once she has regained consciousness, an altered manner:

> Her voice was so strange a contrast to what it had been before she had gone into the fit, that Susan hardly recognised it; it was now so unspeakably soft, so irresistibly pleading, the features too had lost their fierce expression, and were almost as placid as death.[89]

Prostitute and angel in the house, biological mother and mother-substitute are blended. Lizzie's transformation through a symbolic process of death and resurrection allows Gaskell to reintegrate her into society. Her sins have been washed away by a pure woman, an interesting interpretation of Unitarian Christology, in which Christ, the perfect human being, is gendered as female. Lizzie's first words after her 're-birth', 'I am not worthy to touch her,'[90] are ones of contrition which are an echo of the words in the Prayer of Humble Access at an Anglican Holy Communion, 'We are not worthy so much as to gather up the crumbs under thy Table.'[91] Susan's response, 'my God, have mercy on her, and forgive, and comfort her,' reinforces the spiritual message.[92] Lizzie's dead child is laid in her arms and Lizzie sleeps that night in Susan's bed. Gaskell integrates a religious message of compassion and acceptance and a powerful challenge to conventional morality and gendering into the narrative structure of this short story.

The death of Walter from croup in 'Mr Harrison's Confessions' (1851) is described in some detail, and the tone and language is more emotionally engaged than in *Mary Barton*:

the little fellow was struggling to get his breath, with a look of terror on his face that I have often noticed in young children when smitten by a sudden and violent illness. It seems as if they recognised something infinite and invisible, at whose bidding the pain and the anguish come, from which no love can shield them. It is a very heart-rending look to observe, because it comes on the faces of those who are too young to receive comfort from the words of faith, or the promises of religion. Walter had his arms tight round Sophy's neck, as if she, hitherto his paradise-angel, could save him from the dread shadow of Death.[93]

Walter's croup has made him incapable of speech, just like Willie, who was pre-lingual when he died, and Gaskell effectively conveys the feeling of helplessness when faced with the inevitability of death. Walter's death sits strangely in this otherwise light-hearted short story, the precursor to *Cranford*. It does not really contribute to the narrative structure as it is clear that Sophy and Doctor Harrison are married at the beginning of the story, and although Walter's death helps to draw them together, it is not a critical factor. It does not assist with the development of Sophy's character as it enhances traits which are already present, rather than contributing new insights. It seems possible, therefore, that Gaskell was continuing to express in fictional form her constant anxiety about her children and her fears about the possibility of more of them dying, which continued to haunt her. On 30 March 1838 for example, she writes to her sister-in-law Elizabeth Gaskell describing Marianne's serious bout of croup, which necessitated both William and her brother-in-law Sam, a doctor, sitting up all night with the child, and Gaskell herself being up until 2 a.m.[94] The description of Marianne's illness is immediately followed by Gaskell's assertion that she expects to hear at any time of the death of another child who also has croup. Life was indeed fragile and children could not be protected, even within the home.

'The Doom of the Griffiths' was first published in *Harper's New Monthly Magazine* in 1858, but Charlotte Mitchell points out that its composition probably dates from around 1834-5 when Gaskell's oldest daughter was a baby, pre-dating her son Willie's death in August 1846 by about a decade.[95] Although Gaskell claimed that the story was founded on fact, it is a brutal and violent tale, culminating in the death of both Owen Griffiths's baby and his father. Vanessa Dickerson notes that at the possible date of composition Gaskell had suffered a still birth and was, as evidenced by 'The Diary', an anxious first-time mother, and that these facts may have influenced the choice and handling of the subject matter.[96] The story deals with a number of narrative themes frequently found in Gaskell's work, including class conflict, divided families and the decline of landed families, as well as illustrating how early key figures such as the dead mother, the stubborn father and the dangerous second wife enter her fiction.[97] Gaskell made some unspecified alterations to the text before its publication but Felicia Bonaparte is probably right to see a connection between the description of the dead baby and Gaskell's recollection of Willie's death.[98]

It is noticeable that Gaskell rarely deals with the death of young men and never depicts them dying at home. Harry Carson in *Mary Barton* is murdered in a narrow alley, Bellingham/Donne in *Ruth* dies in a hotel, and Osborne Hamley in *Wives and Daughters* has already died when we follow Molly into the old nursery where the body has been laid. The narrative focus is on the grief of the old squire and the enforced changes that will now occur, for which Osborne's death has been the catalyst. Jalland points out that 'early and mid-Victorian Christians most feared sudden death because it allowed no opportunity for spiritual preparation and repentance, depriving them of the potential consolations of a Christian deathbed.'[99] It seems that Gaskell was unable to write a deathbed scene for a young man as this would have meant dealing with her own emotions about the loss of her brother, and perhaps, finally acknowledging that he had died with the complete loss of hope that this would entail alongside any spiritual implications.

In another interesting parallel with Gaskell's own life, young women in her fiction rarely die, but are more likely to be purged by illness: for example, Margaret Hale in *North and South*, Sylvia in *Sylvia's Lovers*, Mary Barton in the eponymous novel and Molly Gibson in *Wives and Daughters*. In the case of Margaret Hale, the boundary between illness and death is further blurred by her exchange of 'gifts' with Bessy Higgins, after Bessy's death. Margaret gives Bessy's sister one of her own nightcaps for Bessy to wear in her coffin, and Margaret chooses a small drinking cup of Bessy's as a memento.[100] Bessy is a narrative double for Margaret, a young girl of the same age, but of a very different social background. Her journey towards death mirrors Margaret's journey towards maturity, and it is the link with Bessy and her family that acts as the catalyst for changing Margaret's perceptions, values, and assessment of the world around her. The exchange of these personal items makes psychological and emotional sense in the context of the novel, but can also be seen as symbolic, in that Margaret has to 'die' and be 'reborn' in the physical world as Bessy believes she herself will die and be reborn in the spiritual world.

This purging of young women mirrors Gaskell's own ambiguous reaction to being a published author and therefore very visible in the public domain, to which she responded either by becoming ill or by leaving home. All these characters become the object of public scrutiny in one way or another, and illness is their reaction to the stress this causes. On a deeper level, it may also suggest some kind of residual guilt following the disappearance of Gaskell's brother. Psychiatrists agree that mourners may find it difficult to come to terms with their grief and to accept death in the absence of a body and that therefore grief may be abnormally prolonged.[101] Gaskell may therefore be punishing herself symbolically for the success as a writer which was denied to her brother, and indeed, to her father, by purging these female characters through illness and suffering.

The rescue compulsion

Critics and biographers have noted the theme of the lost male in Gaskell's fiction but have not explored the links such characters have with home and the fact that for many of them, home is, or becomes, unsafe, either physically, psychologically, or emotionally. Gaskell's relationship with her brother John is acknowledged to be integral to the presentation of these figures, but it has proved very difficult to explore the effect of his disappearance on her other than obliquely through her fiction. John Chapple asserts that the dearth of references to or discussion of her brother 'is almost unbelievable' and suggests that she may have deliberately repressed her memories of him.[102] She writes openly, for example, about the loss of her children though illness or miscarriage, but in later life, barely mentioned the brother to whom she had been so close.[103] I now explore the effect of the loss of Gaskell's brother in a discussion of the rescue compulsion and its influence on Gaskell's fiction.

John was twelve years older than Gaskell, but she met and corresponded with him regularly until the time of his disappearance when she was eighteen. Fourteen letters from John to Elizabeth are held at the John Rylands Library, although only four of these exist as manuscript originals, the rest being typed copies of originals which have since disappeared. The letters, which date from 1819 when Elizabeth was nine years old, are all very affectionate in tone, containing colourful and sometimes gruesome accounts of what John has seen on his voyages to India and the Far East. Nearly all contain references to presents he has bought her and complaints that her letters are too few and too short – a defect she remedied in later life. There is an element of bravado which conceals the fears and anxieties of a young boy. He is told, for example, that nine out of ten who go to the East Indies die there, 'but I must comfort myself in the same manner the officers of the army and navy [...] did when they drunk as their first toast after dinner "A sickly season and plenty of new rum".'[104] In a further letter dated 29 November [1820], he reports that nothing occurred during the voyage which would interest his sister, although 'we lost two men overboard who were both drowned', and in a voyage to India during January and February 1821, he only avoids a couple of days in the stocks in Burma due to the intervention of his captain. In general, the tone and content of the letters suggest that he enjoyed life on board ship and was intrigued by his experience of other cultures although he constantly asks for news from home, and in particular, for letters from Elizabeth, who, by 1827, he considered had 'a talent at letter writing, for truly your epistles are remarkably good'.[105]

The character that emerges from these letters shows a remarkable similarity to that of his sister: passionate, impulsive, humorous, and with an immediacy that is both attractive and endearing. In John's penultimate letter to Gaskell of 30 July 1828, he evidently continues a conversation he has been having with her about his future. He wants to become a writer and to leave the Navy, but he cannot afford to do so. Chapple notes that the bankruptcy of Constable and Ballantyne in 1826 had made the publishing world extremely cautious and that this was a probable reason for John's difficulty in interesting a publisher in his writing.[106] John cannot come and see his sister as he will lose his position and clearly, Elizabeth was upset at this news. His reaction illustrates the close bond between them:

> Do not for an instant think it is because I do not like it: how could such an idea come into your head – I would give worlds to see you – to walk with you – to enjoy your conversation – […] seeing you for so short a period – having continually before me the certainty of parting so very soon, of perhaps parting with you for ever – I could not really be happy.[107]

This is the only time in his letters that he talks about seeing his family for the last time and the tone of the letter continues to darken:

> Do you know my spirits have been and are so low that I have not laughed this month and I am getting the name of the Silent man.[108]

His final letter was written on 15 August 1828 and he fears that Elizabeth is still offended by his not coming to see her as she has not written to him. His ship is due to sail the following day and it seems likely that he will remain in India after that. He tells her that he has bought her some tartan silk, a copy of *Friendship's Offering* (given to him by Smith, Elder & Company) and some seeds. He finishes by telling her that he has just got the final answer from Smith, Elder & Company who have refused to take his book 'to end my hopes of being an author'. He signs off:

> And now my dearest Elisabeth [sic] farewell – Should we never meet again, accept my very best wishes for your welfare throughout life and may every blessing attend you -, with love to all enquiring// Believe me to be//Your ever affectionate brother [109]

This extended valedictory and formal superscription is unlike that in any of the other letters which are simply signed 'your affectionate (or 'most affectionate') brother'.

There are a number of theories about John's eventual fate. Gaskell's grandson said that family legend suggested he had been captured by pirates, Ellis Chadwick reports that he was lost at sea and Chapple speculates that he may simply have gone to India to trade and died there.[110] His final two letters clearly indicate that he was both depressed and desperate to remain at home in England, and Gaskell may have felt an enduring guilt that she never replied to his final letter and parted from him on bad terms, hence the suppression of his memory. Gaskell had a deep desire to nurture, and male characters such as Frederick Hale, Peter Jenkyns and John Thornton represent her sublimated wish that she had been able to rescue her brother and to provide him with a safe home.

The rescue compulsion was a strong cultural signifier during the Victorian period, both in life, (for example, the 'rescue' of Elizabeth Barrett by Robert Browning), and in art, (for example the many depictions of St George and the dragon, Perseus and Andromeda and similar myths).[111] Gaskell was familiar with the Domestic Missions, headed up by men, which focused on rescuing women. Rescue could equally occur in male homosocial situations such as battle, and the concept was therefore common in both homosocial and heterosocial contexts. Gaskell explored the rescue compulsion in her fiction and alongside the cultural convention of the return, it helped her to deal with the traumatic loss of her brother.[112]

Personal tragedy triggered the writing of *Mary Barton* (1848), and although the novel opens at the end of a sunny holiday spent in the fields outside Manchester, it quickly darkens, and the tone, atmosphere and plot remain almost unremittingly tragic. The figure of Will Wilson, the sailor, is pivotal to the plot as it is his testimony which saves Jem and enables the novel's various tragedies to be recuperated within a traditional marriage narrative. The fragility of Will's life at sea, and the anxiety and emotional strain felt by his family at home are captured by Gaskell in the character of Alice, Will's foster mother. When she visits the Wilsons, she is 'weary, and sad, and dusty. The weariness and the dust would not have been noticed either by her, or the others, if it had not been for the sadness.'[113] Her sister-in-law immediately guesses the reason for this – she has received no letters. The role of letters in Gaskell's fiction has already been discussed. Here, letters are the tenuous connection between family members which enable them to know the best – or the worst – news about those at sea. Alice voices what Gaskell must have experienced herself: it is the waiting and the uncertainty that are 'very dree work',[114] and she brings this anxiety into the heart of the home.

Domestic rituals are enacted to counteract the dangerous intrusion of the outside world with its potential for tragedy: the kettle is put on, a large loaf is produced and the cheerful sound of rattling teacups is heard instead of the imagined noise of wind and wave. As soon as the domestic space has been made safe, there is a knock at the door and Will, the missing sailor appears. His entrance destabilizes the gathering and facilitates the release of pent up emotions which can now be safely and openly expressed. The description of Will as 'a dashing, bronzed-looking, ringleted sailor, frank, and hearty and affectionate' anticipates that of Frederick Hale in *North and South* (1855), and his personality mirrors that of John Stevenson as it appears in his letters to Elizabeth. The close association between the portrayal of Will Wilson and John Stevenson is further deepened by Gaskell's account of Mary's reaction to his departure on another voyage 'She had always liked Will; but now it seemed as if a sudden spring of sisterly love had gushed up in her heart, so sorry did she feel to hear of his approaching departure.'[115]

Like John Stevenson and Charley Kinraid in *Sylvia's Lovers* (1863), Will Wilson has a fund of sailor's stories to tell. His tale of the mermaid brings a further breath of fantasy into Job Legh's parlour and fulfils the same comic and narrative purpose as the incident of the scorpion discussed in my introduction, where the intrusion of an exotic creature into a domestic setting strengthens and expands the main narrative themes. Will's light-hearted description of the mermaid and his teasing of his sceptical audience are another version of the siren attractions of female beauty and vanity with which both Mary and Esther have to deal. The blending of truth and falsehood in Will's stories is transparent, but he has a serious role to play in the narrative when Jem's life is at stake. Mary's frenetic dash to Liverpool to speak to Will before he sails away seems to be a reworking of Gaskell's last parting with her brother as she would have wished it to be, and is also a nuanced interpretation of the rescue compulsion. Kestner discusses the influence of classical mythology on Victorian art and notes how legends depicting the rescue compulsion were used to promote male heroism and superiority.[116] Common subjects included Perseus and Andromeda and Orpheus and Euridice. Such tales often ended with men subjugating women in marriage. Gaskell's account of a rescue in *Mary Barton* can be viewed as an inversion of this paradigm in which the active role of the rescuer is taken by a woman who then marries the man she has rescued. This inversion also emphasises the shift in the narrative, as Mary moves from a private, domestic world to take on a public role, speaking in court to defend Jem. The balance of power in the relationship has shifted and equalised. Will too, is 'rescued' in that he marries Margaret Legh and is 'domesticated' in the same way that Job's exotic insects are incorporated within the home.

The rescue of Peter Jenkyns by Mary Smith in *Cranford* (1853) is successful and leads to a happy resolution for him and his sister, Miss Matty, despite their changed circumstances. Like John Stevenson, Peter joins the navy, but his letter home is delayed and his mother never sees him again. In the passage which describes his parents' reaction to his departure, it is possible to see Gaskell's own reaction to her brother's departure: pride when speaking to her father about his chosen career, but 'bitter, bitter crying [...] when she was alone'.[117] Like John Stevenson, Peter does come home once, having achieved some success and promotion to the rank of Lieutenant, and Miss Matty recalls that 'My father took him into every house in the parish, he was so proud of him. He never walked out without Peter's arm to lean upon.'[118] The little we know of Gaskell's father suggests that this is an accurate reflection of his relationship with his son. Peter has prospered in India as John Stevenson was meant to do and indeed as Frederick Hale does in Spain.[119] On his return, he resumes his old relationship with his sister, teasing and protective. *Cranford* was Gaskell's own favourite among her novels, the one she always turned to when she was ill, and perhaps one of the reasons for this was that in this text she successfully rescued her brother and brought him home.

Gaskell returned to the theme of the lost brother in *North and South* (1855). Like Peter Jenkyns and John Stevenson, Frederick Hale is an attractive character with a sparkling sense of humour with whom his sister feels an instant empathy: 'she caught the stealthy look of a pair of remarkably long-cut blue eyes, that suddenly twinkled up with a droll consciousness of their mutual purpose of inspecting each other.'[120] Like Peter, he is no respecter of social conventions. Margaret's earliest memory of him is of stealing apples. Although the Hales have plenty of their own apple trees, someone tells Frederick that 'stolen fruit tasted sweetest'[121] and Margaret remarks that his feelings have not changed much since. Margaret's relationship with her brother and her reflection that during his absence at sea, they 'had grown nearer to each other in age, as well as in many other things',[122] mirrors Gaskell's relationship with her own brother. The tone of Frederick's conversations with Margaret, and his use of language as he calls her 'little goose' and telling her 'what a bungler you are',[123] recalls the way in which John addresses his sister in his letters and Frederick's maxim:

> Thinking has, many a time, made me sad, darling; but doing never did in all my life. My theory is a sort of parody on the maxim of "Get money, my son, honestly if you can; but get money."[124]

recalls John's last letter to Gaskell of 15 August 1828 in which he states:

> You yourself seem convinced that nothing is to be done in England – thus it seems I must be contented to be a banished man for what use it is returning and having nothing to do – on three pound [sic] a month what can I save – what can I do – It is better to make up my mind to remain abroad.[125]

Both John and Frederick have no choice but to remain in exile abroad. Frederick's visit and its dangers are foreshadowed in Margaret's dream about Henry Lennox:

> He was climbing up some tree of fabulous height to reach the branch whereon was slung her bonnet: he was falling, and she was struggling to save him, but held back by some powerful invisible hand. He was dead.[126]

The dream is a reworking by Margaret's subconscious of Lennox's proposal and its implications. His climbing of the tree represents his ambition, and Margaret's bonnet, symbol of Victorian femininity, her apparent suitability for a conventional life as his wife. However, it can also be interpreted as Gaskell's own powerful subconscious emotions about her brother being re-worked in her fiction, in that Lennox dies as she feared her brother had. This interpretation complements Jill Matus' argument that Gaskell understood how profound experiences which appear to have been forgotten by the conscious mind are accessible through dreams.[127] Margaret is ultimately unable to save Frederick who has to live his life in exile in Spain. Thematically, this seems to represent a compromise between death or complete disappearance, and an enforced separation where at least Margaret knows that her brother is alive and can correspond with him.[128]

Gaskell's treatment of Kinraid in *Sylvia's Lovers* (1863) is another variation on the rescue theme. Geoffrey Sharps sees Kinraid's capture by the press gang as another version of John Stevenson's disappearance and it certainly indicates the longevity of its effect on Gaskell for this theme to be played out in a novel written two years before her death.[129] Kinraid has much in common with Frederick Hale. Like Frederick, he is introduced into the narrative by reputation. As Frederick led the mutiny against his captain, so Kinraid leads the defence against the press gang who board his whaling ship. Both are impetuous and resist legitimate authority. Both exhibit the violence associated with Carlylean ideas of masculinity, a characteristic shared by John Stevenson:

> One [of] the men employed working on board, being extremely saucy, I kicked him, when he immediately went on shore & lodged an information against me & next morning a guard of soldiers was sent off to take me out of the ship. When I got ashore I was taken before the magistrate [...] & had not our Captain been a very good friend of the government I should not have got off without a couple [of] days confinement in the stocks.[130]

Both men are physically attractive, and their association with lawlessness adds glamour and excitement to their attraction.

Sylvia's first meeting with Kinraid is an ironic inversion of her relationship with Philip. They meet at the funeral of the sailor killed by the press gang and Sylvia, along with several other young girls, breaks into uncontrollable crying. As discussed earlier in this chapter, women in the nineteenth century did not attend funerals as it was considered that they would become over-emotional. However, *Sylvia's Lovers* is set in the historical past and is also concerned with working-class characters for whom cultural norms were different. Gaskell is able to play on these tensions to introduce a nuanced and subtle discussion of the power of sexual attraction while appearing to conform to the cultural expectations of her contemporary readers. Sylvia's loss of control 'became so evident that it attracted the attention of many in that inner circle'.[131] Kinraid assumes that she is a sweetheart of the dead man, and his conclusion is immediately followed by the rattle of gravel on the coffin, completing an association common since medieval times of love, sex and death. This is emphasized by Kinraid's physical appearance 'like a ghost, a-standin' agin a gravestone.'[132] His white and wan face however, unlike Philip's long sallow countenance which repulses Sylvia, marks him out as 'the nearest approach to a hero' Sylvia has seen.[133] As the attraction between Sylvia and Kinraid grows, so too do the images associated with them so that fire becomes the symbol for their powerful feelings for each other.

Kinraid, unlike Philip, has no spiritual side, and this lack foredooms the relationship between him and Sylvia and lays the basis for the tragedy that follows. His rescue by Philip on the battlefield at Acre makes this explicit. Kinraid is feverish as a result of his wound, but nevertheless recognizes Philip. The sailor he sends in search of him fails to find him as Philip himself has been wounded and tells Kinraid that it must have been a spirit sent to help him. Kinraid swears a great oath, insisting that 'It was no spirit, I tell you; and I was in my full senses. It was a man named Philip Hepburn.'[134] This chapter is entitled 'The Recognition' and both the chapter title and the narrative are significant in the thematic context of the novel. Kinraid's statement is critical: it is the first clear acknowledgement in the narrative of Philip's status. He is a 'real' man – a physical presence rather than an incorporeal spirit, and capable therefore of heroic actions, including taking part in the violence of battle and hand to hand combat. Kinraid's naming of Philip affirms his masculinity and completes and rounds off his character, making him sexually a more equal match for Sylvia. The oath he swears gives his statement a quasi-legal status which mirrors the complex meta-narrative in the novel of legitimate and illegitimate power.

Philip's rescue of Kinraid is an example of the way in which such actions occurred in homosocial as well as heterosexual contexts. It is also linked to ideas of chivalry and the medieval revival that occurred during the Victorian period and which became the focus of intense historical interest.[135] Gaskell's use of this medieval trope allows her to explore a complex range of ideas linking sexuality to the rescue theme. As D'Albertis notes, Philip's gendering is unstable: 'he is alternately described as strangely maternal and improbably virile'.[136] His rescue of Kinraid from the battlefield could therefore be viewed as a continuation of this ambiguity: it is either an act of masculine bonding which finally asserts his gender equality with the explicitly heterosexual Kinraid or a feminine, nurturing desire to rescue Kinraid from danger. The destablisation of gender and identity is a major narrative theme in the novel, closely linked to that of spirituality and deceit.

Gaskell's fiction frequently contains presentations of gender which challenge conventional cultural boundaries and expectations. In the next chapter, I discuss her exploration of masculinity in more detail.

2 - A MAN ABOUT THE HOUSE: MASCULINITY IN GASKELL'S FICTION[1]

Gaskell's acute interest in the individual included a willingness to explore the allocation of gender and gendered roles, particularly where these were on the margins of what might be acceptable to contemporary society. This applies in particular to her interest in the traits of character that comprise masculinity and femininity. She uses the intimacy of a domestic setting to provide a contained and apparently safe environment in which to focus on the ways in which gender influences character and behaviour.

Gaskell and cross-dressing

The first evidence that we have of Gaskell's awareness of cross-dressing comes in a letter from her brother John, written in 1827 when Gaskell was seventeen. John describes crossing the equator and tells his sister that Mrs Neptune was 'a handsome young sailor, dressed in a sprig muslin gown & a high French bonnet'.[2] On 22 November 1852, Gaskell wrote to Marianne, her eldest daughter, about a visit from a Mrs Rich. Gaskell was enchanted with her. She had 'never-ending accounts of her life to tell the children; [including] her riding across Asia Minor as a Turkish horseman, turban, pistols & all'.[3] On 17 May 1854, she wrote to John Forster about Rosa Bonheur, the French animalier whom Gaskell knew and liked: 'She is a spirited woman excessively fond of animals & out-door life. [...] to paint this famous horse picture, she dressed herself as a young man, & went & painted it in the greatest livery stables in Paris.'[4] Rosa Bonheur was one of the few nineteenth-century women to obtain official police permission to wear men's clothing, probably for ease of movement and protection.[5] However, when she went out on social occasions or attended official gatherings, she always wore women's clothes. Bonheur had two long-lasting relationships with women but none of her contemporaries ever alleged any impropriety against her. Gaskell was clearly quite comfortable in her company and as enchanted with her stories as she was with those of Mrs Rich.

The Gaskells all enjoyed the fun of disguise and masquerade, including theatregoing – the actor Macready was a personal friend - and like many Victorian families, entertained themselves at home with the performance of charades. On 28 March 1851, Gaskell described to Marianne with great glee a game of charades at Plymouth Grove which intricately combined religious, personal and gender issues:

> They acted in the outer lobby, under the gas; and we stood on the stair-case,\ in the inner hall [,]/and the folding doors were thrown open. The first word word [sic] was Author. Awe – a nun brought before the Inquisition. Tottie (nun) rushed in from the back stair-case door, was caught by Annie and the doors flew open, and displayed the three judges dressed in black with blk masks on (your 3 sisters).[6]

It is possible to over-interpret what was, after all, family entertainment, but it is of interest to note that the first word chosen by Tottie and the girls was 'author', particularly given the conspicuous absence of Gaskell the writer from her list of 'mes', or selves.[7] By March 1851 when the charade was enacted, Gaskell had published her first novel and a number of short stories and pieces of journalism, including regular contributions to Dickens's *Household Words*. The choice of a Catholic theme is also significant as both Gaskells had a strong aversion to Catholicism.[8] During the winter of 1861-2, Marianne Gaskell went to stay with Oxford friends in Rome and became the target of a conversion attempt. Her horrified parents took immediate steps to cleanse her of 'that evil influence'.[9] Here, it is the non-family member, Tottie, who is allocated the role of the nun, and the Gaskell sisters who take the masculine role of judges. Tottie's costume is not described, but the sisters are dressed in black with masks which completely conceal their identity and gender.

In December 1851, Gaskell wrote to Emily Tagart about a repeated bizarre dream she had been having, telling her:

> I dream and dream again of Robert Darbishire as a Bloomer a daughter of mine with a 'pig beard under her muffler', & striding

along in his pettiloons: and you can't think what an uncomfortable dream it is. [.....] I don't know any other young man at all like him.[10]

Robert Darbishire was the son of Samuel Dukinfield Darbishire, a trustee of Cross Street Chapel. The Gaskells and the Dukinfield Darbishires became good friends and their children played together. Gaskell's dream appears to mix cross-dressing, (Robert wears girl's clothes), with issues of gender (his pig beard).

The description of Robert as a 'Bloomer' refers to women who adopted clothing designed by Amelia Bloomer. Bloomer set up a temperance paper called *The Lily* in 1849 and used the journal to promote the causes of women's suffrage, temperance, marriage law reform, and higher education for women. *The Lily* was a great success and quickly built a circulation of over 4,000. In 1851, Bloomer began to publish articles about women's clothing. Female fashion at the time consisted of tightly-laced corsets, layers of petticoats, and floor-length dresses. Bloomer advocated dressing in clothes of the type first worn by women living in the socialist commune, New Harmony, in the 1820s. This included loose bodices, ankle-length pantaloons, and a dress cut to above the knee. Bloomer and other campaigners for women's rights began wearing these clothes and were consistently ridiculed for doing so.[11] Bloomer continued to dress in this way until about 1859 when she said that the crinoline was a sufficient reform, and reverted to conventional female clothing. Gaskell's dream therefore appears to be contemporary with the first emergence of discussion about a more emancipated form of clothing for women and is the more interesting, because there is no further reference to 'bloomers' in her letters, although there are many discussing clothing, new bonnets, the importance of cut in dress, and so on.[12]

Cross-dressing in Gaskell's fiction

Cross-dressing in nineteenth-century fiction, whether the author adopts the narrative voice of the opposite gender or has characters who cross-dress is comparatively rare.[13] Both Gaskell, and her close friend Charlotte Brontë, indeed all the Brontë sisters, were unusual in that they used narrative cross-dressing, that is, they wrote in a male narrative voice. Both Gaskell and

Charlotte Brontë also had characters who adopted some or all of the signifying clothing of the opposite gender. Brontë's De Hamal in *Villette* (1853),
who cross-dresses as a nun, is small but exquisitely formed like a doll: 'So
nicely dressed, so nicely curled, so booted and gloved and cravated, he was
charming indeed.'[14] Gaskell used a male narrative voice in a number of short
stories including 'The Sexton's Hero' (1850), 'The Heart of John Middleton'
(1855), 'Mr. Harrison's Confessions' (1851), 'The Poor Clare' (1856), 'Curious
if True' (1860) and 'Cousin Phillis' (1864).[15] An assumption of masculinity
enabled artists such as Bonheur and novelists such as the Brontës to access
professions and environments denied to them as women.[16] It might be assumed therefore that fictional representations of cross-dressing would focus
primarily on power. I consider instead that Gaskell was more interested in a
subtle and wide-ranging exploration of gender assignment, its effect on the
emotional and psychological development of the individual, their relationship with their families, and, by implication, on what she felt to be necessary
change in wider society.

Cross-dressing first appears in Gaskell's fiction in the third instalment
of *Cranford*, published in *Household Words* on 13 March 1852, and involves
the rector's son Peter, who is introduced to the reader through the letters he wrote home as a boy from boarding school.[17] His full name, Peter
Marmaduke Arley Jenkyns, carries the weight of patriarchal authority and
expectation – he is named after his godfather, Sir Peter Arley – but he is
immediately referred to by Miss Matty as 'poor Peter'.[18] This diminutive not
only makes him accessible to the reader's sympathy, but also suggests that he
is not perhaps the stereotypical strong, masculine figure that his gender and
education might indicate. This impression is reinforced when Mary and Miss
Matty read through his 'show- letters' with their required exhibition of learning and progress interrupted by a 'little sentence […] written in a trembling
hurry, after the letter had been inspected'.[19] Significantly, Peter's request for
cake, (emotional as well as physical nourishment), is addressed to his mother.
Mary's caustic comment on Peter's education – 'I do not know much about
Latin, certainly, and it is, perhaps, an ornamental language: but not very useful, I think', – is a reflection on the lack of emotional (feminine) education that Peter is receiving.[20] The implication is that this imbalance leads to a

decline in his performance, and he writes apologetic letters to his father that parallel the show-letters in their formality without addressing his real concerns. His true emotional state is apparent in his letter to his mother which is a 'badly written, badly-sealed, badly-directed, blotted note'.[21]

Peter deals with his unhappiness by becoming 'captain of the school in the art of practical joking'. His father reacts to this disappointment by 'remedying the matter in a manly way' and reading Latin with his son.[22] The choice of the adjective 'manly' and the activity chosen by the rector are both significant as they reflect the belief that the role of a father was to prepare his son for adult life and to form his character appropriately. John Tosh comments on the various models of fatherhood common among the Victorian middle classes, and notes that the figure of the distant father was far more common in contemporary memoirs than the tyrannical paterfamilias.[23] He argues that this was a psychological reaction on the part of men who feared that their masculinity might be undermined if they displayed emotional warmth towards their children. This was particularly so in the case of a father's attitude towards his son whose masculinity might be compromised by overt displays of affection.

Peter, however, cannot resist playing jokes and cross-dresses as 'a lady that was passing through the town and wished to see the Rector of Cranford, "who had published that admirable Assize Sermon"'.[24] The Rector is so pleased by the attention that he offers to 'copy out all his Napoleon Buonaparte sermons for her'.[25] He allocates this task to Peter, triggering a complex layering of masculine and feminine masquerades. Peter, the male, is asked to copy out sermons for Peter, the female visitor. Peter, the male, wants to go fishing, and curses the female impersonator who has prevented him engaging in this male pastime. His masculine language, ironically, deeply offends his father and reveals a side of Peter's character he has tried to keep hidden, adding another layer of deception to their already difficult relationship.

Peter is very frightened by the ease with which his father is taken in by his impersonation. He did not expect his masquerade to succeed and yet, as Miss Matty points out, if his father had not believed him, the consequences would have been disastrous. His father's failure to recognize his cross-dressed son is also a comment on his failure to recognize and meet Peter's emotional needs.

David Roberts, who read the memoirs of 168 Victorians born between 1800 and 1850, notes that this was a common problem for Victorian fathers, and was the result of a combination of the delegation of child-rearing to servants, coupled with long absences of sons at boarding school.[26] The development of masculinity, a characteristic so prized by early Victorian fathers, was thereby paradoxically hindered. The Rector's failure to acknowledge and meet the emotional needs of his son is destructive, both for Peter's family and for the wider society of Cranford, as it deprives both of a healthy challenge which could produce change and vitality.[27]

Miss Matty is complicit in the tricks her brother plays, and although she is equally terrified of her father's reaction, 'could hardly keep from laughing at the little curtsies Peter kept making, quite slyly, whenever my father spoke of the lady's excellent taste and sound discrimination'.[28] Her comment highlights the comic thread which binds her to her brother, but also illustrates the high level of risk he is prepared to run, and the desperation of his need to be recognised and acknowledged. Peter seeks to challenge the staidness of the town, saying that 'the old ladies [...] wanted something to talk about'.[29] Terence Wright recognizes this as an attempt to subvert authority, but it is far from clear which authority is being subverted, the masculine or the feminine.[30] Peter's choice of disguise as a female who admires the Rector's sermons would seem to be a comment on what was considered suitable reading matter for ladies, which was just as constraining as Peter's masculine education.[31] Their closely prescribed education means that the ladies have little of relevance to discuss. The 'clacking noise there always was when some of the ladies got together' suggests a hard, hollow sound which has little meaning beyond making an unpleasant vibration. Peter seeks to educate the gullible ladies of Cranford and to encourage them to think independently.

His next venture into cross-dressing is profoundly destructive, both for himself and for his family. It is such a terrible tale to tell, that Miss Matty sends the servant out of the house and locks the door after her to ensure that the conversation is not overheard. Peter takes the opportunity, when his father is out visiting the sick and his sister Deborah is away, to go to her room and dress himself in her old gown, and shawl, and bonnet; just the things she used to wear in Cranford, and was known by everywhere; and he made the pillow into a little – you are sure you locked the door, my dear, for I should not like anyone to hear – into – a little baby, with white long clothes.[32]

The broken nature of Miss Matty's recital of this incident, with the pauses in her speech indicated by dashes in the text, and her insistence on complete privacy, underlines the seriousness of Peter's challenge to convention years after he has left Cranford.

Peter's relationship with his other sister, the formidable Miss Jenkyns, is uneasy and full of friction. His motivation for cross-dressing in Deborah's clothes is therefore complex. She is her father's representative, and expects Peter to conform to the standards of masculine behaviour, including a deep seriousness, an application to appropriate study, and 'proper' social behaviour. She applies the same rigorous standards of femininity to herself and her sister, whose thought and behaviour she completely dominates. In choosing to dress in Deborah's clothes therefore, Peter is challenging constructs of both masculinity and femininity. He also blatantly introduces a sexual element into the charade by implying that Deborah Jenkyns has been seduced and given birth. Although he denies that he has any other motive than to give the inhabitants of Cranford something to talk about, the very public nature of his performance suggests a deep seated anger and a desire to shock society out of its complacency. His performance is truly theatrical: 'he went and walked up and down in the Filbert walk – just half hidden by the rails, and half seen; and he cuddled his pillow, just like a baby; and talked to it all the nonsense people do.'[33]

When the Rector returns, he sees a crowd of people peering through the railings of his garden. The rectory, repository of the moral values of the town, has become a place of entertainment, and the role of the rector, to provide spiritual guidance and the underpinning moral values of the community has been superseded by the thrill of illicit sex. The Reverend Jenkyns at first thinks the crowd is admiring 'a new rhododendron that was in full bloom and that he was very proud of'.[34] This image underlines the complex sexual and spiritual message of the charade. Deborah, the daughter who is most like him, and who most clearly represents the accepted mores of society, is in full bloom, but in a diametrically opposite way to the one which he would have expected.

The Rector has considered making a sermon from the 'relation between the rhododendrons and the lilies of the field'.[35] The lilies of the field 'toil not, neither do they spin; And yet I say unto you, that even Solomon in all his glory was not arrayed like one of these'.[36] Gaskell conveys layers of irony in this passing reference. The lily was a symbol of purity, much beloved by the pre-Raphaelite painters. Peter is masquerading as Deborah, the pure female, who is apparently not pure at all, but corrupted. Solomon/Peter, the male, is not as pure as the lilies of the field and he certainly is not 'arrayed like one of these' since he is masquerading in female clothes. There is also an oblique comment on the role of women who 'toil not neither do they spin'. Peter is struggling to find a role, having disappointed his father in his failure to fulfil traditional masculine expectations of an only son. Deborah, of whom nothing more is expected than that she should be ornamental, nevertheless feels she has the right to criticize her brother on his performance of masculinity. N M Jacobs discusses the use of a female persona as a literary masquerade and links it to the female impersonations of drag artists, noting that despite their ironic consciousness of the artificiality of gender behaviour, the drag queen also expresses profound ambiguity about his own failure to fit into a traditional gender category as does Peter in this episode.[37] There is also a burlesque element to his performance. It is easy to overlook the robust nature of Gaskell's humour, described as 'racy' by Susanna Winkworth, which she uses to test the boundaries of propriety.[38]

The Rector reacts to his deception as a stereotypical Victorian father would have reacted to the seduction of his daughter – with intense anger. He immediately and dramatically unmasks Peter: '[he] tore his clothes off his back – bonnet, shawl, gown, and all – and threw the pillow among the people over the railings: [...] and before all the people he lifted up his cane, and flogged Peter!'[39] The violence of the Rector's reaction in the sexualised context of the masquerade, is extreme, amounting almost to symbolic rape, expressed through the actions of stripping and beating with a cane to assert power, authority, and control. It is however ambiguous as to whether this is the symbolic rape of his son or his 'daughter'. The etymon of 'Rector' is the Latin for one who rules or governs. Peter has challenged the Rector's spiritual and paternal authority and, (albeit temporarily and under false pretences), has taken away his power, exposing his father to public ridicule. By undressing Peter and flogging him in public view, the Rector is unhesitatingly re-asserting his authority. At the same time, he is reclaiming his daughter, reasserting her true, feminine nature, and expressing his dominant masculinity while exposing his son to the people of Cranford as not truly masculine.

It is significant to note that *Cranford* was written coterminously with *Ruth* (1853) a novel that openly deals with the seduction and pregnancy of a young girl. In January 1850, Gaskell wrote to Dickens about a young girl, Pasley, who was seduced by a doctor called in when she was ill and who turned, in despair, to prostitution. This episode formed the basis of *Ruth*.[40] The outcome of his 'seduction' for Peter is violent male anger and a beating, and he chooses therefore to remove himself from the family and society in which he can find no acceptable role. Although Peter, as a male, has choices and an independence denied to Victorian females, his experience parallels that of other seduced girls both in Gaskell's fiction and in reality, who encountered anger, rather than understanding, and who were excluded both from their families and from wider society. And, as with other female characters in Gaskell's fiction, such as Lizzie Leigh or Esther, Peter's departure destroys relationships in his family.

Dickens' reaction to this episode is curiously muted. He wrote to John Forster on 9 March 1852: 'Don't you think Mrs. Gaskell charming? With one ill-considered thing that looks like a want of natural perception, I think it masterly.'[41] Judith Flanders points out that 'taste', which is what Dickens seems to imply by 'natural perception', had a moral value for the Victorians, in other words, to be 'tasteful', was to adhere to the moral standards set down by society.[42] It is interesting therefore that, despite this implied lack of conformity with the moral norm, Dickens allowed the episode to appear unedited in his family magazine.

'My Lady Ludlow' was published in *Household Words* in 1858. It is a creative and wide-ranging exploration of social and domestic themes, focusing on change and its effects on society and individuals. Lady Ludlow provides an intriguing female role model for the orphaned girls she takes into her home. After the death of her husband, she returns to her estate of Hanbury and takes on the management of the farms and the village, with the aim of freeing the property from debt for the benefit of her son. Although she is meticulous in recording information and checking facts, her approach is old-fashioned and frequently irritates her steward, Mr Horner. His irritation is compounded by Lady Ludlow's proposal to appoint her own candidate, Miss Galindo, as his assistant, rather than accepting Mr Horner's proposal to employ Harry Gregson, the son of the local poacher. Lady Ludlow's apparent motivation in offering Miss Galindo a job is to assist the impoverished spinster financially, but she is also concerned to retain close control of the management of the estate according to her own clearly stated principles, and to avoid change.

Miss Galindo prepares carefully for her new job. She sits up all night to prepare a selection of quill pens and 'a pair of brown-holland oversleeves, very much such as a grocer's apprentice wears'.[43] She is well aware of her unwelcome intrusion into a masculine role and does her best to modify her gender through her behaviour:

> I try to make him forget I'm a woman, I do everything as ship-shape as a masculine man-clerk. [...] I have stuck my pen behind my ear, I have made him a bow instead of a curtsey, I have whistled – not a tune, I can't pipe up that [...] I have said "Confound it!" and "Zounds!" I can't go any farther.[44]

Unlike the episode with Peter, there is no attempt to disguise the fact that Miss Galindo is a woman. Her masculine masquerade amounts to little more than adopting some minor signifying items of dress and a parodic interpretation of masculine behaviour. Miss Galindo's new role may be viewed as Gaskell's light-hearted contribution to the serious debate that raged in the 1850s about women gaining access to the public sphere, discussed in greater detail, for example, by Gregory Anderson and Barbara Leah Harman.[45]

Her new role, however, has a number of effects on the society of Hanbury. Firstly, she announces that 'Mr Gray [is] taking advantage of my absence to seduce Sally!'[46] Mr Gray, the new young clergyman, is enthusiastic in his pursuit of the establishment of a village school in Hanbury, very much against the wishes of Lady Ludlow. His seduction of Sally is spiritual rather than sexual, but is nevertheless an oblique comment on what happens when women undertake the work of men. Illness and injury intervene and force through the changes which Lady Ludlow opposes. Miss Galindo reverts to her more traditional role of nurse, and the death of Mr Horner opens the way for the appointment of an inexperienced naval officer to administer Lady Ludlow's estates and the eventual partnership with the dissenting baker, Mr Brooke. Miss Galindo's masquerade is comic, rather than tragic, and very much in the spirit of Cranford, but nevertheless, it plays its part in disrupting the established social pattern and moving forward necessary change.

Gaskell returned to the theme of cross-dressing in 'The Grey Woman', a Gothic tale based on Grimms' *Das Mordschloss*, first published in 1861 in *All the Year Round*.[47] Anna, a beautiful, but passive young woman, is pressured into marrying a French count, Monsieur de la Tourelle. His appearance is effeminate: 'His hair was powdered, of course, but one could see from his complexion that it was fair in its natural state. His features were as delicate as a girl's, and set off by two little "munches", as we called patches in those days.'[48] When he speaks to her, Anna is as startled 'as if the angel Gabriel had spoken to me'.[49] The reference emphasises his androgyny. He speaks German with a soft lisp and is far from being a threatening, overtly male figure. Yet, by the end of the evening, Anna becomes 'a little tired of the affected softness and effeminacy of his manners, and the exaggerated compliments he paid me'.[50] Fatigue becomes fright, but Monsieur de la Tourelle is insistent in his courtship of Anna, and she marries him and travels to his remote castle in France, a country far away from her friends and family. In this Gothic setting, with its dimly lit chambers, winding passages and secret rooms, Anna 'soon found out how little I, or, apparently, anyone else, could bend the terrible will of the man who had on first acquaintance appeared to me too effeminate and languid to exert his will in the slightest particular'.[51] This is a challenging interpretation of masculinity and its presentation. Monsieur de la Tourelle appears effeminate, but is actually possessed of a steely will and is the ruthless and bloodthirsty leader of a gang of bandits who do not hesitate to murder anyone who opposes them.

Anna's husband gives her a maid called Amante whose name means 'a lover' or 'beloved' in French. Amante and her mistress are close in social class, and in the loneliness of the chateau, where Anna is frightened of her husband and socially excluded from her neighbours, they form a bond. Amante rescues the pregnant Anna from her husband who plans to kill her after she discovers his true, murderous identity and organises their escape from the castle. Gaskell's description of Amante's behaviour is sexually ambiguous: 'she took me in her vigorous arms, and bore me to my room, and laid me on my bed'.[52] Amante is as active in her rescue of her mistress as Monsieur de la Tourelle has been in marrying her and removing her from her friends and family, whereas Anna remains a passive participant throughout. Amante finds a suit of men's clothes that she uses to construct a complete disguise and to transform her gender:

> she cut her own hair to the shortness of a man's, made me clip her black eyebrows as close as though they had been shaved, and by cutting up old corks into pieces such as would go into her cheeks, she altered both the shape of her face and her voice to a degree which I should not have believed possible.[53]

The reason for this extreme disguise is the physical danger they are in from Monsieur de la Tourelle and his gang of 'chauffeurs', but Anna, who is 'in an almost idiotic state', treats Amante's attempts at disguise with amusement as it if were only a charade.[54] Amante goes to extreme lengths to disguise her mistress, dying her hair and face, thickening her figure with extra clothes and even breaking one of her teeth. They escape and live together for a number of years as husband and wife, looking after Anna's daughter, with Amante earning a living by working as a tailor.

Coral Lansbury suggests that the story is an exploration of transgressive lesbian love.[55] Her theory is given weight in that Amante's assumption of masculine clothes could be said to allow her underlying gender preference freer expression. Heilmann points out the similar links made by Wilkie Collins in *The Woman in White* (1859) between Marian Halcombe's figure, which is undeformed by wearing a corset, and the growing of her moustache, suggesting unstable gendering.[56] An alternative interpretation is that the novella is a reworking of the Bluebeard story, focusing on the issue of men's repressive power over women, particularly in marriage.[57] This is perhaps to miss the other key influence on 'The Grey Woman', that of the sensation novel which peaked in popularity during the 1860s. Gaskell knew Geraldine Jewsbury, who, as a publisher's reader, had to read much sensation fiction. Gaskell was writing to Jewsbury as early as 1849 and also read, (but did not always admire), the work of Wilkie Collins.[58] Lyn Pykett points out the gender instability inherent in all sensation novels and in particular, analyses Collins' exploration of the boundaries between masculinity and femininity.[59] She argues that the reader's perception of Marion Halcombe's 'masculinity' is largely as a result of her presentation through the conventional viewpoint of Walter Hartwright. 'The Grey Woman' is set in a frame story narrated by a visitor of undefined gender to a small town in Germany, but the main narrative purports to be a letter written by the Grey Woman to her daughter. Thus the reader is presented with a woman's perception of the gender transformation of another woman.

Given the Grey Woman's initial attraction to the feminised Monsieur de la Tourelle, it is plausible to suggest that Gaskell was interested in writing about lesbian relationships, but I consider that it is the quality of the relationship that is more important to her and the provision of emotional safety and security within a home. Although 'The Grey Woman' can legitimately be viewed as a sensation novella, building on the Gothic foundations of Mrs Radcliffe and Maria Edgeworth, reworking gender stereotypes within a melodramatic setting, it is also a further example of Gaskell's belief that a stable home, however unconventional, is paramount.

The resolution of this novella, in which Amante is killed and Anna bigamously marries her doctor, is a complex layering of debates around gender as well as an illustration of Gaskell's creative use of the short story format to manipulate older narrative forms. Rose Lovell-Smith rightly claims that the death of Amante at the hands of Anna's husband introduces a new plot element into the Bluebeard story and removes 'a dangerously subversive object', along with the threat posed by the bonding of the two females.[60]

However, as Catherine Craft-Fairchild notes, Gaskell was also following the tradition of novelists between 1790 and 1835 whose cross-dressed female characters were always either socially ostracised or killed.[61] Attitudes to cross-dressing moved from an easy acceptance and even admiration in the eighteenth-century to a marked aversion in the nineteenth. Craft-Fairchild links this gender demarcation to the debate around women's roles and emerging feminist ideas. Upper-class female education in the eighteenth century was designed to display women to their best advantage in the marriage market, with an emphasis on display and appearance. In the nineteenth century, this emphasis was replaced with training women for a domestic role in which they would become the moral and spiritual guardians of the family. Cross-dressing was therefore regarded as one of the most flamboyant ways of drawing attention to oneself, and, in that sense, as a refusal to succumb to an appropriately controlled domesticity. In this context, Rosa Bonheur's wearing of dresses in a social setting is understandable, particularly if she did not wish to draw attention to her private life.

Gaskell's interpretation treads an uneasy boundary between acknowledging the courage and practicality of Amante, without which, Anna would not have survived, and ultimately sacrificing her in the interests of conventional domesticity. Cross-dressing, and the loss of chastity, as Craft-Fairchild asserts, are two transgressions that cannot be redeemed by marriage.[62]

In the next section, I examine Gaskell's portrayal of feminised men in the social and cultural context of the radical Unitarian movement.

Feminised men in Gaskell's fiction

In *Cranford*, Gaskell used the cross-dressing of Peter Jenkyns to explore the construct of masculinity and its impact on relationships within the home. Foucault argues that in the nineteenth-century, sexuality was apparently carefully confined within the home, contained by the family unit for the sole purpose of reproduction.[63] However, what he describes as 'illegitimate sexualities' flourished, and the supposedly self-contained family unit was in fact 'a complicated network, saturated with multiple, fragmentary, and mobile sexualities.'[64] Gaskell was well aware of this dichotomy between the public and the private, and the complexity of gender allocation. She was interested in the interstices where power and sexuality met, and in the negotiations which were carried out on a daily basis within the confines of the home. She explored these issues in the context of the group of reforming activists whom Kathryn Gleadle calls the 'radical Unitarians' who campaigned in the 1830s and 1840s.[65]

The Unitarian movement was tightly knit and Gaskell knew many of the key activists in the radical Unitarian group based around William Fox's South Place Chapel.[66] Fox's daughter, Tottie, was a close friend, as were Harriet Martineau and the Shaen sisters. Charles Dickens, who was also part of Fox's entourage, published three of the works considered in this chapter in *Household Words*, and William and Mary Howitt, who by the mid 1840s had established themselves at the centre of the radical Unitarian circle, published 'Clopton Hall', Gaskell's first piece of journalism. John Relly Beard, who trained with William Gaskell and was a close friend, shared Fox's views on education for women and supported the Working Women's College.[67] As Kathryn Gleadle has demonstrated, this group of radical Unitarians formed the basis of the women's rights movement of the 1850s with many of whose activists Gaskell also had strong connections.[68]

However, the aims of the radical Unitarians in the 1830s and 1840s were not simply confined to issues of women's rights. By the late 1840s, they had developed 'a powerful social, political and cultural critique of modern society, and women's role within it.'[69] While they certainly demanded the right to equal treatment with men, they articulated this within a wider concept of radical transformation, seeking a rational social model in which individuals were motivated by mutual concern, and where reform was undertaken in a number of key areas including universal suffrage, national education, and new ways of social organisation.[70] According to their Unitarian principles, home remained the primary focus for change which would then radiate out across society, and they celebrated the contribution women made to domestic and family life. John James Tayler encapsulated this belief and its grounding in associationist psychology when he stated: 'home is the source from which the virtue, the religion and the happiness of a community mainly flow.'[71] Radical Unitarians, unlike other contemporary socialist movements such as the Owenites, sought to improve and consolidate monogamous marriage. The novelist Mary Leman Grimstone, a leading figure in the early feminist movement, set out in fiery terms, the cataclysmic consequences to the home of a lack of sympathy between husband and wife:

> There are many homes in which happily, the fiend Discord is un-known; yet to which, from want of intellectual sympathy between the husband and wife, Vapidity finds its way. Discord is an incendi-ary, who fires the house over one's head, and Love, if not insured, is burnt out without remedy or redress. Vapidity is an under-miner who saps the foundation; the house falls, and Love, if not dug out in time, is buried alive.[72]

Grimstone's dramatic metaphors link the physical and emotional structures of the home and illustrate how the radical Unitarians sought to realign family life to achieve a more democratic, egalitarian balance in which both sexes had an equal partnership.

Yet as both Watts and Gleadle have shown, the liberal, rational Unitarian movement was as conflicted as the rest of nineteenth-century society. While they publicly campaigned and supported the call for women's rights, both men and women behaved very differently within the privacy of their own homes. Gaskell's letters contain a continuing dialogue with her close friends in radical Unitarian circles as she seeks to unravel the dilemma of balancing her life as a practising writer with her other varied domestic duties.[73] Her access to reading material was through William's membership of the Portico Library: 'With a struggle and a fight I can see all the Quarterlies three months after they are published: till then they live on the Portico table, for gentlemen to see. I think I will go in for Women's Rights.'[74] She was shocked when two members of Cross Street Chapel censored their wives' reading by burning their copies of *Ruth*, and a third forbade his wife to read it.[75] Yet, despite such internal conflict, Gaskell also had considerable freedom within her marriage and was able to buy The Lawn, a large house in Hampshire as a retirement home, and to keep its purchase a secret from William. John Seed claims that a patriarchal structure was normal within Unitarian families, despite publicly expressed views on the importance of education for both men and women.[76] Education for women after all, was intended to make them better mothers, and, as Seed points out, the only divine being Unitarians recognised was God the father, enabling the role of fathers within families to be appropriately sanctified.[77] Watts links the apparent contradiction between the radical views of Unitarians on the role of women and the actual circumscription of their lives to the anathema with which they were viewed by contemporary society:

> because of their anxious quest for 'respectability' in a world which anathematized their religious beliefs, they tended to mind the proprieties which restricted the lives of middle-class women, the class to which many of them belonged.[78]

One way in which women in particular were able to articulate their views and frustrations at the constraints that surrounded them was to write, and literature, as Gleadle notes, became an important weapon for the radical Unitarians.[79] George Henry Lewes, another member of Fox's radical circle, stated firmly that 'The object of Literature is to instruct, to animate, or to amuse. Any book which does one of these things succeeds; any book which does none of these things fails.'[80] An anonymous reviewer of *Ruth*, writing in the radical *Prospective Review*, claims that 'literature, while it reflects the character of the age in which it is produced, becomes, in its turn, one of the most powerful agencies by which that character is modified.'[81] However, although the moral and transformative ability of literature was important, it was the power of the written word to reveal the truth beneath the mask of convention that was its vital function.[82] The crucial truth which early feminists wanted to expose through literature was the status of women, and the way in which their characters were oppressed and malformed by social conditions.

Their work and thought was widely disseminated, and by the 1840s, writers including the Howitts, who later received civil list pensions from the government, were 'no longer perceived as an eccentric minority, but were well-known esteemed figures with a large mainstream audience.'[83] While Gaskell sympathised with the views of the feminists, supported them to a certain extent and corresponded with them as a way of trying to resolve some of the personal tensions she experienced between her domestic life and her life as a writer, she nevertheless remained conflicted and ambivalent, lingering on the borderland between convention and radical transformation. The dialogue she conducted with her friends in her letters is transmuted into her fiction, particularly in her portrayal of some feminised male figures which I regard as her contribution to the feminist debate.

I first consider Gaskell's characterisation of Tom Fletcher in 'Hand and Heart', an apparently straightforward moral tale published in the *Sunday School Penny Magazine* in 1849.[84] Tom is the only child of a widowed mother who has to work in order to support both of them. The issue of women's work was contentious, but feminists insisted that it needed to be addressed, and the short story and the novel were popular ways of exploring such ideas.[85] The focus in Gaskell's story is not on Tom's mother, but on the effect of her working on both Tom and her home. The customary view of women working was that it would lead to neglect of the home and children, but Tom's home is spotless and Tom is a boy motivated principally by his desire to do good deeds for others. It is significant that Gaskell has chosen to make the widow's only child a boy, not a girl, as this enables her to comment on the role of men and boys within the home.

Tom goes to help his neighbour, Ann Jones, who does not work, but is struggling to manage both her domestic chores and her children. Unitarians placed great emphasis on harmony within the home as this would encourage the positive associations needed to develop moral and spiritual character. Tayler addressed the parents and children at Lower Mosley Street school directly on this issue:

> a bad home, the neglect of domestic duties, the want of harmony and affection in families, the estrangement of parents from their children, and of children from their parents – is the great seat and source and principle of sin – the rank hotbed of misery and crime.[86]

Violence was abhorrent, but Ann Jones has not only lost control of her domestic duties, she also hits her children. The contrast in gender roles is made explicit: Ann Jones' behaviour has made her daughter as inept as she herself is. Her daughter, who should have been helping her mother by looking after the younger children, has failed to stop them getting a knife and cutting themselves, and she then stands by passively, too afraid to help. Ann Jones contrasts her daughter's behaviour with that of Tom: 'I wonder how it is your mother has trained you up to be so handy, Tom; you're as good as a girl; better than many a girl.'[87] The failure however is the mother's, not the daughter's.

Ann Jones, whose focus should be her home and family, has failed to train her daughter and to set her an example by association, whereas Tom's mother has trained him to undertake a feminine role so that he can be more useful in a domestic setting. Gaskell is setting out in fictional form, the views of the radical Unitarians such as Grimstone, who stated: 'Till the respective discipline under which male and female children are trained begins to operate, no dissimilarity is discernible.'[88] Tom has been feminised, and in the context of 'Hand and Heart', this is viewed as a strength.

Tom's mother dies and he goes to live with his uncle and his family. His uncle, 'a rough kind of man', is critical of Tom's upbringing which has made him 'too nesh for a boy;'[89] Tom's aunt is similar to Ann Jones: she is a tall, large woman, who speaks angrily to her children and whose house is dirty and unkempt. Tom's introduction to his uncle's house may be viewed as his transition to adulthood in that the values and training his mother gave him are now tested in the wider world. John Tosh argues that this transition was difficult for nineteenth-centry males, partly because of the emphasis on the importance of maternal nurture, and partly because of the increasing rigidity of codes of manliness which were intolerant of any feminisation.[90] Manliness meant that 'boys became men not just by growing up but by acquiring a variety of manly qualities and manly competencies.'[91] Although these qualities included chivalry and the protection of women, manliness was essentially a set of values and behaviour by which men judged each other in a public arena. Tom has however been trained by his mother in an exclusively domestic setting, and prepared for adulthood as a girl would be. His entry into his uncle's house precipitates a clash of gender roles and cultural expectations.

Tom undertakes the feminine role for which his mother has trained him and this begins to have a positive effect on the family. The critical transition point is reached when he accidentally breaks a window in trying to let fresh air into the foetid bedroom. Lack of attention to basic domestic duties and hygiene has poisoned the family who have headaches from breathing in constantly recycled air, a metaphor for the unhealthy habits in which they are trapped. Tom's remodelling of gender roles offers a new, better model of domestic living. This is not an easy rite of passage. Tom is beaten for breaking the window and prepares himself for this by praying. There is a complex iteration here of gendered roles and an association with martyrdom. Tom has explicitly fulfilled a feminine role in the home and is physically punished as a result. He accepts this with spiritual resignation and continues to seek a feminine, maternal role which will meet his need to nurture, physically and emotionally.

'Hand and Heart', in many respects, is typical of the genre of evangelical children's stories best epitomised by Mrs Sarah Trimmer which, as Claudia Nelson notes, brought their heroes and heroines to spiritual perfection through physical, mental or emotional suffering.[92] Gaskell departs from this model in her questioning of gender roles in a domestic setting. Her presentation of gender aligns both with specific Unitarian beliefs and with the arguments presented by radical Unitarians. Her insistence on the importance of men and women working together to create a spiritually and emotionally harmonious home to ensure the proper development of children is consistent with mainstream Unitarian philosophy: 'The first thing which is sure to mar the proper upbringing of children, is the want of mutual love and courtesy between the husband and the wife.'[93] Her feminisation of Tom enhances rather than detracts from his status in the household. His uncle, the titular head of the family,

> really respected him for the very qualities which are most truly 'manly'; for the courage with which he dared to do what was right, and the quiet firmness with which he bore many kinds of pain.[94]

In 'Hand and Heart', therefore, Gaskell offers a transformative model of domestic behaviour, which, as the radical Unitarians argued, re-educated men and showed how they could embrace domestic values and re-evaluate their role within the home.

Gaskell continued to explore the connections between spirituality and masculinity in her portrayal of three clergymen: Thurstan Benson in *Ruth* (1853), Mr Hale in *North and South* (1855), and Mr Gray in 'My Lady Ludlow' (1858). Historians and critics have increasingly questioned to what extent the nineteenth-century separation of public and private life, the 'two spheres', was a theoretical concept rather than something that was rigorously applied to everyday living. Tosh, for example, points out that men were able to pass freely between the two settings and that this was integral to the social order.[95] Clergymen, like William Gaskell, worked from home and in Chapter 1, I discussed the ways in which this impacted on family life. I suggest here that in her fictional representation of these clergymen, Gaskell was continuing to explore the arguments of the radical Unitarians about the need for reform across a wide range of social issues and to analyse how this impacted on the roles and domestic relationships of men and women.

The introduction of Thurstan Benson into the narrative of *Ruth* is destabilising. Ruth is crossing a stream, and Gaskell uses the landscape as a metaphor to comment obliquely on her situation as Bellingham's mistress. The water of the stream runs 'high and rapidly, as busy as life, between the pieces of grey rock.'[96] Ruth's sexuality is at its peak, but in her innocence, she has no fear and does not see the hidden dangers of her situation. The rushing water, like the clacking tongues in *Cranford*, represents the noise of gossip and chatter, and the rocks the hidden dangers for those who diverge from the accepted social model. In the middle of the stream however, is a great gap, and Ruth hesitates, her ears filled with the sound of rushing water and her eyes on the current which would sweep her away. This is the critical moment in the novel when she first becomes aware of how her position as Bellingham's mistress has excluded her from the rest of society. There is a gulf between her and the rest of the world, one she will be unable to bridge without help. The landscape in *Ruth* at this point is reminiscent of that in spiritual autobiography such as John Bunyan's *Pilgrim's Progress*. Ruth must cross the river and go through the woods to reach the pasture land beyond. She is so intent on her dilemma that she neither sees nor hears Benson who startles her by appearing before her on one of the stones and offering his help.

Benson's unexpected entrance into this allegorial landscape gives him a quasi-mythical status similar to the effect produced by Job Legh surrounded by his cabalistic instruments in *Mary Barton* (1838). The effect is enhanced by the description of his physical appearance:

> She looked up and saw a man, who was apparently long past middle life, and of the stature of a dwarf; a second glance accounted for the low height of the speaker, for then she saw he was deformed.[97]

At this point, the narrative almost tips from realist fiction to fairytale, or what could be described as an early example of magic realism. Benson's quotation from Keble's poem, 'St Matthew', from *The Christian Year*, locates the reader in contemporary spirituality, but his reference to a Welsh legend about a foxglove, while in keeping with Unitarian belief that everything forms part of a spiritual chain of association, also suggests his links with magic and a pagan past.

Benson's physical appearance and disability can also be related to the sometimes agonized contemporary debate that revolved around issues of masculinity and androgyny.[98] Ruth's attention is captured not just by Benson's stature and deformed back – which imply that he is not sexually active, less of a man – but by his beautiful face with its spiritual light in the eyes. Nelson points out that some religious writers made the case for an androgynous Christ and God, and suggests that this platonic equation of androgyny and divinity was particularly attractive to mid-Victorian moralists.[99] I consider that Gaskell's portrayal of Benson is also a fictionalised account of the changes that were occurring in Unitarian belief during this period. James Martineau, who was a friend of the Gaskells, introduced a more introspective form of the Unitarian faith, profoundly influenced by German romanticism, that encouraged action based on the examination of inner feelings.[100] Kay Millard argues convincingly that Gaskell was attracted to the renewed interest in personal spirituality preached by Martineau, and the American Transcendentalism of which her close friend, Charles Eliot Norton, was a leading exponent.[101] Martineau's grounding of the spiritual in the everyday, his argument that 'a soul occupied with great ideas best performs small duties' and his contention that even the highest intellects benefit from carrying out minor domestic tasks, appealed to Gaskell's own insistence on the importance of practical charity, a characteristic which found a natural outlet in her lifelong work with Sunday Schools.[102]

Benson's 'feminine morbidness of conscience' predisposes him to look inwards and to follow his own personal and ideological convictions, and this is both a strength and a weakness.[103] Benson has strong nurturing instincts which are associated both with a caring God who acts as father to his children, and also with the nineteenth-century adoration of the figure of the mother.

As a pastor, Benson views Ruth's pregnancy and motherhood as a way to bring her back to a spiritual life. As a man, his reaction to the news of her seduction is feminised. He blushes at the realisation of her 'profligacy' and is so passionate in his defence of Ruth that 'The tears were full in his eyes: he almost trembled in his earnestness. He was faint with the strong power of his own conviction.'[104] Benson has spent the afternoon contemplating the problems Ruth is facing and this more reflective, transcendental approach to spirituality is in line with the radical Unitarian view that God resided within the individual.[105] This is a feminised form of spirituality, based on emotion and insight rather than the earlier rational approach founded on the harsh necessarianism of Priestley.[106] Benson's passionate outburst can therefore be viewed as an active portrayal of the new approach to Unitarianism.

However, Benson's feminine, nurturing traits and his emotional reaction to Ruth's pregnancy also make him weak. His ability to decisively assert his moral and spiritual authority is affected by his quasi-maternal instinct to protect Ruth's unborn child. His sister Faith persuades him to pass Ruth off as a widow to avoid scandal and in succumbing to this temptation, Benson offends against the Unitarian belief in the primacy of truth. As William Gaskell was to point out in a sermon of 1862, it is those who 'with brave outspoken sincerity denounce what they believe to be wrong and maintain what they hold to be right, that ever most effectually move and reform the world'.[107]

Faith's influence over her brother also raises questions about gendered relationships within the home. Benson is small of stature because of his deformity, and in some respects, this has infantilised him and given Faith a quasi-maternal role in relationship to him. He lacks the maturity and unquestioned authority within the home to which as the adult male, he would be entitled. As an early reviewer of *Ruth* pointed out, his decision 'was the pivot on which moved the destiny of years, and he turned it wrong.'[108] However, this pivotal moment in the novel is more complex than a decision made by one individual, and at this point of tension between the public and the private, within the privacy of the home, it is internal domestic relationships that most affect external public behaviour. It is the feminised Benson who agonises about the spiritually correct way to deal with Ruth's dilemma and the forthright Faith, guardian of the home, who persuades him to modify his beliefs to supply a more socially acceptable solution.

Mr Hale in *North and South* (1855) also faces a spiritual dilemma which has a direct impact on his family and domestic relationships, and he too, is presented as a feminised male. He is fine boned, and his physical similarity to his daughter Margaret is marked. His weakness is made explicit by his habit of 'half-opening his mouth as if to speak, which constantly unsettled the form of the lips, and gave the face an undecided expression.'[109] He has always been shy and withdrawn and his college friends treat him 'with something of the protecting kindness which they would have shown to a woman.'[110] Anxiety is his dominant emotion, antithetical to cultural expectations of his role as a man and as a member of the clergy which would require him to act with authority and decision.

Jill Matus notes how powerful emotion is not conventionally gendered in *North and South*.[111] A number of male characters including Frederick Hale, John Thornton and Nicholas Higgins are unafraid to openly express profound emotion in contrast to contemporary codes of masculinity which emphasized a cerebral containment of emotion.[112] Mr Hale's femininity is not a weakness in itself, rather, it is his anxiety and his failure to manage it which contributes to his failure to support his family, and the decline and eventual death of both his wife and himself. Mr Hale's unconventional gendering is balanced by that of Margaret who is increasingly forced to take on a parental and adult role within the home, and to make authoritative decisions about where and how the family will live. Her journeys around Milton and her visits to the Higgins family may be viewed as a version of the pastoral role her father undertook in Helstone as well as a comment on the role of the domestic visitor.

In her characterisation of Mr Hale then, Gaskell seems to be contributing to the arguments of the radical Unitarians in a number of ways. The group supported the views and actions of enlightened manufacturers such as the Greg brothers and others known to Gaskell, who sought to establish new ways of working intended to meet the wider needs of their employees and to improve labour and class relations.[113] This discussion is a key narrative theme in the novel, and Mr Hale plays an important part in assisting the two sides of the debate to be articulated. On a more intimate, domestic level, Gaskell explores the possibility of a balanced harmonious gendering which accepts the unacknowledged feminine within men, and allows a wider, more public role for women. This was part of the argument the radical Unitarians were making for transformative change for both men and women.

Mr Gray in 'My Lady Ludlow' (1858) is openly campaigning for radical change based on education for the working classes, a key component of the Unitarian faith. He is described as 'A very pretty young man.'[114] His physical appearance is more feminine than masculine; he is small of stature and blushes easily. He is verbally as well as physically awkward, and finds it difficult to speak without choking and coughing. However his radical tendencies are evidenced by his hair, which is frizzy, red and unpowdered. The colour and texture of the hair suggests an innate energy, and the lack of powder, as the narrator carefully explains, is 'reckoned very revolutionary and Jacobin'.[115] He is more sensitive than the young women who live with Lady Ludlow, blushing redder than ever at the sight of them while they composedly curtsey to him. Like Mr Hale and Thurston Benson, he is very emotional, and tears of passion are in his eyes when he tries to persuade Lady Ludlow to intervene with the magistrates on behalf of the poacher, Job Gregson. In his anxiety to speak to Lady Ludlow, he is oblivious to social boundaries and bursts out with his request in the public space of the entrance hall, rather than waiting to be conducted to Lady Ludlow's parlour where she would normally conduct the business of the estate.

Mr Gray's transgression can be interpreted in two ways. It illustrates his determination to transform local society by breaking down boundaries of class and hierarchy. He insists that Lady Ludlow listens to his account of the miscarriage of justice against Job Gregson which has occurred because of class and social relationships among the magistracy rather than evidence of guilt. He educates her just as he wants to educate the working-class people on the estate by making her aware that 'good family' does not automatically imply good judgement.

A parallel interpretation is to view the incident as a comment on gendered roles in society. Mr Gray may be a feminised man, but he is nonetheless both powerful enough to defy convention, and determined enough to insist on being heard. He confronts Lady Ludlow, the representative of social order and class-based hegemony with courage and dignity, drawing himself up to his full height to speak to her: 'Little as was his stature, and awkward and embarrassed as he had been only a few minutes before, I remember thinking he looked almost as grand as my lady when he spoke.'[116] The physical characteristic most associated with Mr Gray is the blush and his dominant emotion is tears. Yet despite the continuous allusions to his size and feminised appearance and behaviour, it is Mr Gray who remains absolutely true to his ideals and his moral purpose, and who unswervingly keeps to the goals he has set himself. It is he who is the catalyst for fundamental change in the feudal society run by the benign dictatorship of Lady Ludlow.

3 - SEX, SECRETS AND STABILITY: DOMESTIC ARTEFACTS AND RITUALS

The interior of a nineteenth-century home was full of coded signifiers that provided spatial representations of their inhabitants. It was a showcase in which the taste and domestic skills of the occupiers could be displayed to public view, so that visiting or any kind of social contact became a performative art. In 'Company Manners', Gaskell describes the range of preparations that contributed to a successful social occasion from cleaning the house, to the selection of guests and the choice and presentation of food. Even apparently informal and specifically gendered events, such as a tea party 'nominally private to the ladies', becomes a site for negotiating more intimate relationships that challenge conventional cultural boundaries.[1] Thematically, some objects or settings recur in Gaskell's fiction, for example, the use of fire and windows as symbolic representations of morality and repression. Gaskell also uses domestic objects to comment obliquely on sexuality or to indicate intimacy. The history of domestic objects mirrors that of their owners: for example, inherited artefacts such as Squire Hamley's watch represent stability, a link with the past and the security of continuity, whereas the loss of the Bartons' possessions as their economic fortunes decline is a stark symbol of the social and emotional displacement of poor families. I begin this chapter with the codified messages contained in the detailed descriptions of domestic interiors in *North and South* (1855).

In *North and South*, Gaskell uses descriptions of domestic interiors to 'place' Margaret Hale socially and to chart her journey from a sheltered childhood to an adult appreciation of a wider social and cultural environment. Margaret's progress towards maturity mirrors Gaskell's own move from the sheltered middle-class comfort of Knutsford to her first home in Dover Street, Manchester, on the edge of the working-class district of Ardwick.

When Henry Lennox visits Margaret in Helstone to assess her suitability as his possible wife, he makes a careful appraisal of the drawing room into which he is shown:

> The little drawing-room was looking its best in the streaming light of the morning sun. The middle window in the bow was opened, and clustering roses and the scarlet honeysuckle came peeping round the corner; the small lawn was gorgeous with verbenas and geraniums of all bright colours.[2]

The open window, with the sun streaming in reflects the simplicity and honesty of the Hales. The colour and vibrancy of the plants suggest Margaret's exotic sensuality and fecundity, emphasised by the way in which the plants intrude into the house through the open window. This, together with Margaret's nostalgic attachment to Helstone as a pastoral idyll, leads Lennox to misread her character as that of a conventional 'angel in the house', just as Thornton will later similarly misread her. But the bright light also illuminates the intrinsic financial poverty of the Hales:

> The carpet was far from new; the chintz had been often washed; the whole apartment was smaller and shabbier than he had expected, as the background for Margaret, herself so queenly.[3]

The drawing room was simultaneously one of the most public rooms in the house and yet the most intimate in terms of its decoration. It was the space into which visitors were shown, and was therefore an important showcase for objects such as furniture and paintings that indicated the wealth and social status of the family. It was also an essentially feminine and intimate space, used as a private retreat by family members, in which tasteful artefacts made by women could be displayed as signifiers of their skill and ability to create an appropriate domestic environment. A whole industry developed around the production of these objects. A single volume of *Cassell's Household Guide* includes a plethora of articles on leather work, diaphanie (the art of imitating stained glass), imitating marble busts and statuettes in wax, paper flower-making, feather screens and clay modelling.[4]

The Hales' drawing room is clean: the upholstery is faded but washed, and the sunlight does not show up any dust or marks. Gaskell was typical of her contemporaries in persistently and explicitly associating cleanliness with high moral standards.[5] It is clear, therefore, that the Hales, although poor, are ethically immaculate. Yet there is no indication of the drawing room being used as a setting for Margaret's decorative needlework, artwork, flower arrangements or any of the expected ornamentation. It is simple, uncluttered and old-fashioned, a comfortable domestic setting for the family. It becomes clear later in the novel, when Margaret visits the Thorntons, that she has remarkably little in the way of traditional feminine accomplishments, her only apparent talent being for sketching.[6] Gaskell thus subtly indicates from the start of the novel that this is no conventional heroine, taught, like her cousin Edith, to display herself to her best advantage in the marriage market by the acquisition of suitable, decorative skills. In Gaskell's detailed description of the Hales' drawing room, it is the absence of objects, rather than their presence, that is telling.[7]

Instead, like Phillis Holman, Margaret is more interested in educating herself and in the rigours of debate, since, like Gaskell herself, she loves a good argument. Gaskell discusses the presence of books in a room in 'Company Manners', arguing that books should be part of the indispensable furniture of a successful salon, not something artificially chosen and displayed simply when visitors are expected.[8] Dante's *Paradiso* is naturally integrated into the domestic furnishings of the Hale's drawing room, lying next to a dictionary and some vocabulary which Margaret has copied out.

This simple collection of objects however contains a number of coded messages. Helstone appears to be a rural paradise, and Margaret's reading of the *Paradiso* is therefore an apparently apt choice.[9] The edition is an old one, 'in the proper old Italian binding of white vellum and gold'.[10] The binding indicates serious scholarship and authenticity. This impression is confirmed by the list of vocabulary lying alongside it that Margaret has copied out for further study. Lennox thinks the list dull, an indication both of his own superficiality, and of his misreading of Margaret, who is willing to apply herself so that she can understand the text at more than a superficial level. Margaret's willingness to engage with the *Paradiso*, and the linking of the text with her immediate surroundings, prefigures the way in which she will engage with her new home in Milton, in an environment that appears at first to be socially and culturally alienating, and where she also has to learn a new industrial language. Finally, the appearance of the book suggests an association with the past and 'old money' for as Lennox remarks to himself, 'the Beresfords belong to a good family'.[11]

Lennox's cold-blooded scrutiny of the Hales' circumstances is the reaction of a worldly London lawyer. Margaret's powerful sexuality is indicated by the fact that he 'has been carried out of his usual habits by the force of a passion'.[12] This is contrasted with John Thornton's first visit to the Hales at their new home in Milton, where Gaskell's detailed description of the drawing room consolidates and deepens the developing narrative themes. Coral Lansbury notes that Froude, whom Gaskell met when he was working as a tutor for her friends, the Darbishires, recognised the Hales' drawing room as a mirror image of his own, and asserts that Froude gave his employees in Manchester the same traditional scholarship that Thornton receives from Mr Hale:[13]

> Here were no mirrors, not even a scrap of glass to reflect the night [...] a warm, sober breadth of colouring, well relieved by the dear old Helstone chintz-curtains and chair covers. An open davenport stood in the window opposite the door; in the other there was a stand, with a tall white china vase, from which dropped wreaths of English ivy, pale-green birch, and copper-coloured beech-leaves. Pretty baskets of work stood about in different places; and books, not cared for on account of their binding solely, lay on one table, as if recently put down. Behind the door was another table, decked out for tea, with a white table-cloth, on which flourished the cocoa-nut cakes, and a basket piled with oranges and ruddy American apples, heaped on leaves.[14]

Mirrors were an essential feature of Victorian drawing and dining rooms. They were usually incorporated into an overmantel placed above the fireplace so that the overmantel became the dominant decorative feature.[15] Mirrors and gilding were intended to provide a decorative effect, particularly at night when the glow of gas and candle light would be reflected off their surfaces. Here, Thornton is aware only of softness, and a lamp which 'threw a pretty light into the centre of the dusky room, from which with country habits, they did not exclude the night-skies and the outer darkness of air'.[16] Unlike Lennox, who saw the drawing room at Helstone in the full glare of afternoon sunlight, Thornton enters a seductive nest, similar to the drawing room in Harley Street, where Margaret finds her cousin curled up asleep on the sofa in a tumble of muslin and blue ribbons. The shift from early afternoon to early evening suggests that Margaret has already progressed into a more adult role, as indeed she has, by taking on full responsibility for finding and moving the family into their new home.[17] It is she who has taken the decision to light the lamp, indicating her position of authority in the household. The shabby, much washed covers have become 'the dear old Helstone chintz-curtains and chair covers', and the sober colouring suggests the moral seriousness and social status of the Hales in contrast to the 'vulgarity and commonness' of the wallpaper that was previously in the room – 'Pink and blue roses, with yellow leaves!'[18]

Margaret's reaction to the floral wallpaper reflects contemporary discourse about colour and pattern as wallpapers and carpets began to be mass-produced and took over from stencilling, which had virtually disappeared by the mid-1870s. From mid-century onwards, there was a proliferation of publications offering advice on interior design ranging from articles in professional magazines such as *The British Architect,* to guidance in manuals like *Cassell's Household Guide.*[19] This was a response to the Great Exhibition of 1851, after which issues of taste and design began to be widely discussed.[20] Charles Eastlake and Owen Jones were two influential writers who inveighed against the way in which fashion dictated taste. Jones was instrumental in founding the Department of Practical Art in 1852 which sought to improve the design and production of domestic objects.[21] Eastlake outlined the basic tenets of good design, insisting on a flat design for a flat surface such as wallpaper and carpets:

> commonsense points to the fact, that as a wall represents the flat surface of a solid material, which forms part of the construction of a house, it should be decorated after a manner which will belie neither its flatness nor solidity. For this reason all shaded ornament and patterns, which by their arrangement of color give an appearance of relief, should be strictly avoided. Where natural forms are introduced,

they should be treated in a conventional manner, i.e. drawn in pure outline, and filled in with flat color, never rounded.[22]

Jones gives a vivid picture of the sort of wallpapers Margaret found so offensive, complaining about the difficulty of finding a wallpaper that was not both three dimensional and luridly unnaturalistic:

> Either we have large masses of conventional foliage, in high apparent relief, surrounding masses of unbroken colour, or representations of flowers, fruits, and ribbons twisted into the most unwarrantable of positions: nothing is more common than to find strawberries and cherries, or other equally impossible combinations, growing on the same stalk; and although great pains are taken to make the fruits and flowers as much like nature as the paper-stainer's art can make them, this imitative skill only increases the inconsistency.[23]

Wallpaper should act as a background, 'and nothing on it should be obtrusive or advancing to the eye,' he stated, advice that was reiterated in *Cassell's Household Guide* which informed its readers that although wallpapers were generally provided by landlords for their tenants, 'a landlord's tastes in art matters are by no means to be implicitly relied upon', and

> it is not improbable that this gratuitous decorative feature will be one which it would be unwise to regard as the key-note, [...] By far the wiser plan, therefore, if the paper be of an unsatisfactory design, [...] is to have it immediately replaced with one which is in every respect, agreeable, and based on the sound principles already explained.[24]

The seasonal display of leaves in the drawing room signifies a tasteful response to nature, illustrating not only Margaret's personal nostalgia for the lost paradise of Helstone, but also a wider need within Victorian society to maintain connections with the natural world that were threatened by the industrial revolution and the concomitant loss of a rural past. Gaskell's friend, Harriet Beecher Stowe advised her readers:

> If you live in the country, or can get into the country, and have your eyes opened and your wits about you, your house need not be condemned to absolute bareness. Not so long as the woods are full

of beautiful ferns and mosses, while every swamp shakes and nods with tremulous grasses, need you feel yourself an utterly disinherited child of nature, and deprived of its artistic use.[25]

Gaskell was familiar with *The Language of Flowers*, originally published in France in 1818, which spawned over 150 similar dictionaries.[26] In the language of flowers, ivy represents fidelity and friendship, suggesting the positive benefits of a connection between Margaret and Thornton.

The Hales' drawing room is an essentially feminine space, typical of the period with its scatter of small tables and workbaskets. The open davenport and books, clearly being used and read, indicate a family actively engaged in literary activities:

> In a parlour, books ought to have an honoured place. It is where the family work and play; and instead of being allowed to appear untidy and neglected, it should represent that culture and refinement which is now happily within the reach of almost every one however poor.[27]

However, the choice of food on the table is interestingly exotic. The piles of fruit on leaves echo Lennox's visit to Helstone when Margaret 'made a plate for the pears out of a beetroot leaf, which threw up their brown colour admirably',[28] a stylistic presentation admired by Mrs Loftie who asserted that 'if fresh leaves of the fruit can be had as garnishing they are a great addition.'[29] Oranges and coconuts are visual evocations of far-flung destinations in the Empire, and in this context, can also be seen as an early hint of Frederick's return from exile.

The Thorntons' home, where Mrs Thornton sits in a 'grim handsomely-furnished dining-room' is in sharp contrast to that of the Hales.[30] There are no books 'with the exception of Matthew Henry's Bible Commentaries, six volumes of which lay in the centre of the massive side-board, flanked by a tea-urn on one side and a lamp on the other.'[31] The reference to Henry, an authoritative non-conformist theologian, may have hinted at the modelling of Thornton on Samuel Greg, the Gaskell's industrialist friend, who was a distant relative of Henry.[32] The choice of spiritually improving reading matter, God, the water of life and the light of the world ironically positioned between mundane domestic objects, raises questions about the uses of traditional literacy in a mercantile world.[33] The biblical commentaries also emphasise the rigid conventionality of the Thorntons and are perhaps, in addition, a comment on what was considered suitable reading material for women.[34] The solidity of the furnishings and the harsh functionality of the room suggest a masculine environment in which Mrs Thornton, with her large-boned frame, is competently at ease. Her prosperity is indicated by her 'stout black silk, of which not a thread was worn or discoloured.'[35] Yet the fine needlework in which she is engaged requires a delicate and sensitive touch that hints at a more empathetic side to the character of the firm, dignified woman whose face and character are apparently equally impassive and unyielding.

Gaskell, like Mrs Loftie, is acutely aware of the way in which domestic objects, such as table linen, are imbued with memory and history: 'In old times a lady took pride in her linen closet, and knew every table-cloth by name. Each piece had its story.'[36] Mrs Thornton's table cloth is of the finest texture and requires 'her delicate care.'[37] Gaskell indicates in this detail that the Thorntons too have a long and proud history. She would be aware, just as Mrs Loftie was, that:

> Home-grown, hand-spun, hand-woven, sun-bleached flax wore for so many years that with the care it received it descended through many generations. The mending of precious damask was not left to servants, but attended to by the lady of the house, whose deft fingers could weave the ravellings she kept for the purpose into the exact pattern of the worn piece.[38]

Angus Easson notes how in Gaskell's writing, objects are often used to project and focus emotion which might otherwise have to be conveyed more self-consciously in a way that would compromise dramatic integrity and the carefully constructed realism of her settings.[39] He notes the poignancy of the similar scene, later in the novel, when Mrs Thornton unpicks the initials on her table linen in preparation, as she thinks, for the marriage of her son to Margaret. It is the only point at which Thornton's father is given a name, and as Easson notes, a whole subtext of their lives together is alluded to. The forward narrative, he asserts, is suspended and the narrative is enriched and deepened in a manner which is psychologically and emotionally apt.

Thornton's experience of the Hales' drawing room seduces him, and causes him to reinterpret the style and presentation of his own home.[40] However, it has the opposite effect on his mother. On her first visit to the Hales, Margaret is embroidering some cambric for a dress for Edith's baby, which Mrs Thornton despises as non-functional, preferring Mrs Hale's practical double knitting. She notes that: 'The room altogether was full of knick-knacks, which must take a long time to dust; and time to people of limited income was money.'[41]

Thad Logan quotes a domestic manual of 1889 which estimates that a thorough daily cleaning of the drawing room would take about three hours, since 'all the ornaments have to be removed to another room or packed on a central table and covered with a clean dust sheet.'[42] Since *Cassell's Household Guide* suggests allocating approximately half of a household's annual income to housekeeping, including laundry, this puts Mrs Thornton's disdain into pragmatic focus.[43] The appearance of the room and its contents reinforce misunderstandings and highlight the clash of cultures. Unfavourable first impressions continue with Margaret's visit to Mrs Thornton's drawing room:

> The walls were pink and gold: the pattern on the carpet represented bunches of flowers on a light ground, but it was carefully covered up in the centre by a linen drugget, glazed and colourless. The window-curtains were lace; each chair and sofa had its own particular veil of netting, or knitting. Great alabaster groups occupied every flat surface, safe from dust under their glass shades. In the middle of the room, right under the bagged-up chandelier, was a large circular table, with smartly-bound books arranged at regular intervals round the circumference of its polished surface, like gaily-coloured spokes of a wheel. Everything reflected light, nothing absorbed it.[44]

Logan notes how domestic manuals give conflicting advice about the use of the parlour or drawing room. One for example states that 'Many families breakfast in the dining room, and remain there till after dinner, only using the drawing-room in the evening.'[45] The dining room was therefore a multi-functional room for most middle-class families, and of course, Gaskell herself wrote in the dining-room at Plymouth Grove.[46] Mrs Loftie declares confidently that:

> In the same way that in small houses the drawing-room cannot be
> spared for the exclusive use of afternoon callers, so the room de-
> signed by the architect for feeding is generally too good to be set
> apart and only inhabited for about three hours of the twenty-four. It
> thus arises that the eating room, perhaps the best in the house, must
> in large families often serve either as parlour, study or schoolroom.[47]

Mrs Thornton clearly is of the same opinion, and the spending of her
days in this cold, uncomfortable room reflects the iron control she has had to
take over her life. It is a public statement of her moral rectitude.[48]

Mrs Thornton's economical and practical approach to domestic chores
ensures that the whole room has been bagged up, both to protect the furniture and ornaments from the constant dust and grime of central Milton and
the adjoining factory, and to save time and money on unnecessary cleaning,
following the advice of the redoubtable Mrs Loftie:

> It is provoking to find how much money it costs [...] to prevent
> rooms from assuming that dingy tone which robs all delicate fabrics
> of their charm. Smuts and fogs are dreadful enemies to cope with,
> unless a long purse and plenty of servants can be brought into the
> field. Much however may be done to fight this dragon of dirt by
> providing plenty of clean dust-covers to throw over the furniture
> at night, and to remain on until the rooms have been thoroughly
> cleaned in the morning.[49]

In his article on *Cranford* and its similarities to the kinds of decorative objects
produced by Victorian women, Tim Dolin describes the need the Victorians
had to encapsulate and contain objects and information through the use of
categories, lists and buildings such as the public museum.[50] He argues that
the Crystal Palace under its glass dome was perhaps the crowning expression of this 'concern with congregation'.[51] As the tone of the preface to the
*Official Descriptive and Illustrated Catalogue of the Great Exhibition of the Works of
Industry of All Nations* (1851) makes clear, there was also a fundamental underlying anxiety to control disorder and chaos through classification and explanation.[52] The alabaster groups under their glass domes in the Thorntons'

dining room are a miniature version of the Crystal Palace, and also reflect the hard industrial focus of the family. The catalogue of the Great Exhibition records a display of various specimens of stone, including alabaster from Derbyshire, so the Thorntons' choice of ornament is appropriately local, particularly since during the 1840s and 1850s, wax flowers, displayed under glass, were the height of fashion.[53] As *Cassell's Household Guide* points out, there were also good practical reasons for keeping ornaments under glass. In the case of alabaster, they would need cleaning about twice a year with a solution of acqua fortis and water if they were not kept under a shade.[54]

The room is also resonant with a number of other coded messages. By the mid-nineteenth century, technological advances made the mass production of consumer goods possible on a hitherto unrealised scale. This was accompanied by a plethora of domestic manuals providing advice on a range of issues associated with the rituals of daily life, often illustrated by advertisements which preyed on consumer fears.[55] The Thorntons have acquired the appropriate fixtures and fittings to showcase their wealth and status. However, they do not feel able to enjoy their home, unlike the Hales, whose comfortably worn furnishings suggest confidence in their social position. When the covers are removed for the Thorntons' dinner party,

> the apartment blazed forth in yellow silk damask and a brilliantly-flowered carpet. Every corner seemed filled up with ornament, until it became a weariness to the eye, and presented a strange contrast to the bald ugliness of the look-out into the great mill-yard.[56]

Gaskell's description of the Thorntons' dining room and the social occasion of the dinner party neatly captures the period's social mobility and the discourse around the nature of gentility.[57] The well-known photograph of Mrs Gaskell's drawing room at Plymouth Grove shows an interior that, although cluttered to modern eyes, is more akin to the Hales' parlour in terms of ornamentation and comfort.

> Over the years it had become more cluttered. During Elizabeth's time the crinoline was fashionable so furniture needed more space between pieces. [...] the paintwork was a shade of cream with gold leaf on the cornice and door panel [...] Elizabeth possessed several

Paisley shawls where the colours used tended to be warm [...] several of these colours occur in the wallpaper. [...] The chintz she mentions had rosebuds and carnations, presumably pink.[58]

Gaskell is making a value judgement about the Thorntons' decorative style which has followed the dictates of contemporary fashion rather than personal taste. The fixtures and fabrics are of the highest quality, bought to demonstrate their wealth, but the effect is sterile as well as garish. The knowledge contained in their books is not valued: they are for ornament only. The physical environment of the room has shut down all debate and any possibility of contentious conversation. It is a carefully set stage that reflects the aspirations of its owners rather than their character, a safe context, within which the very rigidity of accepted rules and rituals offers protection to those who are socially uncertain.

Gaskell also uses domestic objects in *North and South* to comment obliquely on sexuality or to indicate intimacy. As Hilary Schor observes, perhaps the most interesting innovation in *North and South* is the way in which Gaskell eroticises economic and social issues.[59] The focus of Margaret's sexuality for Thornton is her hands and arms, and Gaskell uses the single ornament of the bracelet, continually slipping down Margaret's arm, to draw the reader into Thornton's fascination and to create a moment of intimacy:

> Mr Thornton watched the re-placing of this troublesome ornament with far more attention than he listened to her father. It seemed as if it fascinated him to see her push it up impatiently, until it tightened her soft flesh; and then to mark the loosening – the fall. He could almost have exclaimed – "There it goes, again!"[60]

The slipping bracelet suggests the tightening and loosening of corseted clothing and enables Gaskell to subtly indicate a moment of considerable eroticism. Thornton then watches Margaret's father, 'who took her little finger and thumb in his masculine hand, and made them serve as sugar-tongs'.[61] Their byplay acts as a substitute for Thornton's desire to capture Margaret as her father captures her fingers, thus eliding the closeness of Margaret's relationship with her father and his innocent unawareness of her maturity with her sexuality.[62]

Sylvia Robson's father in *Sylvia's Lovers* (1863) uses her 'little finger as a stopper to ram down the tobacco – a habit of his to which she was so accustomed that she laid her hand on the table by him,'[63] Sylvia and her father are both passionate and headstrong, and this moment of domestic interplay with its easy intimacy enables Gaskell economically to illustrate their strong bond at the same time as enhancing the credibility of her characters' setting and behaviour. She also hints at Philip's lack of masculinity. He does not smoke, and unlike Thornton, has no sexualised reaction to Daniel's use of Sylvia's finger to tamp his pipe. He would prefer to continue the debate about the French, and knows that he will not get a chance to speak unless Daniel has his pipe in his mouth.

Such interactions take place within a domestic setting whose physical features also contain coded messages. On her return to her former home at Helstone, Margaret sees that the parsonage is altered. New windows have been added to open up the view:

> From it the wandering sheep of her husband's flock might be seen, who struggled to the tempting beer-house [...] his parishioners [...] had need of quick legs if they could take refuge in the 'Jolly Forester' before the teetotal Vicar had arrested them.[64]

The opening up of the building reflects the way in which the new Vicar is keen to actively enter his parishioners' lives and provide for their spiritual care. His muscular Christianity, 'brisk, loud-talking, kind-hearted, and not troubled with much delicacy of perception'[65] is not subject to the scruples that tormented Mr. Hale. When the Hales lived at Helstone, the character of the family was reflected in their home where even a stray rose-leaf on the lawn 'seemed like a fleck on its exquisite arrangement and propriety'.[66] Elegance and sensitivity have been replaced 'with signs of merry, healthy, rough childhood'.[67] Gaskell uses her descriptions of the parsonage to comment obliquely on the scruples and sensitivities of the Hales. Neither Mr nor Mrs Hale are able to make the transition successfully to Milton: they belong to a gentler, more stable, romanticised past in which a rose-leaf out of place is of more concern than the villagers Margaret sketches living in an uninhabitable cottage. Margaret, who starts her journey with arrogance and prejudice, exacerbated by her enforced expulsion from the paradise of Helstone, learns to tolerate difference and to accept change.

The fireplace, the central feature of any nineteenth-century room, symbolises the core of the domestic ethos and Gaskell fully exploits this contemporary metaphor. Logan notes that

> The hearth had for Victorians a practical and symbolic centrality in the home and thus was a site at which both functional and ornamental objects were concentrated.[68]

and Philippa Tristram comments that 'One might with only slight exaggeration claim that firelight illuminates virtually every positive page in Victorian novels.'[69] The title of Alexander Boyd's advertising pamphlet published in 1874, *The English Fireplace: Its Advantages, its Objections and its rivals. Considered with a view to utility and economy* illustrates how the marketing of products was blended with practical advice on the best type of fire and fuel for each room of the house.[70] The Stowe sisters devote two entire chapters of their domestic advice manual to 'Scientific Domestic Ventilation' and 'Stoves, Furnaces and Chimneys'.[71]

A well-kept fire and a clean hearth conveyed a range of messages about the morality of the house's inhabitants, a woman's domestic competence, and the wealth and physical security of the family. In *Mary Barton* (1848), for example, the damped down fire keeps a perpetual form of life in the house, a Lares and Penates, that represents the health of the family and its relationships, whereas Alice Wilson's 'damp coals, and half-green sticks' are an economic shorthand for her constant struggle to keep alive despite her poverty and deprivation.[72] When the elder son in 'The Half-Brothers' (1856) is dying from exposure on the moors in a snowstorm, he thinks about his family 'sitting round the warm, red, bright fire'.[73] This is the only spot of colour in a bleak, monochrome story of family estrangement and jealousy. The fire represents the brother's realisation of the importance of his family and his desire to return home and re-build his relationship with them. The image associates fire as a source of heat at the centre of the house, and links it to the heart, which circulates heat around the body and is traditionally associated with emotion.

Gaskell's personal preference was for a wood fire, which she saw as a living companion:

> A wood-fire has a kind of spiritual, dancing, glancing life about it. It is an elvish companion, crackling, hissing, bubbling: throwing out beautiful jets of vivid many-coloured flame.[74]

She loved the intimacy of firelight, the atmospheric possibilities it offered for telling stories and the fun and informality of cooking over a fire, even when this had unexpected consequences: 'We set the fat on fire & had to run out of doors out of the window blazing pan in hand, amidst screams of children.'[75] Fire was often the most economical way to light as well as heat a room, and Gaskell understood how the exchange of confidences was easier in the warmth and soft glow of firelight. In 'The Moorland Cottage' (1850) for example, Maggie and Frank are unable to talk about the death of Frank's mother:

> Maggie shut the casement, and put a log of wood on the fire. She sat down with her back to the window; but as the flame sprang up, and blazed at the touch of the dry wood, Frank saw that her face was wet with quiet tears.[76]

Maggie closes the window, just as Miss Matty shuts and locks the door in *Cranford* when she is telling Mary Smith the story of Peter's expulsion from the town, to exclude the outside world and ensure privacy. She throws wood onto the fire knowing that the light will reveal her emotions because she is willing to share her grief with Frank, and understands his need to hear about his mother's final illness.

Fire is a living thing, and its fluctuations can represent the ebb and flow of emotion. In 'Martha Preston' (1850), when the doctor confirms that her brother is mentally affected, Martha sits all night in front of her dying fire. The 'gray embers among which the sparks ran to and fro' represent both her internal struggle as she decides whether or not to marry Will Hawkshaw, and the final extinguishing of her hope of marriage and fulfilment as she accepts that her duty is to care for her brother.[77] More subtly, Gaskell uses fire in *Sylvia's Lovers* to suggest sexual attraction.[78] Kinraid entering the room was

like that which you may effect any winter's night, when you come
into a room where a great lump of coal lies hot and slumbering on
the fire; just break it up with a judicious blow from the poker, and
the room, late so dark, and dusk, and lone, is full of life, and light,
and warmth.[79]

The fire imagery is continued, and interwoven with the theme of the sea,
when Sylvia dreams all night 'of burning volcanoes springing out of icy
southern seas.'[80] The opposite metaphor of the dying fire and the guttering
candle is an oblique commentary on Philip and Sylvia's marriage:

The wick of the candle grew long and black, and fell, and sputtered,
and guttered; he sate on, unheeding either it or the pale gray fire that
was dying out – dead at last.[81]

Fire then, as a living thing, can symbolise death as well as life. *Sylvia's Lovers*
begins with a funeral and Sylvia's marriage is a living death. In 'Morton Hall'
(1853), Miss Phillis lies dead in front of a cold hearth: 'No fire. Grey wood
ashes lay on the hearth.'[82] The ashes indicate that she is too poor for coal and
has had to rely on gathering wood. The fire would have provided heat for
cooking, so the dead fire indicates that she has starved to death. The story is
a harsh forerunner to 'My Lady Ludlow' (1858), in which the constraints of
a hierarchical class system inhibit the lower class sisters' offering of a gesture
of common humanity to Miss Phillis, and prevent Miss Phillis asking for help
until it is too late.

The death of Squire Hamley's wife in *Wives and Daughters* (1866) not only
deprives the household of effective domestic management, but also exposes
the flaws in the relationship between the Squire and his sons. The cold, hun-
gry Squire enters the drawing-room where the clock has stopped because
no-one has wound it up, and the fire, also neglected,

was now piled up with half-dried wood, which sputtered and smoked
instead of doing its duty in blazing and warming the room, through
which the keen wind was cutting its way in all directions.[83]

The clock and the fire are potent physical reminders to the Squire of the
loss of his wife. The inefficiently made fire is unable to protect him from the

draughts, just as his wife is no longer there to act as a buffer between him and his sons, smoothing out the 'state of feeling between the squire and his eldest son, which, if it could not be called active discord, showed at least passive estrangement'.[84]

Domestic objects and personal possessions also carry coded messages and help to strengthen character and narrative themes. Much of Gaskell's writing focuses on change and tensions between past and present. Personal possessions, including books and letters, act as a link to the past, integrating their owners into their settings and suggesting longevity and stability. They provide a sense of time and continuity which acts as a counterbalance to the pressure for the social and cultural changes that Gaskell recognizes are necessary for the creation of a healthy society. Equally, they can show the destructive effect of the passage of time.

In *Mary Barton,* the Wilsons and the Bartons have few possessions but use these to bring order and structure into their insecure lives. The Bartons have a cupboard

> full of plates and dishes, cups and saucers, and some more nondescript articles, for which one would have fancied their possessors could find no use – such as triangular pieces of glass to save carving knives and forks from dirtying table-cloths.[85]

Keeping a house clean took a great deal of time and effort, so Mrs Barton's glass stands are a practical necessity as well as being a pragmatic copy of the more luxurious knife stands used in wealthier homes. Gaskell was intensely practical herself, describing for example, how she and her friend, Mrs Barton, taught Marianne 'the decencies of civilized life, how to use her napkin at dinner; to make a piece of bread serve for fork &c'.[86] The amount of furniture crammed into the room illustrates that the Bartons are relatively prosperous and that work is plentiful. Some objects are highly decorative as well as functional, such as the gaily coloured oil-cloth on the floor, the 'bright green japanned tea-tray, having a couple of scarlet lovers embracing in the middle' and the 'crimson tea-caddy, also of japan ware'.[87] Japanning is a method and style of decoration that started in England at the beginning of the seventeenth century to imitate Japanese laquerware. Tin or papier-mâché bases were the most frequently used, although some items were made of wood. Colours originally followed the Japanese gold and black, but later, reds, greens and blues were all introduced as variations. It is unclear what base is used for the Bartons' japan ware.

The catalogue of the Great Exhibition shows that items made from papier-mâché, including tea trays, tea caddies and even large items of furniture such as pianos, were ubiquitous, and the range suggests that many of them might have been accessible to factory workers when work was good.[88] Angus Bethune Reach, who visited several of the better-class houses in Hulme, Manchester between 1849 and 1851 to report on the conditions of the working classes on behalf of the *Morning Chronicle*, describes homes that are strikingly similar to Gaskell's fictional interiors.[89] He reports that 'A conspicuous object is very frequently a glaringly painted and highly glazed tea-tray upon which the firelight glints cheerily.'[90] *Cassell's Household Guide* has an item on re-japanning old metal tea trays, which gives an indication of their popularity.[91] Mary Elizabeth Braddon describes a similar set of iron-based japanned tea trays in a working class parlour in *Lady Audley's Secret* (1862), suggesting that this is the likeliest material for the Bartons' tea tray and caddy.[92] Certainly the ready availability and range of such objects would have enabled people to assert their own sense of style and taste.

The presence of the tea tray, the tea caddy and the oilcloth also illustrates how domestic interiors had become commodities in their own right, opening up entrepreneurial opportunities that were richly exploited by retailers. An oilcloth on the floor for example indicates both prosperity and modernity.[93] Bethune Reach reports that a piece of battered oilcloth was laid down in the passage of one of the houses he visited.[94] The Bartons' choice of japanware is also significant in the visual message it conveys. Its exotic colour and subject matter suggests a family who are interested in and capable of moving outside the limited geographical sphere of their enclosed court. In that sense, the objects fulfil a similar function to Job Legh's collection of insects. The japanware also provides a narrative link to the east where Gaskell's brother John disappeared, and to the sailor, Will Wilson, who is to play such a critical role in uniting the lovers, Mary Barton and Jem Wilson, whose relationship is hinted at by the lovers represented stylistically on the tea tray.

Domestic objects become personalised. In *Mary Barton*, for example, the Bartons move to their home just after their son has died, and the home is associated with hope and a fresh start. John Barton has therefore

> taken more interest in the details of the proceeding than he otherwise would have done, in the hope of calling her forth to action again. So he seemed to know every brass-headed nail driven up for her convenience.[95]

The stripping away of his possessions as the economic climate worsens and Barton declines into opium addiction, further fuels his anger and violence, and is a stark symbol of the social and emotional displacement of poor families. The Bartons' possessions, that have such rich associations, become mere commodities after the death of Mrs Barton. They are sold to fuel John Barton's opium addiction since they no longer sustain him emotionally.[96]

Lady Ludlow, by contrast, is surrounded by possessions which link her not only to previous generations of her own family but also to the distant past. Change is observed from the central perspective of Lady Ludlow.[97] The drawers of her bureau are like memory boxes filled with broken objects, torn scraps of letters and shards of marble. The narrator, Margaret Dawson, is 'puzzled to know why some were kept at all'.[98] As the drawers are emptied and the contents revealed, it becomes apparent that Lady Ludlow is taking Margaret on a journey back through her life. The scraps of notes and the broken riding whip are mementoes of her youth, and perhaps of her first love affair. Alongside these in the drawer are pieces of Roman tesserae brought back from her Grand Tour. Lady Ludlow had intended to make these into a table, giving them a new use and setting in which to appreciate their decorative qualities. They lie however in the drawer, symbolic of fading hopes and dreams, still covered with the soil of the onion field she collected them from. This is made more poignant by the next revelation of the 'locks of hair carefully ticketed, which my lady looked at very sadly; and lockets and bracelets with miniatures in them,'[99] which belong to her dead children. Lady Ludlow, for all her apparent status and privilege, is a lonely, isolated woman, trapped in the past, 'looking ever onward to her death'.[100]

Squire Hamley is another character in a position of power who is apparently frozen in time. His nature and status are represented by his 'old steady, turnip-shaped watch'.[101] The watch has been given to him by his father, and 'had given the law to house-clocks, stable-clocks, kitchen-clocks – nay, even to Hamley Church clock in its day'.[102] The watch is worn near the Squire's heart, beating in time with it. The symbolic act of pulling out the watch to check the time enables the Squire visually to assert his authority and power over his home and estate. The weight of his responsibilities is suggested by the size of the watch and the effort he has to make to extract it from his waistband. The Squire's word and his time-keeping are law in the world he controls. It is his responsibility to wind up the watch, unlike the clock over the mantelpiece in his drawing-room, which no-one has remembered to wind up since his wife died. Time, in this feminine space, is out of control. The Squire's watch, like himself, is 'plain, but steady-going', unlike Osborne's dainty little French watch.[103]

Time-keeping becomes the focus for the Squire's discontent with his eldest son. Osborne 'always moved slowly'. The Squire interprets this as his lack of commitment to his inheritance, but it is in fact due to the heart defect that ultimately kills him. The Squire, already irritated by his tardiness, reacts to Osborne's innocent questioning of the accuracy of his father's watch as an attack on his personal power, and, by extension, on his quasi-legal jurisdiction of his home, since the Squire's watch is value-laden with the weight of inherited authority:

> Poor Osborne might have known better than to cast this slur on his father's flesh and blood; for so dear did he hold his watch![104]

The fact that Osborne's watch is French enhances the impression of his effeminacy and his frivolous attitude to responsibility. Squire Hamley's opinion of the French is coloured by his memory of the French Revolution and by his violent antipathy to Catholicism, and these feelings are transferred to Osborne's French watch. The physical appearance of the two watches points up the contrast between the two men and indicates Osborne's underlying frailty. The dainty little watch will simply not have the stamina to be passed down to Osborne's son, unlike the robust turnip-shaped watch. The choice of adjectives also underlines the difference in character and interest between father and son. Osborne's dainty French watch is decorative and reflects his interest in poetry, literature and the arts. The Squire's turnip-shaped watch on the other hand, is in harmony with its environment, the estate and lands which the Squire loves so much, its very nomenclature redolent of soil and produce.

4 - THE DISCOURSE OF DIFFERENCE: HOMELESSNESS IN GASKELL'S FICTION

There are very few characters in Gaskell's fiction who are literally without a home or some sort of shelter, however poor or tenuous this may be. A downturn in the economy for example, means that Davenport in *Mary Barton* (1848) is out of work, and he and his family are living in the utmost squalor. Gregson, in 'My Lady Ludlow' (1858), lives in extreme poverty on the edge of the common, existing as best he can by poaching. However both the Davenports and the Gregsons are known to their communities, and are visited and helped. Gregson's son Harry finds a way out of poverty through education and employment. Other potentially homeless children are rescued and find loving homes, for example, Leonard with the Bensons in *Ruth* (1853) and the Boucher children with Nicholas Higgins in *North and South* (1855). The only truly homeless characters in Gaskell's fiction are Esther in *Mary Barton* and Lizzie Leigh, and even Esther retains strong ties with her family and neighbours. It might appear then that Gaskell is unwilling to address the issue of homelessness which exercised and threatened her contemporaries.

To be homeless is to be rootless, detached from family relationships, and excluded from society. Homelessness necessitates constant movement, precisely because a homeless person has no fixed abode, no secure sanctuary in which to feel safe from external threats. Contemporary social commentators, such as Henry Mayhew and George Godwin reflected on the homeless state of the millions of poor who flooded into the newly created cities, and who could not, or would not be incorporated within the physical boundaries of a home or contained within the emotional enclosure of a family.[1] The 1851 Census stated that: 'It is so much in the order of nature that a family should live in a separate house, that 'house' is often used for family in many languages'.[2] This alignment of the concept of 'house', a physically contained space, with 'family' a domestic unit, was an attempt to deal with the physical and psychological pressures experienced in an increasingly urbanised environment. The need for privacy in this overcrowded society became paramount, for rich and poor alike. As the century progressed, the courts in which the working classes lived were opened up, and external space became something to be used for access, rather than a leisure or domestic amenity. The middle classes retreated into a more private residential style, and outdoor life ceased to have a social purpose and disappeared behind walls and hedges.[3] The concepts of 'homes' and 'homelessness' therefore acquire a psychological, emotional and spiritual dimension rooted in the difficult transition between the agrarian, romantic age of the eighteenth century, and the industrialised, urban centered dynamic of the nineteenth century.

Gaskell recognised the distinction between a physical, and a psychological and social space in her fictional representations of homes, and her exploration of what constitutes homelessness is nuanced and compassionate. She is interested in those who are excluded and cut adrift from society and in her letters and her non-fiction, as well as in her fiction, argues for tolerance and acceptance. For Gaskell, homelessness is better defined as a psychological, social, and emotional separation, rather than the literal lack of a physically enclosing space, and in this sense, it is linked to her own contested and ambiguous experience of home. By foregrounding characters such as the Davenports and the Gregsons, Gaskell makes them visible as individuals and places them in a wider cultural, spiritual, and social discourse.

Homelessness, for both William and Elizabeth, was linked to their Unitarian beliefs, the principles of associationist psychology, and the importance of individual and social responsibility clearly articulated by William in his sermons:

> For the joys and solace of friendship, for the pleasures and endearments of home, for the thrill of our souls when sharing the enthusiasm of a multitude, for the inspiring themes of our country's history, for the rich treasures which the world's struggles have accumulated for our use, for all that distinguishes us from the poor shrivelled victim of isolation, we must acknowledge ourselves under deep obligation to Society.[4]

The expansion and contraction of the focus of this sentence between the intimate relationships of home and wider social experiences, makes clear the critical importance of the ties between the individual and society. Those who are isolated become 'shrivelled': engagement with society is vital for individual health and well-being as well as for the creation of a morally balanced society. William's sermon continues with a vivid metaphor describing how society and the individual are linked:

> As the boughs of the forest trees interlace, so all the ramifications of family and kindred connect us, more or less, with the great public. We can none of us move in the world without making a larger or a smaller current there.[5]

Gaskell addressed the question of tolerance and the danger of prejudice in her non-fiction essay 'An Accursed Race'.[6] This essay originally appeared in 1855 in *Household Words* and Gaskell chose to include it in the collected edition of stories entitled *Round the Sofa* (1859). The topic, and its inclusion in a volume of fiction, makes it of interest in a consideration of homelessness, defined as 'exclusion from society'.[7] *Round the Sofa*, as the title suggests, consists of six stories told by a group of acquaintances during long winter evenings in Edinburgh. By including 'An Accursed Race' in this intimate domestic setting, Gaskell is bringing the theme of an oppressed, dehumanised race into the heart of the Victorian home. In addition, as Julian Wolfreys notes, although each of the stories is appropriate to the teller, there is a minimal attempt to define their individual characters, enabling Gaskell to focus more effectively on her wider social message.[8] All the narrators speak an accented English, suggesting the possibility of an integrated community which both respects and celebrates difference.[9]

There are many parallels between the Cagots, who are the subject of this essay, and the dispossessed Victorian poor. Contemporary descriptions of the homes of the working-class poor portray them living in conditions which bear little resemblance to human habitations. James Kay-Shuttleworth for example comments: 'Home has little other relation to him than that of shelter. [...] it chiefly presents to him a scene of physical exhaustion from which he is glad to escape.'[10] The Cagots are associated with infection and 'bad blood',

a theme to which Gaskell would return in 'Lois the Witch'.[11] They are stigma-
tised by bearing the mark of a duck or goose foot stitched prominently to the
front of their clothing. They are excluded from taking a full part in the mass,
and are therefore barred from the spiritual life of the community. Ironically,
it is the French Revolution that 'brought some good out of the fermenta-
tion of the people: the more intelligent among them tried to overcome the
prejudice against the Cagots.'[12] Gaskell brings her message of tolerance and
compassion firmly, if somewhat heavy handedly, home with an epitaph from
a gravestone in Stratford–upon–Avon:

> What faults you saw in me,
>   Pray strive to shun;
>   And look at home: there's
>   Something to be done.[13]

Gaskell believed in the importance of family and, by extension, the integra-
tion of individuals into a home and wider society. A clear thread of concern
runs through her letters, particularly about the fate of children who are homeless. She writes to an unknown correspondent on 14 April 1852 (or 1863)
about her concern for some children who, like the Boucher children in *North
and South*, have no alternative but to go to the workhouse after the drowning, (possibly suicide), of their father unless some relatives can be persuaded
to give them a home.[14] A letter of 4 March 1854 to Lady Kay-Shuttleworth
illustrates the way in which her views reflected her Unitarianism, placing particular emphasis on the importance of association and the moral and spiritual
education which can be provided within a secure home:

> It seems to me so very desirable to surround an orphan with some-
> thing of the love & duties of a home, to place her as nearly as pos-
> sible in the relation of a daughter, and to secure for her the nearest
> approach to the domestic relationships of which she has been de-
> prived, that I think I should consider this education of the affec-
> tions, and the domestic duties that arise out of them, as more than
> an equivalent for the accomplishments & languages which she would
> learn by the other plan, and the superior station in society which a
> governess may assume.[15]

The girl in question appears to be about fifteen. She had intended to be a dressmaker, and it is possible that Gaskell, following the publication of *Ruth* in 1853, was particularly sensitive to the implications of her vulnerability and lack of protection. Every approximation 'to God's ordinance of a 'family' is surely to be desired' she tells Mary Robberds in a letter of June 1861.[16]

In accordance with her Unitarian faith, Gaskell also believed in the importance of individuals and in an individual's power to transform society. She had 'a grand quarrel' with Florence Nightingale over the question of children being brought up in crèches rather than by their mothers, asserting to Emily Shaen in a letter of 27 October 1854 that Nightingale was 'too much for institutions, sisterhoods and associations' and rather unconvincingly following this with the comment that 'this want of love for individuals becomes a gift and a very rare one, if one takes it in conjunction with her intense love for the race'.[17] It is therefore unsurprising that her portrayals of homelessness focus on individuals, and on the individual's dissociation from society and its consequences.

Private space, even within relatively spacious middle-class homes was often difficult to find. The need for psychological and emotional space within the home caused a type of homelessness, a detached, albeit temporary, wandering from the constraints of domestic ties. The opening pages of *Mary Barton* describe how Victorians flooded out of the cities into the countryside on public holidays, where 'the artisan, deafened with noise of tongues and engines, may come to listen awhile to the delicious sounds of rural life'.[18] Once she became a successful writer, Gaskell seized every opportunity to escape from Manchester, where, as she told Tottie Fox in a letter of April 1850, 'we have no great external beauty either of nature or art the contemplation of which can put calm into one; and take one out of one's little self – and shame the demon (I beg its pardon) Conscience away; or to sleep.'[19] There are two parts to Gaskell's comment: one half of her sentence refers to her attachment to the past, her happy upbringing in Knutsford and her nostalgia for a rural idyll common to many of her contemporaries. The other, perhaps more interesting half, refers to the psychological pressures of home and family, and what became an increasingly urgent need to escape from their constraints, to wander and to travel. While Gaskell of course was never homeless in the strict sense of the word, she was certainly aware of her own need for psychological space to reconcile the 'warring members' of her multiple 'mes' described in the same letter to Tottie Fox.

Esther (*Mary Barton,* 1848)

Esther, the pretty girl who is seduced, gives birth and is then forced to live on the streets as a prostitute, provides a moral mirror for the heroine of Gaskell's first novel, Mary Barton. Despite her homelessness and apparent lack of power, Esther plays a pivotal role in the plot. The opening of *Mary Barton* is deceptive in its pastoral simplicity, but the language, from the outset, inscribes a sense of conflict and division.[20] The first words spoken in the novel are a question from Wilson to Barton about Esther: 'Well, John, how goes it with you? And in a lower voice, he added, 'any news of Esther, yet?'[21] Wilson's voice, lowered so that Mrs Barton does not hear his query, indicates that Esther is a cause of dissent within the family. Esther's story is a common one, told economically by Barton, that encapsulates contemporary fears about the dangers of factory work for girls, with its exposure to sexual temptation, freedom from domestic constraint, and financial independence. Esther's beauty and her spirit have not been moderated, and her presence in Barton's home has been the cause of tension between him and his wife. Gaskell implies that Esther's position in the family is tenuous. She has no parents, we never learn her full name, and she does not appear to have a role in the domestic unit. In these opening pages, Gaskell uses the story of Esther to establish the main narrative themes of poverty, temptation, class struggle and death within the domestic setting of the Bartons' home, and the traits of character that will drive the plot.

Esther's disappearance from the Bartons' lives is swift and dramatic and from Barton's point of view, precipitates the crisis of his wife's death, his own decline into radicalism and opium addiction, and his daughter's exposure to the same temptations that attracted Esther. Jill Matus notes how the death of Barton's wife, the maternal centre of the home, marks the loss of moral direction for both Barton and his daughter.[22] In a later essay, she develops this point, setting out the connection between John Barton's lack of self-discipline and the pathology of his physical and psychological disintegration, arguing that Gaskell was using a common contemporary trope which associated this with class difference.[23] Esther and Barton share a common pathology, and the crisis point in their relationship is marked by Barton tearing the old nail on which Esther used to hang her bonnet out of the wall and throwing it into the street. This is both a symbolic eviction of Esther from her home and family and a metaphor for the loss of Mrs Barton, the 'peg' on which the whole family depended, and without whom the physical, emotional and spiritual environment of the home rapidly disintegrates. The nail acts as a substitute for Esther who, by leaving home voluntarily, has deprived Barton of the traditional male role of driving her from home like so many disgraced Victorian girls. Esther has taken the power which would normally reside with a man. Since Barton also blames Esther for the death of his wife, tearing out the nail is the only way he has of expressing his violent anger and resentment.

Esther's next appearance marks the depth of her decline, and is the first time she appears in person in the novel, speaking directly to Barton instead of having her actions and words reported. She is bedraggled, soaking wet and ill, but persists in trying to warn Barton about Mary's relationship with Harry Carson. Their meeting at night not only emphasises the truth of Barton's prediction that Esther will become a street walker, but also illustrates his own decline. Barton has no work and no motivation to get out of bed in the morning. He faces a choice between eating or opium, and chooses the latter to which he is addicted. When he meets Esther, he is returning from an illegal Trade Union meeting. The night-time meeting between two desperate people, one excluded from society and the other a member of a quasi-secret society, begins with their inability to communicate and ends violently in a foreshadowing of the failed negotiations of the Chartists and the murder of Harry Carson. Matus rightly argues that the decline of each arises from strong feelings unmitigated and undisciplined by education or wisdom, that should come from the moral guidance provided by a mother/wife.[24] Barton's later reaction to their meeting however is an inversion of the conventional plot in that he regrets his anger, and recalls Esther's humility and 'her tacit acknowledgment of her lost character'.[25] He remembers his wife who has acted as a mother to Esther, and, in a reversal of conventional gender roles, sets out, like Lizzie Leigh's mother, to search for Esther.

Although the narrative illustrates how poverty and misfortune shape character as much as moral choice, Gaskell does not pursue this possibility for the redemption of both Barton and Esther.[26] Instead, Barton repeats the pattern of his behaviour towards Esther with his daughter: 'he upbraided her with the loss of Jem Wilson till she had to bite her lips till the blood came, in order to keep down the angry words that would rise in her heart.'[27] As Barton becomes increasingly powerless and voiceless, Esther turns to Jem Wilson in an attempt to protect Mary. As she did with John Barton, Esther places a restraining hand on Jem's arm. This is not simply a gesture to attract his attention: her 'firm and unusual grasp' also symbolises Esther's desperate desire to prevent Mary from pursuing a relationship that will detach her from friends and family.

Amanda Anderson argues that this gesture illustrates Esther's entrapment within the romance genre, noting the allusion to Coleridge's Ancient Mariner and his compulsive story-telling.[28] While *Mary Barton* is at times an uneasy blend of romance, melodrama and social reform, Esther plays a much more active part in the narrative than that of a stock figure. When she lived with the Bartons, her presence in the home created tension, in that she and Barton competed for the attention of his wife – Esther's substitute mother. In the novels, and particularly the short stories that followed *Mary Barton,* Gaskell repeatedly portrayed unconventional family structures in which children were given a home by strangers or single women and a successful and integrated unit was created, described by Patsy Stoneman as 'functional cooperation'.[29] In her first novel, she is still finding her narrative voice and exploring the most effective way in which to evoke her readers' sympathy for the social issues with which she is concerned, and she therefore adopts a conventional trope to portray Esther's fall.

Nevertheless, her interest in alternative patterns of mothering is illustrated by Esther's social interactions. Esther is only able to speak to Barton, the patriarchal figure, in a whisper. Her relationship with Jem is different, poised somewhere between that of an authoritative substitute mother figure and an older sister. In speaking to Jem, Esther is able to tell her own story in full for the first time, a story Gaskell was to revisit in *Ruth,* where an alternative family structure is portrayed as a compassionate and viable alternative to a life on the streets. Esther describes her night wanderings in which she becomes a shadowy protector for Mary. Her position on the outside of the family is symbolised by her peering into the house through a chink in the window shutters. At the end of her confession, Jem offers her a home, but Esther refuses, telling him that she uses drink, as Barton uses opium, because, 'If we did not drink, we could not stand the memory of what we have been, and the thought of what we are, for a day.'[30]

Esther's poignant description of her night time visions of the dead shades from delirium tremens to a morbid consciousness of her failures:

> 'There they go round and round my bed the whole night through. My mother, carrying little Annie (I wonder how they got together) and Mary – and all looking at me with their sad, stony eyes; oh Jem! It is so terrible! They don't turn back either, but pass behind the head of the bed, and I feel their eyes on me everywhere. If I creep under the clothes I still see them; and what is worse,' hissing out her words with fright, 'they see me.'[31]

The boundary between dreaming and waking, memory and reality is blurred. As Matus notes in her discussion of *The Mystery of Edwin Drood*, Gaskell's account here does not accord with contemporary views of drunkenness which suggested that 'there are two states of consciousness, which never clash, but each of which pursues its separate course as though it were continuous instead of broken.'[32] Instead, Esther's traumatized mind is no longer able to distinguish accurately between past and present, the conscious and the unconscious, memory and reality.

The legal relationship between Esther and the Bartons is underpinned throughout the novel by the more subtle ties of shared character traits and physical appearance. Mary Barton the mother, Esther, and Mary's daughter all share the same striking beauty, and Esther and her niece are both spirited and independent. Deborah Denholz Morse comments on the significance of the three names, arguing that the Biblical allusions, together with the blending of the identities of the three women, allow Gaskell to blur the sharp distinctions between mother, falling and fallen woman.[33] As the narrative progresses, and the focus moves from John Barton to Mary, Gaskell becomes increasingly interested in the psychic links between the family and in the effects of emotional shock and trauma. Matus appropriately places Mary's collapse after her defence of Jem Wilson in open court in the borderland between bodily and psychic disorders.[34] However, Gaskell begins to explore the effects of shock and trauma on Mary earlier in the novel when Mary realises after Jem's arrest for murder that she loves him. Her agony and confusion are expressed in a passage of indirect speech, a tumble of questions and reflections. Like Gwendolen Grandcourt after the drowning of her husband, shock has affected Mary's memory. Her mental turmoil, in which she veers wildly between revulsion at the murder, passionate love for Jem and self-blame for her behaviour which she believes has driven him to commit murder, is only partly relieved by tears. The passage concludes by specifically linking the physical and the psychological: 'Oh! She was going mad; and for awhile she lay outwardly still, but with the pulses careering through her head with wild vehemence.'[35] Mary retreats into memories of the past, and falls asleep remembering happier times.

As Matus notes in her discussion of *North and South*, Gaskell's use of dream is revelatory of psychological states.[36] Here, Gaskell recognises the healing power of sleep in times of emotional crisis:

> And then Heaven blessed her unaware, and she sank from remembering, to wandering, unconnected thought, and thence to sleep. [...] and she dreamt of the happy times of long ago, and her mother came to her, and kissed her as she lay, and once more the dead were alive again in that happy world of dreams.[37]

Gaskell describes with sensitivity and precision the gradual relaxation of Mary's physical and emotional tension, but the passage also elides dream and reality, so that there appears to be continuity between the mind when fully awake and the unconscious mind.

This blurring of the dreaming and waking worlds continues when Mary wakes suddenly from her dream, her hair and face still wet with tears. The physical, external world is also curiously poised between night and day. It is after midnight, the time traditionally associated with ghosts and spirits, 'but the moon shone clearly in at the unshuttered window, making the room almost as light as day, in its cold ghastly radiance'.[38] The emotional turmoil Mary has just experienced is reflected in the narrative style and tone, which slides from a story firmly rooted in contemporary realism to the unreality of a ghost story:

> There was a low knock at the door! A strange feeling crept over Mary's heart, as if something spiritual were near; as if the dead, so lately present in her dreams, were yet gliding and hovering round her, with their dim, dread forms. And yet, why dread? Had they not loved her? – and who loved her now?[39]

This change of narrative form, if taken out of context, might seem bizarre, but Gaskell uses the trope of the ghost story as the most effective way to portray Mary's trauma, vulnerability and isolation. This is emphasised when the knock at the door is followed by a call:

> 'Mary! Mary! Open the door!' as a little movement on her part seemed to tell the being outside of her wakeful, watchful state. They were the accents of her mother's voice; the very south-country pronunciation, that Mary so well remembered; and which she had sometimes tried to imitate when alone, with the fond mimicry of affection.[40]

The ambiguity as to whether the voice calling Mary is human or spirit derives from the reference to Mary's dead mother, but the passage is also psychologically consistent. In her grief for her mother, in the extreme crisis she has just passed through, lacking the protection and understanding of her father, Mary has tried to recall the sound of her mother's voice in an attempt to recapture the emotional stability and security of which she has been deprived.

The boundary between the real and the unreal, the physical and the spiritual, ghost story and realist narrative collide and are blended as Mary throws herself into her aunt's arms. Esther, the homeless outcast, is the character who is able to reconcile and heal misunderstandings and emotional pain, and who can bring Mary and Jem together in a way which offers a positive future. As Stoneman notes, at this point in the narrative the parental impulse is more important than parental identity.[41] Whereas John Barton shakes off her restraining arm, Jem shakes Esther's hand when he recognises her, and Mary embraces her. This physical contact symbolises not only their acceptance of Esther's moral message, but also their more tolerant and compassionate attitude to her homeless and fallen state. Their reaction reflects the views of Gaskell's acquaintance, the Unitarian preacher James Martineau that 'even wandering guilt must be sought for and brought home; and penitence that sits upon the steps must be asked to come within the door'.[42]

Esther also gives Mary the physical evidence which would convict her father of murder. This transient domestic object, a scrap of paper torn from a Valentine given to Mary by Jem Wilson, has been used by Barton to prime the gun with which he shot Harry Carson. The shock which Mary receives on recognising the paper and the realisation of what it implies dislocates her thoughts and disrupts her growing interest in Esther and the possibility of re-establishing links with her aunt:

> As if, according to the believers in mesmerism, the intenseness of her wish gave her power over another, although the wish was unexpressed, Esther felt herself unwelcome, and that her absence was desired.[43]

Gaskell uses the language and rhetoric of contemporary psychology to explore the connections between the conscious and the unconscious, and the ways in which shock affects action and behaviour. By linking this to an apparently trivial physical object, she suggests the ways in which the physical and psychological are intimately linked.

Superficially, the torn scrap of paper, an expression of love, becomes the link between Mary's family, who fail to protect her, her lover who seeks her as a passing amusement, and her disregarded admirer Jem, who has the courage and stability the others lack. It is also a metaphor for damaged relationships between individuals. As Esther's bonnet nail has been torn from the wall and thrown into the street, so a piece of the Valentine from Jem, whom Mary does not value, has been torn off and used to destroy another human life. In this sense, it also becomes symbolic of wider relationships and the destructiveness of a society where class divisions and intolerance are rife.

The homeless Esther therefore performs a critical role in the novel. Her appearances in the narrative act as a continual warning to point out the dangers of a family life without a clear moral focus. As the locus of dissent and tension within the Barton family, Esther is viewed by John Barton as the catalyst for the series of disasters which strike his family and lead to its dissolution.

John Barton's subsequent radicalism and substance misuse put Mary at risk by his failure to protect her and to provide her with a clear moral framework. Mary herself, like Esther, is almost destroyed by her wilful independence and lack of responsibility. Despite her anti-domestic lifestyle however, it is Esther's persistence in keeping hold of her family ties and her continuing sense of responsibility for Mary that eventually lead to redemption and resolution for Mary and Jem. The rapid deterioration of Esther's physical appearance enables Gaskell to use her interventions in the narrative to explore the effects of shock and grief on Mary's psyche. Esther's physical insubstantiality, her invisibility as a homeless prostitute, mean that she inhabits a shadowy borderland between the world of the real and the supernatural: 'They rushed outside; and, fallen into what appeared simply a heap of white or light-coloured clothes, fainting or dead, lay the poor crushed Butterfly – the once innocent Esther [...] naught but skin and bone, with a cough to tear her in two.'[44] Like John Barton's guilt, Esther's homelessness can only be resolved by death, but as in *Ruth*, her story is not without hope in that she has enabled the next generation to establish itself in a more congenial environment.

Lois ('Lois the Witch', 1860)

Death is also the resolution for the homeless Lois in 'Lois the Witch' (1860). Gaskell's choice of witchcraft as a narrative subject is not unusual in the period.[45] Maureen Moran notes the ubiquity of the Victorian interest in witchcraft and sorcery, including the fashion for spiritualism and mesmerism, used as a means to explore cultural and social issues of class, gender and power.[46] Gaskell had already used the cat-roasting incident in *North and South* (1855) to highlight the need for education as a means of counteracting superstition. In 'Lois the Witch', she uses the landscape and society of seventeenth-century America to explore an isolated, inturned and hostile community in which Lois, the homeless orphan daughter of a Warwickshire parson, finds not sanctuary with her aunt and uncle, but vilification and hanging as a witch.[47]

Instability is one of the key themes of this novella and the tone is set from the opening sentences. Lois steadies herself on the stable land after weeks of being on the rocking ship that has carried her from the Old World to the New. Yet, 'It seemed as strange now to be on solid earth as it had been, not long ago, to be rocked by the sea.'[48] She has no point of reference in the strange landscape she sees before her and she shivers in the 'piercing wind, which seemed to follow those whom it had tyrannised over at sea with a dogged wish of still tormenting them on land'.[49] She is destablised physically and emotionally. Like Margaret Hale after the death of her parents, Lois is at a 'breathing-time of her life', but unlike Margaret, who has matured and is able to plan for her future independent life, Lois recalls the past, her home in the peaceful Warwickshire countryside and her childhood as the vicar's daughter.

As in the opening of *Mary Barton,* Gaskell subtly erodes the apparently idyllic setting of the rose-covered parsonage and the security of Lois's home. She is the only child of elderly parents. Her parents and her old nurse are all dead; 'they slept, calm and still, in Barford churchyard, careless of what became of their orphan child, as far as earthly manifestations of care or love went'.[50] Lois is isolated and vulnerable. Love and death are inextricably associated with her in the opening pages of the novella, and are presented in an extreme and violent form. Her lover, Hugh Lucy, swears 'a great oath unto the Lord' that he will find Lois 'sooner or later, if she was still upon the earth,'[51] a telling phrase which hints that Lois may not survive long. Lois's mother wishes that Lois was dying with her; 'Such was the selfishness of conjugal love: she thought little of Lois's desolation in comparison with her rejoicing over her speedy reunion with her dead husband!'[52] Later, when Lois is living in Salem, her cousin Manasseh insists that 'If I wed not Lois, both she and I die within the year. I care not for life: before this, as you know, I have sought for death.'[53]

Dissent, distrust and conflict have split Lois's family: one uncle was killed in the Civil War, another was a schismatic who quarrelled with his brother, Lois's father, and left with the Puritans for America. Barriers of class and social status, coupled with extreme passion also mark Lois's relationship with

Hugh Lacey, a relationship which similarly threatens to divide his family and to further isolate Lois:

> [He] told her, in one great burst of love, of his passionate attachment, his vehement struggles with his father, his impotence at present, his hopes and resolves for the future. And, intermingled with all this, came such outrageous threats and expressions of uncontrolled vehemence, that Lois felt that in Barford she must not linger to be a cause of desperate quarrel between father and son.[54]

Lois, as she will be later in Salem, is the unwilling focus of this maelstrom of violent emotion. The dominant tone of the novella therefore, even in what appears to be the romantically imagined pastoral past of rural England, is one of florid and extreme emotions associated with anger and violent death.

Blood is used as a metaphor for disease and decay both in individual families and in the wider community. 'Blood is thicker than water', says Lois's dying mother, but the uncle to whom she proposes to send her orphan daughter, has separated himself from his family both spiritually and geographically. When Lois arrives in Salem, her uncle is bed-ridden and powerless, and her aunt's reception of her is hostile. The first words spoken by her aunt are a denial of any knowledge of Lois's existence, by implication, a denial of any blood relationship.[55] Her next speech asserts her complete control of the household and is an active attack on Lois's father, reigniting the religious dissent caused by the Act of Uniformity which led both to the schism within Lois's family and to the Puritans being ejected from England. Lois's forthright response to the implied insult to her dead father means that her first words to her aunt are angry and challenging:

> Lois and her aunt gazed into each other's eyes unflinchingly for a minute or two of silence; but the girl felt her colour coming and going, while the elder woman's never varied.[56]

Here, blood, which causes Lois to change colour, is a metaphor for the differing characters of the two women. Grace Hickson is not related by blood to Lois and is unmoved by her homeless plight, rigid and unbending. Lois's eyes fill with tears, whereas her aunt maintains an almost inhuman stare, 'dry and unwavering.'[57] Together with her tall, large stature, her voice which is almost as masculine as her son's, and her dominance over the household, this suggests an unnatural gendering which in turn can be seen as indicative of a degenerative inheritance and diseased blood. The language used to describe Lois's uncle, and his relationship with her, is similarly grounded in anatomically precise metaphor. Gaskell comments that 'Lois's heart often bled at the continual flow of contemptuous reproof which Grace constantly addressed to her husband', and that his 'first flow of action towards Lois was soon exhausted', a phrase which suggests an ineffectual pumping of the heart.[58] Indeed, it is a stroke which finally kills him.

Blood is also associated with religion and superstitious beliefs. Lois describes the drowning of a witch she witnessed as a child and recalls old Hannah's face as 'bloody and black with the stones and the mud they had been throwing at her'.[59] Her account of this incident immediately precedes her arrival in Salem, and reveals Lois's unease with the way her community turned on an isolated and vulnerable old woman who lived not only outside society but on the borderline of starvation. Difference breeds intolerance and Lois's dramatic telling of the brutal and violent end of old Hannah prefigures her own life and death in Salem. Lois's emotions, like that of the crowd who attack Hannah, spiral out of control as she tells her tale so that her eyes are full of tears. Her dream that she has herself become a witch and is drowning in the pond is a premonition of her eventual death in Salem. The men 'hating her with their eyes', offer an ironic inversion of the accusations that Lois has bewitched Manasseh and others with her glance. Captain Holdernesse describes the attack on Marblehead by French Papist pirates and the murder of a woman prisoner when 'the blood of all who heard the [dying] cry ran cold with terror', and Nattee's wild stories have a similar effect on Lois.[60] The Indian who attacks the settlers under cover of darkness, is shot, and leaves 'a long stream of blood lying on the grass.'[61] Violent death and religious and civil conflict are inextricably intertwined, impacting on both individuals and the wider community, within a narrative blend which combines realism with gothic fantasy.

Religious belief, like other emotions, is also taken to extremes in the enclosed world of Salem, and presents a more direct threat to Lois in the disturbing presence of her cousin Manasseh, whose behaviour, fuelled by his

prophetic visions, spirals increasingly out of control. Early indications of
Manasseh's limitations are given when Lois arrives at her new home and no
gleam of intelligence enters his face at her unexpected entrance. The book
which is always open on his knee becomes a symbol for his disrupted consciousness, as he increasingly retreats from the world around him and enters
a fantasy world of dreams and visions. Eventually, as his monomania dis-
places his rationality, he does not even see the printed letters on the page.
In an ironic inversion, his hermeneutic study of 'godly books', instead of
providing spiritual insight, merely feeds his obsession: 'I saw no letters of
printers' ink marked on the page, but I saw a gold and ruddy type of some
unknown language, the meaning whereof was whispered into my soul; it was,
"Marry Lois!"'[62]

Manasseh's physical appearance, described fully after his first proposal of
marriage to Lois, suggests his increasing insanity:

> He might be good and pious – [...] but his dark fixed eyes, moving
> so slowly and heavily, his lank black hair, his grey coarse skin, all
> made her dislike him now.[63]

Gaskell's use of physiognomy is a common novelistic device and her description of Manasseh and of his behaviour calls to mind Alexander Morison's
thesis:

> The appearance of the face is intimately connected with and depend-
> ant upon the state of the mind; the repetition of the same ideas and
> emotions, and the consequent repetition of the same movements of
> the muscles of the eyes and of the face give a peculiar expression,
> which in the insane state, is a combination of wildness, abstraction,
> or vacancy, and of those ideas and emotions characterising different
> varieties of mental disorder.[64]

Religion is the trigger which destabilises Manasseh's mind, and Gaskell clearly associates his mental illness with his excessive spirituality, his 'sick soul'.

Manasseh's descent into madness, and the concomitant threat to Lois,
is paralleled by increasing hysteria in the enclosed community of Salem as
accusations of witchcraft burgeon. The plot operates as a series of miscom-
munications, misunderstandings and misreadings, all of which embroil Lois

further in a morass of false accusations as the community turns on itself, seeking victims in outsiders such as Lois, and Nattee and Hota, the American Indians. The only characters who maintain a sense of balance, rationality and perspective are the Widow Smith and Captain Holdernesse, both of whom live outside the settlement. After her initial challenge to her aunt, Lois tries to form a bond with her cousins, but her innocent stories of Halloween only serve to increase their paranoia and suspicion. Lois, like the American Indians, is a cultural 'other' who cannot be trusted.

Vanessa Dickerson reads the narrative as a commentary on paternalism and female helplessness, noting that Old Hannah, the witch of Lois's child-hood, is only the first in a series of women in the story whose unsatisfactory relationships with men are transferred into negative emotions and actions against another woman – that is, Lois. The drama, she notes, is a quintes-sentially female one: Manasseh, the only male who can 'save' Lois, offers her a choice between death or an unacceptable marriage.[65] However, while the accusation and hanging of an American Indian woman as the first witch in Salem is historically accurate, Gaskell enriches the blend of themes in her novella by allowing Lois, a white English woman, to share equally the Indian women's experience of persecution and their ultimate fate. The Hicksons, in their narrow view of religion, are as intolerant of Lois's beliefs as they are of the beliefs of the American Indians.

While 'Lois the Witch' displays characteristic elements of sensation fic-tion in that Lois's new home is the site of terror and madness, it is Gaskell's interest in socio-cultural issues which is of primary importance. The narra-tive form is simply a convenient way of presenting serious concerns in an entertaining manner, given the cloak of authenticity because it is, in large part, a rendering of real events. Time and historical events are manipulated by the characters in the novella allowing Gaskell to further critique sectarian-ism and intolerance. The past is never allowed to lie forgotten, but becomes elided with the present. Grace Hickson accuses Lois by implication of being ungodly; her inheritance is the sin of her father who took the oath of alle-giance to Charles Stuart. Lois's innocent glance back at the toddler who falls over as Lois is driving into Salem, becomes in retrospect, an instance of her casting the evil eye on the child.

Gaskell uses the landscape, as she does in 'Cousin Phillis', as a metaphor for a range of cultural and individual instabilities.[66] Her description of American roads, with the stumps of trees blocking the most direct route, logs of wood laid across boggy ground and the deep green forest which continually threatens to overwhelm the track, is factually accurate, compared for example to Fanny Trollope's account of her travels in America, but also suggests the difficulties the settlers have in controlling both the environment and the Indians, who represent a physical and a spiritual threat. The Indians are always 'lurking' but never seen, the distant cries of strange birds may be the war-whoops of their 'deadly painted enemies', and their invisibility adds to the atmosphere of terror.

The physical and spiritual worlds are blended until they are indistinguishable, just as they are in Manasseh's disordered mind. Manasseh's wanderings in the surrounding forests are a challenge to the Indians whose spiritual beliefs are intimately connected to the natural world around them. His behaviour also illustrates his recklessness and lack of contact with reality. While his mother publicly boasts of his courage and disregard of danger, in private she warns and reproves him. As in 'Cousin Phillis' where the failure of the engineers to lay a railway track across the boggy myrtle represents a wider failure of men to understand women, so the failure of the settlers to respect and work with the landscape and indigenous inhabitants is used by Gaskell to critique colonialism and to argue for toleration of difference. In a rare narratorial intervention, she insists:

> We can afford to smile at them now; but our English ancestors entertained superstitions of much the same character at the same period, and with less excuse, as the circumstances surrounding them were better known, and consequently more explicable by common sense than the real mysteries of the deep untrodden forests of New England.[67]

The tone and language here has echoes of the opening of 'An Accursed Race':

> We have our prejudices in England. [...] We have tortured Jews: we have burnt Catholics and Protestants, to say nothing of a few

witches and wizards. [...] To be sure, our insular position has kept us free [...] from the inroads of alien races; who, driven from one land of refuge, steal into another equally unwilling to receive them: and where, [...] their presence is barely endured, and no pains is taken [sic] to conceal the repugnance which the natives of 'pure blood' experience towards them.[68]

Gaskell, as Wolfreys notes, feels compelled to narrate against the emergence in the 1700s and 1800s of 'racist, religious and biologically determinist forms of brutality'.[69] It is notable that there are occasions in 'Lois the Witch' as in 'An Accursed Race', when the narrator intervenes directly to comment on intolerance. The argument in both texts is the same: resistance to oppression, an implied criticism of the inability of the English, (or in the case of 'Lois the Witch', the community of Salem), to open itself to self-enquiry and internal criticism. The metaphor of bad blood is used in both texts to symbolise what Gaskell views as the inevitable outcome of intolerance, the death of both individuals and society.[70]

'Lois the Witch' is a highly internalised exploration of homelessness and its concomitant effects on a vulnerable young girl. Lois's home in England is superficially stable, but proves to be fragile, and the exploration of various forms of instability becomes a key theme in the narrative. Gaskell uses the tropes of sensation fiction to examine how the unstable and disordered minds of individuals not only threaten the domestic environment, but also spill out into the wider community to create a destructive and violent vortex. Positive emotions associated with home such as the love and protection of a family and blood relatives become poisoned and degenerate, and spiritual beliefs, which should bind civil society together, become instead a source of hysteria leading to violent death, a perverse inversion of martyrdom. The landscape, time and historical events are all used to create a toxic blend through which Gaskell can explore the psychology of collective and individual hysteria in this unremittingly dark novella.

Philip Hepburn (*Sylvia's Lovers*, 1863)

Philip Hepburn in *Sylvia's Lovers* (1863) makes himself homeless, driven from Monkshaven by the realization that his marriage to Sylvia, which was based on a lie, has failed. Homelessness is the punishment he inflicts on himself for deceiving his wife about the fate of Charley Kinraid, the man she loves. Philip is not an attractive character. His physical appearance is a complete contrast to Charley, the specksioneer:

> The sight he saw in the mirror was his own long, sad, pale face, made plainer and grayer by the heavy pressure of the morning's events. He saw his stooping figure, his rounded shoulders, with something like a feeling of disgust at his personal appearance as he remembered the square, upright build of Kinraid; his fine uniform, with epaulette and sword-belt; his handsome brown face; his dark eyes, splendid with the fire of passion and indignation; his white teeth, gleaming out with the terrible smile of scorn.[71]

Sylvia's Lovers however, is not a simple tale of opposites although Philip's physical weakness certainly reflects the narrowness of his moral and spiritual outlook.[72] Sylvia, like Charley Kinraid, is lively and passionate, and her desire for a red, rather than a gray cloak, suggests her visible sexuality which Philip tries vainly to control and hide under what he considers to be a more sober and suitable colour.[73] The tone of their relationship is immediately set as one of conflict in which Sylvia 'would not have yielded to Philip in anything that she could help'.[74] Her recklessness, defiance and uncontrolled emotions make her dangerously unstable, and Philip physically holds her back from joining the crowd going to protest against the press gangs, telling her that it is the law and she can do nothing against it. Philip's forcible removal of Sylvia from the public arena and public debate, his persistent attempts to contain her within the safe confines of the home and to give her a suitable education are however as futile as trying to control the elemental power of the sea with which Sylvia has such a strong bond.

Philip continues in his courtship of Sylvia 'with the patient perseverance that was the one remarkable feature in his character', despite her clear aversion to him, because he believes that he can teach and guide her to behave in a more appropriate, conventional way.[75] The futility of his obsession is underlined by the vignettes and old tales of doomed lovers that are scattered throughout the narrative: Alice Rose's unhappy marriage, mad Nancy and Guy of Warwick all emphasise Phillip's tenuous grasp on the reality of his desires.[76] Like Manasseh, Philip's desire for possession of Sylvia can be described as monomania, in that it is 'exclusive, fixed and permanent'.[77] His obsession is similarly confused and elided with his spiritual beliefs. Philip, a Quaker, whose religion insists on plainness of dress and worship, confesses on his death bed that he has made Sylvia his idol. Not only that, as Marion Shaw asserts, the lie which finally brings about his marriage 'is motivated by a desire for possession so strong that it cancels the promptings of conscience in an otherwise virtuous young man'.[78]

Philip's marriage to Sylvia does not bring him the happiness he expects. The omniscient narrator asks:

> Did it enter into Philip's heart to perceive that he had wedded his long-sought bride in mourning raiment, and that the first sounds which greeted them as they approached their home were those of weeping and wailing?[79]

Philip's guilt at the lie he has told breaks through in dreams, and Sylvia too dreams that Kinraid is alive. Dreams and reality, and the physical and mental health of both Philip and Sylvia become interwoven in a downward spiral of increasing mutual unhappiness. The birth of their daughter, which immediately precedes the crisis in their marriage, at first seems to offer hope. Sylvia learns to love Philip as well as to like and respect him, and Philip 'reached the zenith of his life's happiness.'[80] However, Sylvia's health declines after the birth of her baby, and she develops a fever in which she loses her grasp on reality. She calls out for Charley Kinraid, and her distressed exclamation, 'Oh, who's there?', as Philip enters the room, leaves the reader in doubt as to whether she mistakes her husband for her former lover or imagines she sees Kinraid.[81] Her explanation that she imagines she has seen Charley Kinraid and that he is still alive triggers an angry response in her husband and inflicts what Matus calls a 'psychic wound' on Sylvia.[82] The power of Philip's turbulent emotions made his heart beat so wildly, and almost took him out of himself. Indeed, he must have been quite beside himself for the time, or he could never have gone on to utter the unwise, cruel words he did.[83]

Gaskell here recognises that an altered state of consciousness, an 'out of body' experience, can cause people to act in ways which would be described as 'out of character' with their normal or accepted behaviour. Philip's unconscious has overcome the restraint of his conscious mind. Sylvia's reaction is immediate: she lies down 'motionless and silent', exhaustion and depletion, as Matus notes in her analysis of *North and South*, being the after affects of extreme shock.[84] Again, as in *North and South*, Sylvia's reaction to Philip's speech is associated with dream and trance: 'her steady, dilated eyes had kept him dumb and motionless as if by a spell'.[85] Gaskell uses the language of mesmerism to describe Sylvia's suspended consciousness following the shock she has received. Equally, it reinforces the unconscious and certainly unwilling spell she has cast over Philip, the fatal attraction which has led to this critical point in their relationship.[86] The title of this chapter, 'Evil Omens', and the quasi-spiritual language threaded throughout, also emphasise Philip's misplaced adoration. Philip is 'stung with remorse': he implores forgiveness on his knees and must have Sylvia's pardon, 'even if they both died in the act of reconciliation.'[87] The psychic wound Philip has inflicted is constantly replayed in Sylvia's mind:

She used to shudder as if cold steel had been plunged into her warm, living body as she remembered these words; cruel words, harmlessly provoked. They were too much associated with physical pains to be dwelt upon; only their memory was always there.[88]

The physical and mental, conscious and unconscious are inextricably linked, and the marriage of Sylvia and Philip – founded on a lie on one side and desperation on the other – finally becomes intolerable. It is at this point, that Philip too, begins to suffer from dreams and visions:

Philip used to wonder if the dream that preceded her illness was the suggestive cause that drew her so often to the shore. Her illness consequent upon that dream had filled his mind, so that for many months he himself had had no haunting vision of Kinraid to disturb his slumbers. But now the old dream of Kinraid's actual presence by Philip's bedside began to return with fearful vividness. Night after night it recurred; each time with some new touch of reality, and close approach; till it was as if the fate that overtakes all men were then, even then, knocking at his door.[89]

The sea, which is such a powerful and continuous symbol throughout the narrative, becomes Sylvia's refuge. She can retreat into the past and lift her depression by remembering happier times. The sea offers her the freedom and solitude which she cannot find in the dark, oppressive confinement of her home. The sea also represents her growing spirituality, recalling a passage from one of James Martineau's discourses:

> We must go in contemplation out of life, ere we can see how its troubles subside and are lost, like evanescent waves, in the deeps of eternity and the immensity of God.[90]

But for Philip, the nightly recurrence of his dream of Kinraid, seems to put the same remorseless pressure on his conscious mind as the waves breaking on the shore. This theme is continued into the subsequent chapter, with its title 'Rescued from the Waves' when Philip's dream becomes reality and Kinraid returns.[91] While as Shaw notes, the return of one who is supposed dead was a popular theme in mid-century fiction, Gaskell combines this with the idea of dreams acting as premonitions of events to come.[92] By further aligning dreams with Philip's disrupted conscience, she seems to imply that he has somehow willed Kinraid's reappearance. In the dramatic confrontation between the three protagonists, it is only the remembrance of her child which stops Sylvia from leaving with Kinraid.

In despair, Philip chooses to make himself homeless, leaving home in an act of self-punishment that turns into a pilgrimage. Critics have commented both on the topographical specificity of *Sylvia's Lovers* and the curious disjunction of the enclosed world of Monkshaven with Philip's experiences in the Holy Land.[93] Patsy Stoneman, for example, links Philip's journey and his stay at St Sepulchre's with the wider narrative theme in the novel of power, in particular, controlling masculinity and subservient femininity.[94] If Philip's wanderings are however viewed as an Odyssean continuum of internalised experience and personal growth, and as part of a narrative which includes the telling of personal stories and fables of adventures far away from Monkshaven, then this episode is consistent both with the psychology of the characters and with the narrative structure. Although the story opens with a description of the small town of Monkshaven, bounded by the moors on three sides and the sea on the other, the links to the whaling community suggest an active, exploratory, adventurous life beyond that prescribed by the narrow physical, emotional, and spiritual confines of Monkshaven. In part, therefore, Philip's elective homelessness arises from his need for psychological and emotional freedom as a way of dealing with his obsession with Sylvia, his guilt at the secret he has kept for so long, and his grief at the collapse of his marriage.

Felicia Bonaparte suggests that Philip is imprisoned in a daemonic doubling with Kinraid and argues that he needs to die as Philip Hepburn in order to be reborn 'in his full daemonic character'.[95] She links this to Gaskell's own internal daemon, the divided self which both rejoiced in freedom from domestic constraints and acutely missed her children, the 'many mes' which did not include Gaskell the writer. This challenging interpretation is certainly consistent with Philip's literal and metaphorical journey, but his flight also fits the pattern outlined by Jean Esquirol in his description of the effects of erotic monomania:

> Like all monomaniacs, those suffering from erotomania, are pursued both night and day, by the same thoughts and affections, which are the more disordered as they are concentrated or exasperated by opposition. Fear, hope, jealousy, joy and fury seem unitedly to concur, or in turn, to render more cruel the torment of these wretched beings. They neglect, abandon, and then fly both their relatives and friends. They disdain fortune, and despising social customs, are capable of the most extraordinary, difficult, painful and strange actions.[96]

While Gaskell was tolerant of a wide range of behaviour, she also sought balance and harmony. Philip's extreme passion cannot be reconciled either with accepted codes of social behaviour or within the confines of his own home, and death therefore is the only acceptable resolution.

Homelessness in *Sylvia's Lovers* and in 'Lois the Witch' is considered in the context of an obsessive passion which destabilises behaviour and conscience. In both works, this occurs within a society which is equally destabilised. In Salem, this is the result of spiritual conflict which leads to mass hysteria. In Monkshaven, the community lives under the constant threat of press gangs that descend unannounced to snatch male breadwinners from their families in an ironic inversion of law and order. Gaskell's use of dreams and visions in *Sylvia's Lovers* enables her to explore psychic states beyond the ordinary, and adds richness and depth to her interest in the unconscious mind and its connection with the physical body.

5 - THE INVISIBLE HAND: SERVANTS IN GASKELL'S SHORTER FICTION

Gaskell's fiction is almost exclusively concerned with the portrayal of working and middle-class lives. In this context, it is servants who straddle the cultural and social divide between the classes. They share domestic space and tasks in an often uneasy relationship that negotiates a tenuous path between the vulnerability and intimacy of both employers and employed. Gaskell uses the unique position of servants within the Victorian home to comment on a range of social relationships and a changing society.

The nineteenth century saw an expansion in the demand for domestic servants to meet the needs of the emerging middle classes, who viewed the employment of servants as an essential mark of their newly acquired social status.[1] Service was the largest occupational category after agricultural work, and more people were employed in domestic work than in factories or in any other sector of the economy.[2] Census returns for 1851 show that large numbers of employers were small tradesmen who mostly employed a maid-of-all-work. By 1871, almost two-thirds of the 1.2 million female servants, (nearly 13% of the female population of England and Wales), were classed as 'general', that is, maids-of-all-work.[3] The solitary working environment of these women was very different from that of servants who were employed in a large, hierarchically ordered establishment.[4] Isabella Beeton recognised their isolation and drudgery: 'The general servant, or maid-of-all-work, is perhaps the only one of her class deserving commiseration: her life is a solitary one, and, in some places, her work is never done.'[5]

Such servants played a crucial role in the Victorian home, protecting the occupants both from the war against dirt, which was relentless, unremitting and physically gruelling, and from the intrusion of the outside world.[6] Culturally, therefore, servants may be viewed as occupying an ambiguous

interstitial space between the internal and the external, the seen and the un-
seen. Most servants lived with middle-class families and were necessarily an
intimate part of family life, yet were expected to be 'socially invisible'.[7] As
Margaret Hale observes in *North and South* (1855):

> There might be toilers and moilers there in London, but she never
> saw them; the very servants lived in an underground world of their
> own, of which she knew neither the hopes nor the fears; they only
> seemed to start into existence when some want or whim of their
> master and mistress needed them.[8]

Karen Chase and Michael Levenson point out that this ambiguity expressed a discourse of tension associated with servants. They were drawn
from the working classes, who, en masse, posed an uncontrolled and apparently uncontrollable social, political and economic threat. Yet, as servants,
they infiltrated into the heart of the domestic refuge, acting as 'a disciplined
squad [...] whose role was to protect home life from the very disruptions
which they exemplified.'[9] In larger, more aristocratic homes, this tension was
managed by rendering servants anonymous. Employers thought nothing of
changing servants' names arbitrarily, or of giving the same name to successive holders of a position, whatever their real names might be.

Servants were also marked out by their uniforms. Maids were put into
uniform for the first time in the nineteenth century as a means of differ-
entiating them from their mistresses, particularly those in the aspiring middle classes who had newly entered the servant-keeping classes. Leigh Hunt's
light-hearted account of a common complaint about servants' dress and
appearance perhaps masks a more complex discourse about the effects of
exposing young working class girls to the social and cultural expectations of
the middle classes:

> In her manners, the maid-servant sometimes imitates her young mis-
> tress; she puts her hair in papers, cultivates a shape, and occasionally
> contrives to be out of spirits.[10]

Maids were often given their mistress's cast-off clothes as well as lengths of
cloth to make their uniforms, initiating a series of confused and conflicting
tensions around power and control versus individual freedom.[11] Sometimes,

cast-offs must have been preferable to the painful clash of cultures and taste at which Gaskell, probably among the more liberal of employers, visibly winced – 'Caroline has on an <u>atrocious</u> print today, great stripes of crimson, blue & brown'.[12] In general, nineteenth-century employers sought to control every aspect of their servant's identity and appearance, including their religious beliefs.[13]

Increasingly, even fairly modest homes attempted to physically separate servants from their employers, and this paradigm was incorporated into theories of design such as those of the architect Robert Kerr:

> Let the family have free passageway without encountering the servants unexpectedly; and let the servants have access to all their duties without coming unexpectedly upon the family and visitors.[14]

In Gaskell's own house in Plymouth Grove, the dining room has three doors, one of which leads into the kitchen and servants' quarters. There are back stairs and a separate entrance for the delivery of goods so that the servants can indeed perform their tasks invisibly. The differentiation of the door in the dining room which leads into the servants' quarters is very subtle. Like the other two doors in the room, it is four-panelled, but the panels have no moulding. The ceilings in the kitchen and servants' quarters are also lower than those in the rest of the house.

It was the servant who negotiated and facilitated the social interactions of the family and who had to become familiar with the often complex codes of visiting, including the elaborate etiquette associated with visiting cards.[15] They were often present, even in middle-class homes, at key events in the lives of the families they served. Julie Nash describes the way a team of servants gently and tactfully informed Maria Edgeworth about the death of her friend, the Duchess of Wellington, and Gaskell's son Willie died in a servant's arms.[16] Yet at the same time, many employers like the Gaskells, particularly those in smaller, middle-class homes, were not comfortable with the intrusion of a live-in servant, even when they offered exceptional skills and experience. In a letter to her daughter Marianne of 22 November 1852, Gaskell remarks:

> We did think of a very first rate German governess, […] who could teach music & singing, German, French Italian & what not, – but

we dislike having a governess in the house to break our privacy as a family.[17]

Gaskell's comment illustrates the daily tensions which had to be negotiated in the contract between servant and employer. As Elizabeth Langland points out in her reassessment of the cultural discourse around Victorian politics and economics, the presence of servants in the home meant that women, far from being protected within the domestic sphere, were in fact dealing with complex issues of labour management that were part of a wider debate in the nineteenth century as society grappled with the emergence of a capitalist economy.[18] The majority of middle-class women who employed servants would have had to undertake daily face-to-face negotiations with their employees. The continuing dialogue throughout *North and South* about the supply and demand of labour, the management of conflict, and the proper treatment of employees therefore finds a direct counterpart within the confines of the home.

The employment of even one servant was an essential mark of social acceptability and Gaskell's light-hearted fictional accounts of the familiar relationship between single women and their sometime far from competent maids recognises this.[19] Yet this did not preclude mistresses from having to undertake some domestic work themselves, since most households only employed one servant, and the work was too much for one person. Mrs Ellis was no doubt making a virtue of a necessity when she stated that if a woman:

wishes to stand at the head of her household, to be respected by her own servants, and to feel herself the mistress of her own affairs, [...] she must be acquainted with the best method of doing everything upon which domestic comfort depends.[20]

Gaskell's letters contain a constant thread of commentary on the domestic chaos caused by the absence of servants on holiday, (she decides to try to do without fires to save work), new servants arriving, (pots and pans have to be scoured before the new cook comes), or the washerwoman not turning up, keys being lost and having to manage a stream of visitors.[21] It is hardly a picture of domestic calm.[22]

It was not only the management of servants that was a potential cause of tension. Contemporary writers such as Sarah Stickney Ellis recognised the importance of focused activity as a means of warding off affective depression triggered by domestic confinement and social and cultural expectations:

> I have strongly recommended exercise as the first rule for preserving health; but there is an exercise in domestic usefulness, which, without superseding that in the open air, is highly beneficial to the health, both of mind and body.[23]

Ellis is alluding to the dangers inherent in employing servants that could make women overly dependent, resulting in the atrophy of emotional, intellectual, and physical powers. Ellis is firm in her advice:

> I am aware that I incur the risk of being considered amongst young ladies as too homely in my notions […] when I so often recommend good old-fashioned household duties; yet, I believe them, nevertheless, to be a wholesome medicine to both body and mind.[24]

This advice is echoed by Mrs Loftie, whose reliably robust views link practicality with the familiar trope of domesticity as an enhancement of feminine beauty and attractiveness. The lady of the house, she asserts:

> must not be ashamed of being seen in a cooking apron or even with a duster in her hand. Mr. Ruskin thinks every young lady should take charge of a corner of the dining-room, and keep it as bright as a bit of a Dutch picture for her own sake as well as for an example to the housemaid. Certainly the best way to have good servants is to show them we care enough about order and cleanliness to take the trouble to secure it with our own hands if necessary.[25]

Gaskell is clearly of the same mind, for example, in her depiction of Mrs Carson in *Mary Barton* (1848):

> Mrs Carson was (as was usual with her, […]) sitting up-stairs in her dressing-room, indulging in the luxury of a head-ache.[…] Without education enough to value the resources of wealth and leisure, she was so circumstanced as to command both. It would have done her more good than all the ether and sal-volatile she was daily in the habit of swallowing, if she might have taken the work of one of her own housemaids for a week; made beds, rubbed tables, shaken

carpets, and gone out into the fresh morning air without all the para-
phernalia of shawl, cloak, boa, fur boots, bonnet, and veil, in which
she was equipped before setting out for an 'airing,' in the closely
shut-up carriage.[26]

The passage encapsulates the experiences of a woman in the newly emerging middle classes. There is little difference in class, education, and upbringing between Mrs Carson and her servants. Her new-found wealth inhibits
her rather than releasing her to develop a richer and more fulfilling life. She
uses self-medication both to dull her feelings and to cope with the boredom
of her daily life. The smothering layers of clothes she puts on before entering the enclosed world of the carriage further prevent her from engaging in
any real contact with the external world. Her life is the epitome of the gilded
cage in which so many Victorian women were trapped, and Gaskell's robust
comments indicate her own impatience with the paradigm. The passive act
of swallowing numbing medicine is contrasted with the vigorous actions of
shaking and rubbing, and throwing off the restrictive clothing which prevents ease of movement and vision.

Gaskell's own relationship with her servants and her management of her
home was both warmer and more active, and in this sense, more typical of
the eighteenth than the nineteenth century.[27] Like many of her contemporaries, she tended to recruit servants who were already known to her through
personal contacts.[28] She formed a warm and close bond with many of them
and took a personal interest in their lives. By the time the Gaskells were established in Plymouth Grove, they had acquired 'five women-servants, and
an out-of-doors-man, or gardener' including the invaluable Hearn, the governess 'as much one of the family as any one of us'. Hearn stayed with the
Gaskells for over fifty years, (long after Gaskell herself had died), and became
the backbone of the family. She provided practical care and support and
continuity during Gaskell's increasingly frequent absences from Manchester.
Hearn was present when Gaskell died and it is her name that appears on the
death certificate as the informant of her death.[29]

Critics and historians have recognised that the feudal ideal of paternalism
on which the hierarchical social structure of previous centuries was based,
metamorphosed in the nineteenth century into a form of social paternalism

in which wives, children and servants could all be described as dependent upon the figure of the paterfamilias.[30] Certainly, Gaskell was a passionate advocate of an inclusive relationship between social classes in line with her Unitarian principles, but, at the same time, she displays an interesting ambivalence in her essay 'French Life'. She approves of the Parisian style of families and servants living in a large apartment on one level, which not only means saving the cost of at least one servant, but also has the moral advantage of mistresses and their servants living more like a family.[31] However, she moves on to recall a young married lady who came to live in London from the country, bringing with her, two of her Sunday school scholars as servants. She is unhappy with their living conditions 'in the depths of a London kitchen' and prefers to keep them 'under her own eye without any appearance of watching them; and besides this she could hear of their joys and sorrows, and by taking an interest in their interests induce them to care for hers.'[32]

There is an ambivalence in this passage with its suggestion that servants are essentially untrustworthy and therefore need watching, and the artificial creation of a relationship based on need rather than mutual regard. The tension lies in the fact that the employer/servant relationship is essentially a contractual one, masked here by a layer of paternalistic concern. While there is no doubting Gaskell's personal and genuine interest in her servants, equally, she could be ruthless when necessary in terminating their employment when they no longer met her needs. Thus she calls the doctor for Hearn when she is ill, tells Marianne that she must write home to ensure that the servants make the new housemaid welcome, and sends the maid off immediately to see her fiancé, whose leg is crushed in an industrial accident.[33] But she has no hesitation in dismissing her governess, Ferguson, when she feels that her teaching of her daughters is inadequate, even though it was in Ferguson's arms that her son Willie had died.[34]

The children's nurse

The children's nurse is an important figure in both nineteenth-century fiction and society. Leonore Davidoff asserts that in households with young children, even when only one servant was employed, most of that servant's time would be taken up with caring for the children.[35] In many cases, the nurse

would be a young girl, from a different background from that of her employers, but who nevertheless exercised an immense influence over the children
in her care. This could lead to tension. Gaskell says that William tells her
she is 'not of a jealous disposition' but notes, rather ruefully, that her eldest
daughter, Marianne, 'shows a marked preference for Betsy; who has always
been as far as I can judge a kind, judicious, and tender nurse'.[36] As with her
earlier comments in 'French Life', the phrase 'as far as I can judge', displays
a certain ambiguity and doubt as to how Betsy behaves when Gaskell is not
with her. In a sense, the issues of power, conflict, and trust which underlie
the employer/servant relationship could be said to coalesce around the figure
of the children's nurse, since it is she, more than any other servant, who mirrors her employer, being, as Jonathan Gathorne-Hardy remarks, 'half-parent,
half-servant'.[37]

This duality is found in the figure of Nancy, the old servant in 'The
Moorland Cottage' (1850). Critics have identified the Wordsworthian influences in the isolated setting and the importance of the landscape in the
emotional lives and development of the characters, and Gaskell herself acknowledges her debt to 'German forest-tales'.[38] The story opens in the idyllic setting of the Browne's isolated farm as the family make their way to
church. Nancy is introduced to the reader as 'Old Nanny' and although she
walks behind Mrs Browne and Edward, 'they were all one party and all talked
together in a subdued and quiet tone, as beseemed the day'.[39] These few
sentences set the tone and narrative themes of the story. Mrs Browne and
her son are the powerful figures in the family and lead the way. The grouping together of Nancy and Maggie, although a realistic reflection of their
relationship, (Nancy, as Old Nanny, looks after Maggie), also suggests that
child and servant hold a similarly powerless position within the hierarchy of
the family. They walk behind Mrs Browne, the titular head of the household,
and her son, who, as the only male, will assume proprietorial rights over both
the property and its inhabitants. Gaskell underlines this in the next sentence,
by confirming that Mrs Browne is a widow. The opening paragraphs, which
seem to present a calm, pastoral paradise, in fact contain an unconventional
family grouping already holding within itself the seeds of the elemental catastrophe with which the story concludes. In terms of the social paternalistic

paradigm, there is no paterfamilias, and it is Mrs Brown and Nancy therefore who must provide moral and spiritual guidance for the children.

The death of Mr Browne has had financial consequences for the family. They can only afford to keep one servant, the minimum necessary for social respectability, and this has practical implications:

> The cow, the pig, and the poultry took up much of Nancy's time. Mrs. Browne and Maggie had to do a great deal of the house-work; and when the beds were made, and the rooms swept and dusted, and the preparations for dinner ready, then, if there was any time, Maggie sat down to her lessons.[40]

As a Unitarian, Gaskell would be concerned at the low priority given to Maggie's education. It should be the responsibility of Mrs Browne to give Maggie lessons to prepare her for adult life, and she is clearly neglecting this as Mrs Buxton notices later, and takes steps to remedy the situation. Edward (Ned), on the other hand, 'who prided himself considerably on his sex, had been sitting all the morning, in his father's arm-chair in the little book-room, 'studying,' as he chose to call it.'[41] The theme of Maggie's hierarchical and gender based treatment and exclusion from her proper place in the family is further developed when she spills the water she is carrying:

> Perhaps I am clumsy. Mama says I am; and Ned says I am. Nancy never says so, and papa never said so. I wish I could help being clumsy and stupid. Ned says all women are so. I wish I was not a woman. It must be a fine thing to be a man. Oh dear! I must go up the field again with this heavy pitcher, and my arms do so ache![42]

Nancy is aligned with Maggie's dead father as a source of kindness and emotional support. She recognises and acknowledges Maggie's innate qualities and characteristics. Yet as a servant, she does not have the authority to alter the balance of power within the family, although she does challenge Mrs Browne's assumption that she does not know how to deal appropriately with visitors. Neither does she have the formal education to meet Maggie's needs. Maggie's internal dialogue therefore expresses a complex pattern of unmet need and the paradox of her situation: she is 'clumsy' and 'stupid' because she has not been educated, not because of her gender or innate inability. She has not been educated because she has to carry out the hard and heavy work of a servant. Of the two people who could help her, one is dead and the other, a servant, has limited power and authority.

The arrival of Mr Buxton marks a significant change in Maggie's life and his entrance into the house weaves together and further develops the narrative themes. Mrs Browne and Edward have disappeared to make themselves presentable for the visit, leaving Maggie and Nancy bustling in and out of the dairy and kitchen. Mr Buxton, finding the front door open, makes his way past the public space of the parlour, which is empty, through to the working area of the kitchen. Although Gaskell points out that an open front door is customary in country places, it is nevertheless the job of the servant to mediate the entrance of visitors into the family. Mr Buxton's uninvited presence in the home has echoes therefore of the fairy-tale romance, prefiguring the role his family will have in 'rescuing' and rehabilitating Maggie. He is a large male presence in this family of women and children, and his well nourished appearance indicates his power, status and authority. The working kitchen, into which Mr Buxton squeezes his substantial frame, is physically demarcated from the public areas of the farmhouse by a low lintel, and it is significant that Mr Buxton is able to make the transition with pleasure, if with a little physical discomfort:

> he stood there, stooping a little under the low-browed lintels of the kitchen door, and looking large, and red, and warm, but with a pleased and almost amused expression of face.[43]

His treatment of Maggie may be interpreted as a continuation of the fairy tale theme. Like Cinderella, she is 'disguised' as a servant when he first sees her, but he recognises her true self: 'And so, you are a notable little woman, are you?'[44] Mrs Browne re-enters at this key moment, having not only changed her cap, but also her gown, leaving Maggie to retreat to the kitchen, reasserting their respective roles. Nancy immediately rebalances the power by smoothing Maggie's hair: 'it was all that was needed to make her look delicately neat'.[45] This is of course precisely the maternal role which Mrs Browne should have fulfilled and reinforces the themes of disguise, jealousy, and resentment which constitute the dynamics of relationships within the family.

Gaskell's choice of adjectives, 'delicately neat,' subtly indicate that Maggie's true nature and status cannot be concealed or buried, however harsh her treatment, and this is borne out as the narrative develops.

The pivotal role Mr Buxton is to play in Maggie's life is indicated in his next conversation with her where her roles, as maid-of-all-work and daughter of the family, are elided, and the transition from the one to the other suggested:

> Suppose you come to my house, and teach us how to make [gingerbread.] And we have got a pony for you to ride on, and a peacock and guinea fowls, and I don't know what all.[46]

She will gain entry to his house through her practical skills, but once there, will take on her true role as the equal to his own children. Mr Buxton's visit precipitates a family conference which includes Nancy. She takes an important part in the discussion and also in the narrative as she is able to provide additional information for the family and for the reader about the Buxton family.

Nancy's role as surrogate mother continues during Maggie's visits to the Buxton household, easing her transition from quasi-servant to young lady. It is Nancy who persuades Mrs Browne to allow Maggie to take rides with Frank Buxton, and Gaskell is disingenuous in her authorial assertion that 'I don't know why Mrs Browne should have denied it for the circle they went was always within sight of the knoll in front of the house, if any one cared enough about the matter to mount it, and look after them.'[47] There is a scarcely concealed criticism implicit in the phrase 'if anyone cared enough about the matter' that strikes at the heart of Mrs Browne's self-indulgent and careless mothering. Mrs Buxton mirrors Nancy in providing an alternative mother figure for Maggie, but one who is more appropriate to her social status and who can supply the gaps in her education which Nancy cannot.

Nancy's parallel role as surrogate mother is illustrated by her full participation in the discussions about Maggie's engagement to Frank Buxton. It is significant that she is the person who has embroidered the linen and, like Mrs Thornton when she thinks her son will marry Margaret Hale, will be the one to alter the initials embroidered in red cotton. It is Nancy who tells

Maggie the truth about her brother and his excessive spending, as a result of which, Maggie, like Margaret Hale, is forced to take on parental responsibility, and write to Edward to remonstrate with him. Nancy and Maggie work together to reduce the household expenditure and to deal with the crisis brought about by Edward's eventual prosecution. Nancy's role in the family and her dual position as both servant and surrogate mother is recognised and respected by the Buxtons. Erminia, acting as their representative says: 'I've come to take care of your mother. My uncle says she and Nancy must come to us for a long, long visit.'[48] Nancy and Mrs Browne are accorded equal status in the linking of 'mother' with 'she and Nancy'.

In 'The Moorland Cottage', Gaskell explores the intricately entwined figures of servant and parent, their roles and responsibilities and the effect of this on children. While the focus of this discussion has been on Nancy's influence on Maggie, the parallel theme within the story is the disastrous effect of Mrs Browne's weak parenting of her son. Throughout the story, Gaskell weaves a thread of implicit and continuing criticism of Mrs Browne as a mother, expressed indirectly through the actions and responsibilities undertaken by Nancy, the faithful servant who has been with Mrs Browne since her marriage.

Parental authority and control are also a central theme in 'The Old Nurse's Story' (1852). The narrator is once again, a faithful old servant, a children's nurse who is telling her charges about their family history. The opening sentence is reassuring:

> You know, my dears, that your mother was an orphan, and an only child; and I dare say you have heard that your grandfather was a clergyman up in Westmoreland, where I come from.[49]

The story will be a comfortable re-telling of things the children already know, by the familiar, secure adult of the title: the old nurse. Only the passing mention of the fact that their mother was an orphan, with its suggestion of isolation and sadness, and that their grandfather comes from a county unknown to them, hints at darker themes. Hester, the narrator, looks back to when she was 'just a girl in the village school.'[50] It was common for girls to begin work as young as seven or eight, usually with simple cleaning jobs, and by the early 1880s, approximately one third of girls between the ages of fifteen and twenty, most of them country born and bred, were employed as domestic servants.[51] In *North and South*, for example,

> Dixon's ideas of helpful girls were founded on the recollection of tidy elder scholars at Helstone school, who were only too proud to be allowed to come to the parsonage on a busy day.[52]

Dixon's preference for a literate young servant, like the choice of Hester as nursemaid, is, as Jean Fernandez notes, 'teasingly ambiguous'.[53] The professionalisation of domestic management supported by innumerable advice manuals meant that by mid-century, literacy was a desirable qualification for a servant. Yet as Fernandez asserts, literacy needed to be domesticated and controlled:

> The cult of domesticity that established the home as a spiritual and cultural sanctuary suggested a possible space where a wholesome literacy could be acquired and practiced by the working classes, transforming them into an amenable citizenry.[54]

Hester's proudly acquired scholastic skills therefore are juxtaposed against a much older oral tradition in which she fulfils a traditional and accepted role as a benign quasi-maternal narrator of bedtime tales. This already compromised trope is further unsettled by the transformation of a family history into a horrific supernatural tale of feudal violence. Fernandez further notes the complex inversion of a number of narrative expectations: it is the aristocrat rather than the servant who is seduced and gives birth secretly, hiding the child in a farmhouse, and the father of the child who is an employee of the family:

> Hester's proficiency in uncovering such a narrative intimates to the Victorian reader the sinister side to class relations within the domestic sphere, and its consequences for the reworking of conventional plots, when the household employees exceed their masters in knowledge, skills, and social grace.[55]

The unsettled nature of the narrative is suggested from the beginning of the story. Hester's job initially is a happy one. She and her mistress form a close bond and when both of her employers die suddenly, little Miss Rosamond, now aged four or five, is left in her care, even though Hester herself is not eighteen. Gaskell moves the story, in its opening paragraphs, from life to death, from a stable, happy home environment for both employers and servants, to the isolation of a young girl, left alone with a small child.

The unfolding narrative illustrates Hester's powerlessness to influence events, since, 'before we had well stilled our sobs, [...] somehow it was settled' that she and Miss Rosamond would go to Furnivall Manor House in Northumberland.[56] However, Hester's own status is considerably enhanced by this move: she will be a 'young lady's maid', one of the most coveted of positions in a household and she is 'well pleased that all the folks in the Dale should stare and admire'.[57] At the end of the second paragraph of the story therefore, another of the major narrative themes is introduced: that of pride linked to social status.

The narrative is further destabilised by Hester's discovery that they are not to live in the house in which Rosamond's mother grew up, but are to be sent instead to the unknown Furnivall Manor House. Hester obtains this information from Lord Furnivall's manservant, who does his best to reassure her by describing the Manor House as 'a very grand place' and 'very healthy'.[58] His description appeals both to Hester's personal ambition and to her anxiety for Rosamond. The family's lack of care for Rosamond, or indeed for the young servant in whose care she is left, is reinforced by what Hester leaves unsaid as much as by what she does tell the reader. There is no discussion of Rosamond's education or of any provision being made for her beyond that of her entertaining old Miss Furnivall. Lord Furnivall himself never speaks more than is necessary. He leaves his manservant to escort Hester and Rosamond to the Manor House, telling him to be back at Newcastle that same evening 'so there was no great length of time for him to make us known to all the strangers before he, too, shook us off'.[59] The themes of pride and isolation are drawn together in a telling sentence:

> We had left our own dear parsonage very early, and we had both cried as if our hearts would break, though we were travelling in my lord's carriage, which I thought so much of once.[60]

The servant and her young employer are two lonely, grieving, frightened children on their way from a secure, stable home to an unknown destination among strangers. Hester's powerlessness is emphasised when the manservant tells her to wake Rosamond, who has fallen into an exhausted sleep as they drive up to the Manor House, so that she can see the park and house. She is forced to comply 'for fear he should complain of me to my lord.'[61]

The use of the word 'fear' in this sentence is significant. It is the first time Hester has explicitly voiced feelings of anxiety about their change of home, and it is immediately followed by a description of the wild and lonely setting of the Manor House, where nature itself seems to be closing in to destroy the building: 'we saw a great and stately house, with many trees close around it, so close that in some places their branches dragged against the walls when the wind blew'.[62] The house is only clear at the front, suggesting the importance of appearance and status: 'The great oval drive was without a weed; and neither tree nor creeper was allowed to grow over the long, many-windowed front; [...] for the house, although it was so desolate, was even grander than I expected.'[63]

The tone of the narrative continues to darken as Hester and Rosamond enter the hall of the house, which alone is so large Hester thinks they will be lost. The scale of the furnishings and fittings inside the Manor is huge and heavy, emphasising by contrast the emotional and physical vulnerability of the two young girls. The house is dark, without a fire, which contemporary readers would easily decode as meaning a home without warmth and security, and it contains many mysterious doors. An old servant leads them further into the complex internal layout of the manor to meet Miss Furnivall and her companion, the aptly named Mrs Stark, who appears the more formidable of the two:

> She had lived with Miss Furnivall ever since they were both young, and now she seemed more like a friend than a servant; she looked so cold and grey, and stony, as is she had never loved or cared for any one; and I don't suppose she did care for any one, except her mistress; and, owing to the great deafness of the latter, Mrs. Stark treated her very much as if she were a child.[64]

This passage sets up the pattern of doubles and links which are entwined throughout 'The Old Nurse's Story'. The relationship between Miss Furnivall and Mrs Stark mirrors that of Hester and Rosamond. Miss Furnivall's deafness is a metaphor for her pride, selfishness, and lack of care for her sister and her child. Her face, 'as full of fine wrinkles as if they had been drawn all over it with a needle's point' is the living embodiment of her relationship with her sister.[65] The image of the needle etching patterns into her skin vividly captures the torturous and toxic blend of jealousy and guilt which persists after her sister's death. In an ironic reversal of roles, her deafness and age have now made her as helpless as a child and dependent upon her companion. The social and hierarchical distinctions between servant and employer have disappeared, and Hester and Rosamond are left 'standing there, being looked at by the two old ladies through their spectacles'.[66]

After the carefully placed Gothic references, (death, travel to a remote and unknown place, the old and decrepit manor house with its mysterious doors and passages), this is anticlimactic to the point of bathos. However, it is also a very necessary pacing of the narrative so that the climax of the story with its horrific exposure of cruelty and abuse of power within the Furnivall family retains its full impact. The reader, as well as Hester and Rosamond, needs some respite, and this is found in the sanctuary of the old nursery 'with a pleasant fire burning in the grate, and the kettle boiling on the hob, and tea things spread out on the table'.[67] Further reassurance comes from the community of servants: Dorothy and Hester both come from Westmoreland, and Rosamond is soon 'sitting on Dorothy's knee, and chattering away as fast as her little tongue could go'.[68] Hester's experience reverses the trope of the children's nurse suggested by Gathorne-Hardy, that is, that the Nanny was suspended in an uneasy social and cultural limbo between the mother and the rest of the staff, not fully engaging with either.[69] For Hester, the rest of the servants become a quasi-family for both her and Rosamond and provide links to a happier past. The relationship with the servants appears to release Rosamond, who acts as a catalyst to bring the house to life and to forge links between all the inhabitants: 'Kitchen and drawing-room, it was all the same. The hard, sad Miss Furnivall, and the cold Mrs. Stark, looked pleased when she came fluttering in like a bird'.[70]

It is the servant Dorothy who begins to reveal the secret of the Furnivall family. Hester and Dorothy turn round the picture of Miss Furnivall's sister 'that leaned with its face towards the wall, and was not hung up as the others were'.[71] It is at this point in the story that the organ is heard for the first time, as if the servants' talk and actions have unlocked the secrets that the family has tried so hard to contain. Fear dominates the narrative and Hester, once again, has to overcome her pride, and talk to Agnes, the kitchen-maid, 'though I had always held my head rather above her, as I was evened to James and Dorothy and she was little better than their servant', since Dorothy is too frightened to tell her any more.[72] The Gothic elements of the story now predominate as the guilty past is no longer able to be repressed, and Gaskell has to find a narrative form that will allow her to tell a brutal tale of male patriarchal tyranny and violence, female cruelty, class antagonism and gender inequality.

Hester, as narrator, now takes a more distanced stance, simply recounting events as she experiences them as a spectator. It is Rosamond, the living child who sees and communicates with the ghost-child, who takes an active role in the story as it moves towards its denouement. This transfer of narrative power from servant to child is precipitated when Hester loses Rosamond and searches for her frantically throughout the house. In an ironic and complex interplay of symbolic and actual roles in the real world and in the spirit world, Hester, Rosamond's surrogate mother, loses her in the house which belongs to her dead mother's family, who seek both to reclaim her and to destroy her.

In the midst of the Gothic horror, Gaskell subtly inserts a Christian reference, hinting that good will overcome evil, and indicating that Hester's unconditional care for Rosamond will prevail over the destructive rivalry of the two sisters. Hester follows Rosamond's footsteps in the snow and meets a shepherd 'bearing something in his arms wrapped in his maud'.[73] Although the figure of the shepherd is entirely consistent with the reality of the fell landscape, it can also be interpreted as Christ, the shepherd of his sheep. Rosamond is lying under a holly tree, the only bush for miles around, a plant closely associated with the celebration of Christmas, reinforcing the blend of Christian imagery and realistic landscape. Rosamond is 'lying still, and white, and stiff, in his arms, as if she had been dead.'[74] Christ's miraculous power is suggested by the fact that when the shepherd hands Rosamond back to Hester, she returns to life. This short passage is a conspicuous example of the way in which Gaskell's narrative iteration could embrace layers of nuanced references. In this case, a Christian theme runs in parallel with a closely observed description of a landscape and its people.

Rosamond becomes the focus of the power struggle between the Furnivall sisters, one living and one dead, and the means by which their original contest is re-enacted and finally resolved. In this elemental struggle, it is Hester who saves her. It is notable that Miss Furnivall, once again, ignores the claims of the child, linked to her by family ties, and Hester who, although Rosamond is almost convulsed by her efforts to join the spirit child, holds her 'tighter and tighter, till I feared I should do her a hurt'.[75]

The structural narrative pattern of repetition and return, is, as Jill Matus argues in her consideration of Dickens' 'The Signalman', a signifier of unassimilated experience and strong emotion – what would now be described as trauma.[76] Gaskell's concluding sentence, 'What is done in youth can never be undone in age!' underlines the importance of a proper upbringing linked to an appropriate moral education. It neatly joins the narrative circle with the opening of the story which suggests that Hester's actions have ensured that Rosamond has a happy and fulfilling life. Fernandez also notes the continuing ambiguity expressed in the conclusion, in that Miss Furnivall's words could refer equally to the betrayal of her sister and the subsequent death of both her and her child, or to her own desire for the music master, but comments that Gaskell both raises anxieties and soothes them as the servant's narrative is domesticated as family reading within the confines of *Household Words*.[77]

The good and faithful servant

The honesty of servants was a common anxiety in the nineteenth century and fuelled what Chase and Levenson describe as 'a discourse of suspicion'.[78] Huggett points out that thefts by servants accounted for the largest total loss of property in the Metropolitan Police area in 1837[79] and Gaskell ironically comments, 'I am sure that if I were a servant, & suspected and things locked up from me &, I should not only be dishonest, but a very clever thief.'[80] She explores this preoccupation in two of her short stories, 'Right at Last' and 'The Manchester Marriage' both published in 1858, in which servants are wrongly accused of stealing.[81]

'Right at Last' was originally published as 'The Sin of a Father' in *Household Words*, 27 November 1858. The change of title, which occurred when 'Right at Last' became the opening piece in a collection of Gaskell's short stories published in 1860, indicates the real focus of the narrative, which is on the servant-employer relationship. The story opens with the marriage of Margaret Frazer to a young doctor. The marriage is opposed by Margaret's guardians on the grounds that the blandly named Dr James Brown is unknown to them and therefore cannot be 'placed'. Margaret's insistence on marrying him despite their concern isolates her from her guardians and creates the tension and narrative interest necessary to engage the reader.

Money becomes an important issue. There were significant cultural and social pressures on Victorian men who had to establish themselves in a career before they could afford to provide properly for their wives and families. Contemporary readers would therefore immediately understand the implications of the newly-weds setting up home with two servants, including a man-servant. Employers were heavily taxed for the privilege of employing servants, and male servants were taxed more heavily than females.[82] Margaret, who is 'a prudent and sensible girl [...] questioned the wisdom of starting in life with a man-servant; but had yielded to Doctor Brown's arguments on the necessity of keeping up a respectable appearance'[83] and Gaskell subtly conveys unease about this paragon of a servant who is both an excellent practical handyman and carpenter, and domestically accomplished.

Financial pressures, linked to Doctor Brown's insecurity about the status and appearance of the home he is able to provide for his wife, affect the happiness of the newly married couple. These tensions are reflected in a feud between Crawford and Christie, the old female servant who has long been connected to Margaret's family. This domestic power struggle would have been common in Victorian households, and Margaret attributes Christie's vague accusations, which she is unable to substantiate, to jealousy. Although money continues to be an issue, the popular, successful Doctor Brown begins to make good progress in his career. He remains however 'the most anxious person in his family', although he is strangely unconcerned by their household bills which 'amounted to more than even the prudent Margaret had expected'.[84] The climax of the narrative is anticipated by the entry of Crawford bringing tea into the consulting room in which the Browns are sitting 'for the better economy of fire'.[85] He earns a sharp reprimand from Margaret, who is concerned at the size of their debts, for the puffs of smoke coming from the chimney. The scene explicitly ties together the narrative themes of money, the trustworthiness or otherwise of servants, and domestic happiness. It is the first time that Crawford has neglected his duties, and the admittedly unsubtle connection Gaskell makes between the servant and the smoking fire, provides a dual metaphor with diabolic as well as domestic associations.

The following morning however, the fire burns brightly, the sun is shining and all appears to be well, until Doctor Brown discovers that the money he has locked in his bureau overnight to pay their bills has vanished. Suspicion immediately falls upon the servants. The charwoman is quickly eliminated from suspicion, as is the chimney sweep. It is Crawford who is arrested for theft, causing very different reactions in Doctor Brown and his wife. Margaret is more concerned to retrieve the money which has been stolen and thinks she must be very hard hearted not to suffer as her husband is evidently doing. The truth, it transpires, is that Crawford is not only a thief, but a blackmailer who has discovered that Doctor Brown's father is a convicted criminal. The tension Doctor Brown has experienced is a combination of the social stigma of being the son of a convicted criminal, and the necessity of concealing this relationship which, if revealed, would make it impossible for him to earn a living. In addition, he lives with the fear that crime is hereditary.

In this relatively simple short story, therefore, Gaskell explores a number of complex contemporary themes. She uses doubles throughout the story to contrast and illuminate her narrative concerns. Crawford, the apparently competent, but dishonest manservant is mirrored by Christie, the less worldly, but loyal female servant. Crawford's origins, like Doctor Brown's, are unknown. Crawford, outwardly honest and above reproach, is a thief and blackmailer. Doctor Brown, tainted with his father's criminality, is both honest and honourable. Margaret untangles the dilemma by writing to Crawford, telling him that 'No threats can deter your master from doing his duty.'[86] Her signature, Margaret Brown, clearly aligns her with her husband, and the Browns, aided by the faithful Christie, make a new start and finally forge a successful life together. The story, as Charlotte Mitchell notes, is authenticated by the narrator's comment that 'last time I was in London, I saw a brass-plate with Doctor James Brown upon it, on the door of a handsome house in a handsome square'.[87]

The main plot of 'The Manchester Marriage', published in *Household Words* a month later (7 December 1858), anticipates Tennyson's *Enoch Arden* (1864) and Hardy's *The Mayor of Casterbridge* (1886). Like several of Gaskell's stories written during this period, it opens with a frame story which outlines the circumstances of Mrs Openshaw's first marriage, starting with the arrival of the Openshaws in London and moving backwards in time. The opening paragraph shows Gaskell confidently manipulating the tone of the narrative and the perceptions of the reader. Mr Openshaw is presented as a typical Manchester business man whose northern sense of hospitality means that 'he could hardly suffer a visitor to leave the house without forcing meat and drink upon him'.[88] Although Gaskell is gently poking fun at provincial values, the paragraph concludes with the statement that 'Every servant in the house was well warmed, well fed, and kindly treated',[89] a social paternalism of which Gaskell clearly approves.

Norah is the loyal servant who stays with Alice Openshaw all through the difficulties of her first marriage when her husband disappears at sea, forcing Alice and her mother-in-law to take in lodgers, one of whom is Mr Openshaw. Norah's circumstances are as precarious as those of her mistress: she is forced to leave Alice briefly when Alice returns to live with her mother-in-law, but is re-employed when Alice discovers she is pregnant. The vulnerability of a servant's life, as well as the tenaciousness of the relationship between Norah and her mistress is clearly illustrated in this short episode. When Alice marries Mr Openshaw, further tensions arise: 'Norah and Mr. Openshaw were not on the most thoroughly cordial terms; neither of them fully recognizing or appreciating the other's best qualities.'[90]

When Alice's first husband, Frank, returns, having been presumed dead, he comes to the house at night when the Openshaws are out. The servants are no defence, and the housemaid is unable to protect the home and family. Frank easily invades the private areas of the household, and Norah, who initially fails to recognise him, thinks that he is a burglar. When she realises who he is, she is forced to tell him that his wife has remarried and that he has a daughter. Frank is desperate, and Norah fearing both for her own safety and for that of her mistress, can only calm him by showing him his sleeping daughter. She then forcibly turns him out of the house and bolts the door behind him 'as if by bolts to keep out facts'.[91] The encounter shows Norah overcoming her own considerable fear and dealing competently with a half-deranged man she had believed to be dead, who has forced his way into the family home and threatened the stability and safety of her mistress. She has to keep the secret of Frank's return in order to protect her mistress, and is heard speaking harshly to the child, who has seen her father, earning her a rebuke from Mr Openshaw. It is at this moment in the narrative that the point of view shifts from that of an omniscient author relating events to a closer focus on Norah, and the effect on her of keeping her dreadful secret.

Norah's actions and decisions, and her enforced silence about events, lead to a twist in the narrative when she is accused of stealing a valuable brooch belonging to some guests of the Openshaws. The Openshaws think that the mysterious visitor of the previous night was Norah's follower, and that he is implicated in the theft. Followers were discouraged not only because they would distract a servant from her duties, but because the female servant was often used as a decoy to gain entrance into a home which the male accomplice would then burgle.[92] Gaskell here is reflecting some common contemporary fears about servants, not without reason, since, as Horn points out, court records show legal action being taken by employers against servants for the theft of a wide variety of objects.[93] Norah's situation deteriorates with frightening speed from being a long-standing, trusted servant, to being accused of theft and threatened with prosecution and dismissal. Old rifts are reopened with Mr Openshaw, misunderstandings increase, and the narrator is forced to intervene:

> I do not think he had ever really intended to send for the police to
> this old servant of his wife's; for he had never for a moment doubted
> her perfect honesty. But he had intended to compel her to tell him

who the man was, and in this he was baffled.[94]

Rather than reveal the fact of the return of Alice's first husband, Norah leaves home, and is only vindicated when the brooch is found by the Openshaw's visitors and Frank commits suicide. It is Mr Openshaw, the unlikely hero of this tale, who comes to find Norah and apologise to her and with whom Norah then shares the secret she has been keeping.

'The Manchester Marriage' is interesting in several respects, in that it challenges a number of common preconceptions about marriage, servants, class, and gender. Mr Openshaw, who appears to be the archetypal northern male, is shown to be thoughtful and protective of his family and his servants, ensuring that both their emotional and physical needs are met. He shares the burden of carrying the secret of his wife's unknowing bigamy with a servant, and in doing so, learns to modify his behaviour, opinions, and prejudices. Mitchell further notes the significance of his business success and his decision to settle half of his fortune on his wife. The Openshaws' marriage remains invalid, despite the suicide of Frank, and therefore Alice has no legal status as his wife. Mitchell comments that Gaskell's

> apparent endorsement of his silence is interesting as a reflection
> of her views on the sacredness of the marriage tie. There are few
> mainstream mid-Victorian fictions which permit unwed couples to
> live together unpunished. It is conceivable that for some readers the
> implications of Openshaw's new 'reverence' for his wife could have
> included abstinence from sexual intercourse.[95]

Much of the narrative action and the moral argument of the story is carried by Norah, the servant, who becomes the focal point of interest and also mediates between the various members of the family. She is as strong a character as Mr Openshaw, so that, at the end of the story, they are able to take an equal share in bearing the burden of the secret.

The theme of the loyal servant who conceals a secret on behalf of his employer is taken to its extreme in 'A Dark Night's Work' (1863). Linda Hughes and other critics have noted the darkening in several of Gaskell's short stories which appeared around this time and an emphasis on love and betrayal, possibly motivated by the breaking of Gaskell's second daughter

Meta's engagement to Captain James Hill, whose financial position was somewhat ambiguous.[96] 'A Dark Night's Work' appears to be a fairly conventional romantic tale which abruptly swerves into sensation fiction when Ellinor Wilkins' previously respectable father murders his partner in an alcohol induced rage. Ellinor helps her father and the faithful manservant Dixon to conceal the body, until years later, when excavations for the railway uncover the body, and Dixon is charged with murder.

The relationship between Mr Wilkins and Dixon illustrates the tensions caused by the emergence of the middle classes and their struggle to carve out a clear social position. Gaskell uses the short first chapter of 'A Dark Night's Work' to succinctly outline this preoccupation of Victorian society and to suggest the negative impact of restrictive social codes and expectations upon individuals. She charts the progress of the Wilkins family across three generations, from the grandfather, who is a respected attorney, but who probably has no university education, to Mr Wilkins' father, who consolidates the business and becomes the principal lawyer in the county town, 'confidential friend to many of the surrounding families of distinction' but one who 'knew his place', to the education and future career of his son. It is at this point, that the smooth social and financial progress of the family is checked. Mr Wilkins recognises that his business is too successful to be placed in the hands of a stranger and so does not allow his son to receive the university education which would enable him to become a barrister, and thus achieve a higher social status. However, he has already been educated at Eton and it is

> a very severe mortification to him to find that his destiny was changed, and that he had to return to Hamley to be articled to his father, and to assume the hereditary subservient position to lads whom he had licked in the playground, and beaten at learning.[97]

Mr Wilkins senior compensates for this disappointment by providing him with material indulgences, including making the Grand Tour, an experience usually enjoyed by aristocrats, and he returns 'rather too refined for the society he was likely to be thrown into.'[98] Edward Wilkins is in effect a hybrid: overeducated for his station in life, but cleverer and more refined than those to whom he is socially subservient and whom he will have to serve in his role

as local attorney. The potentially damaging effects of this are concealed by
his education and natural abilities, but Gaskell's analysis, which distinguishes
between outward appearance and inward emotions, reflects the social and
cultural dichotomy in which Edward finds himself and hints at the complex
codification of behaviour and manners by which the Victorians attempted to
define and control the concept of a gentleman. In narrative terms, it also provides motivation for his repressed anger which will ultimately end in murder.

The narrative continues with the story of Mr Wilkins' marriage, the death
of his wife shortly after the birth of his daughter, and the gradual decline of
both the business and Mr Wilkins as he increasingly indulges in 'aping the
mode of life and amusements of the landed gentry'.[99] Mr Wilkins decides to
employ a clerk to undertake the routine business and with the introduction
of Mr Dunster, the successful applicant, the point of view of the narrative
shifts to Ellinor, and Dixon, the servant, is introduced to the reader. Dixon

> had been her father's playfellow as a boy, and with all his respect and
> admiration for his master, the freedom of intercourse that had been
> established between them had never been quite lost. [...] he was a
> great favourite, and could say many a thing which might have been
> taken as impertinent from another servant.[100]

Their boyhood friendship has elided the class difference between them and
has placed Dixon in a quasi-family relationship with both Ellinor and her
father.

Dunster, the clerk on the other hand, who is introduced to the narrative
at the same time as Dixon, is a 'quiet, respectable-looking man; you could not
call him a gentleman in manner, and yet no one could say he was vulgar.'[101]
The two men are an interesting contrast and a comment on the complex
codes of gentility. Mr Wilkins finds Dunster offensive. He speaks with 'a
provincial twang which grated on his employer's sensitive ear' and he wears a
green coat which is an 'obnoxious colour'.[102] Yet Dunster is a conscientious
and careful employee. Dixon, on the other hand, although 'out of a completely different class' is also 'as loyal and true and kind as any nobleman.'[103]

As the narrative point of view shifts from that of Mr Wilkins to Ellinor,
so too the focus sharpens on Ellinor's relationship with Dixon and to a lesser

extent with Miss Monro, her governess, who both become surrogate parents to her. The doll's furniture Dixon makes for Ellinor for example, recalls William Gaskell's manufacture of a toy kitchen and kites for his daughter.[104] The loyalty and love Ellinor and Dixon have for each other is contrasted with Ellinor's relationship with Ralph Corbett, who disapproves of her closeness to the old servant. It is Corbett however, who turns out to be faithless, and Dixon, in the crisis of the murder, who takes practical charge of events and acts to protect his master.

The murder of Dunster takes a physical and emotional toll on all three and alters the dynamic of their relationship. The sensational elements of the narrative come to the fore. Mr Wilkins ages overnight, his 'hollow sunken eye seemed […] to have the vision of the dead man before it'.[105] Ellinor becomes ill and Dixon grieves for the loss of his intimate relationship with his master who 'cuts through the stable-yard, and past me, wi'out a word, as if I was poison, or a stinking foumart'.[106] What was once a healthy bond between all three, giving balance to Mr Wilkins's excesses and offering an alternative model of parenthood for Ellinor, has become warped by the secret all three unwillingly share. In this crisis, it is Ellinor and Dixon who become closer, and Mr Wilkins who becomes increasingly isolated from both of them:

> There was a strong bond between Ellinor and Dixon, although they scarcely ever exchanged a word save on the most common-place subjects; but their silence was based on different feelings from that which separated Ellinor from her father. Ellinor and Dixon could not speak freely, because their hearts were full of pity for the faulty man whom they both loved so well, and tried so hard to respect.[107]

Ellinor and Dixon become increasingly responsible for protecting Mr Wilkins and covering up his actions. After her father's death, Ellinor moves to East Chester, but Dixon refuses her offer of a home in order to continue to watch over Dunster's grave to ensure that the body is not dug up: 'I could never rest a-nights if I didn't feel as if I kept the secret in my hand, and held it tight day and night, so as I could open my hand at any minute and see as it was there.'[108] This graphic image articulates the tight control which Ellinor and Dixon have to exercise over their emotions, speech and actions. The secret they share prevents Ellinor from marrying and Dixon from enjoying a secure old age and retirement. The intimate connection between them is expressed in Ellinor's cry when she hears of Dixon's arrest for murder: 'if he dies, I must die too'.[109] When Ellinor visits Dixon in prison, we learn his Christian name, adding pathos to the picture of the frail old man, condemned to death for a murder he did not commit. The ironic resolution of the narrative when Ellinor confesses the truth to her faithless lover, who is now the judge in charge of the case, unlocks the dilemma for both Dixon and herself, enabling her to make a happy marriage and to offer a home to the faithful Dixon.

CONCLUSION

The meaning of home for Elizabeth Gaskell was always contested and ambiguous. The tensions in her own life influenced her fiction in a number of ways, but principally in her depiction of home. Gaskell passionately believed that a stable, secure home was paramount, even if this was not necessarily one which conformed to the expectations of society. Her fiction is replete with constructed families, brought together from pragmatic need, rather than bound by ties of blood or relationship. I have focused on the varied and powerful meanings of home in Gaskell's fiction and now draw some conclusions.

Gaskell's fiction presents a concept of home that often fails to provide a physical place of safety, and where even the architecture of a building militates against a sense of peace and privacy. Doors and windows are potent signifiers of entrapment as well as protective barriers. They are ambiguous openings through which disease, death and those who wish to harm the occupants of the home can enter. Gaskell's treatment of the death of children in particular varies in tone and narrative importance, but as her technique develops, these deaths are used to elide the transition between narrative forms and to give greater impact to her thematic concerns. In a similar way, the figure of the returning or rescued sailor is a recurrent and important character in her fiction, critical to the plot, but on the edge of the narrative action. These characters are linked to the passing of time and often to some kind of destablisation within the home, including the threat of death. Critical events occur during their absence from home, which their re-entry into a domestic setting helps to resolve. While other characters change and develop, these returning sailors remain essentially the same: optimistic, life-enhancing and full of practical good sense. They represent the wider world and, in some respects, Gaskell's own sense of confinement and her thirst for travel and adventure.

The breadth of Gaskell's curiosity about human nature is illustrated by her portrayal of sexuality, in particular, male sexuality. The presentation of men in her fiction is often very far removed from the paterfamilias of contemporary cultural expectations and provides a view of masculinity which is embedded in the domestic and embraces aspects of feminine sensitivity. She is unusual among her contemporaries in the way that she uses cross-dressing to explore the interpretation of character and the potential for change offered by a more ambiguous and flexible allocation of gender. Gaskell uses feminised men in her fiction to explore the issues raised by the radical Unitarians in their campaign for a transformed society and to challenge contemporary concepts of gender and gendered roles within a domestic setting.

Servants were key actors within nineteenth-century homes and Gaskell is fascinated by this ambiguous relationship that combined enforced intimacy with contractual obligations. Only one servant is employed in most of the homes described in Gaskell's fiction, with servant and employer often working alongside each other, sharing domestic tasks. Servants are therefore able to provide an intimate commentary on the action and motives of characters precisely because they are located inside the home.[1] The practical role servants fulfilled in Victorian life of protecting the home by mediating social contact and preserving social status, blends in Gaskell's shorter fiction into an examination of wider domestic and family relationships. The older, feudal model of loyal retainers serving an established aristocratic family develops into a newer concept of social paternalism in which employers are seen to be responsible for the holistic care of their servants, that is, their physical, spiritual, and emotional wellbeing. At its worst, this led to an abuse of power and status as employers sought to control every aspect of their servants' lives. At its best, Gaskell suggests, it is a quasi-family relationship in which strong bonds of affection and loyalty are developed, and the differences between social classes are increasingly elided.

Gaskell's fictional homes are described with close attention to every detail. In the nineteenth century, a range of creative arts represented and expressed reality through the accretion of decoration and the elaborately realistic portrayal of the world around them. This representational tradition derived from Dutch genre painting and was given further impetus by the development of photography.[2] However, detail for a novelist must always have a function, rather than being purely decorative. Gaskell's strength lies in the way in which she uses the contents of domestic interiors and small personal possessions to explore areas of thematic interest in her novels, as paradigms for subjects which were surrounded by cultural taboos and therefore prohibited from open discussion, and as a means of introducing stability into contested or difficult situations. In this way, she was able to extend her creative range while still apparently writing within culturally safe boundaries.

Gaskell's portrayal of homelessness in her fiction is explored through the state of mind of individuals as part of their personal emotional and psychological journeys and is often linked to some kind of destabilisation. It is notable that for Gaskell's homeless characters, the outcome is death. It is as if once an individual has been destabilized beyond a certain critical point, they cannot be re-absorbed into society, and death, therefore, is the only acceptable resolution.

Inevitably, there are other areas related to the concept of home that would benefit from further research. The setting of houses in the landscape is often illuminating and consistently underpins narrative themes. Much of Gaskell's writing begins with a description of a landscape and works into the narrative from the outside. In *Sylvia's Lovers* (1863) and *The Life of Charlotte Brontë* (1857), landscape is intimately integrated with character. Sylvia is a child of nature, her wild and temperamental character with its inflexible core reflects the landscape where she lives, the wild bleak moors that shut in Monkshaven on one side with the sea on the other.[3] Similarly Charlotte Brontë's character was forged in the isolation and wild freedom of the Haworth moors.[4] Jenny Uglow notes how the opening of *Ruth*, with its description of the old assize town, leads us metaphorically through time and society, and the journey through the landscapes surrounding Monkshaven and Haworth has the same effect, drawing the reader back into a society which operated under different laws and customs.[5]

Similarly, the opening of 'Half a Life-Time Ago' (1855) suggests not just Susan Dixon's isolation on the wild fells, but her competence and power. The farmyard is well-organised to support her livestock and herself, and the ancient yew suggests a long-standing settlement in complete harmony with the landscape.[6] The opening of 'The Moorland Cottage' (1850) describes a similarly isolated farm which, as Alan Shelston notes, 'is as much a story of its setting as it is of its characters.'[7] Maggie, like Owen Griffiths in 'The Doom of the Griffiths' (1858) and Sylvia in *Sylvia's Lovers*, has a focal point in the landscape which both grounds her and offers a private space in which to reflect.

Gardens are an important extension of houses. One of Gaskell's great joys in the move to Plymouth Grove was the extensive garden. Even before the move, she wrote to her close friend Tottie Fox on 26 April 1850 telling her excitedly about the garden, the 'great delight in our new house'. It was, she told her, a refuge where she could walk about without a bonnet on.[8] On 10 March 1851, she tells Marianne that she has been spending a great deal of time in the garden setting out vegetables and flowers for later in the year. In early November 1851, she writes to Marianne again telling her about her plans to keep a pig and a cow in the field next to the garden, and of the new roses she has bought. In her fiction, gardens are used to underpin themes and comment on character and plot. Gardens are often a riot of climbing plants, suggesting fecundity, abundance, and sensuality, for example, when Margaret walks with Henry Lennox among the pears and climbing roses. As with the interiors of Gaskell's fictional homes, colour is important. The garden at Helstone has 'scarlet honeysuckle [...] the small lawn was gorgeous with verbenas and geraniums of all bright colours'.[9] In 'Mr Harrison's Confessions' (1851) the garden suggests Sophie's fertility, innate openness of character and domestic capability.

The garden of Mrs Mason's house in *Ruth* (1853) not only records the cumulative redevelopment of the old town where plots have been sub-divided to make a townscape of increasing squalor, but also reflects the way in which Ruth feels trapped by her current circumstances. The larch tree that remains in the garden is confined like Ruth herself. Similarly, the approach to Lady Ludlow's house is a journey back through time as well as through the landscape. Margaret Dawson's difficult journey becomes a metaphor for Lady Ludlow's rigid attitudes and values which are challenged by the younger generation. It is necessary to 'quarter' the lane which approaches the house. Charlotte Mitchell explains that this means locking the wheels of the cart into the quarters of the road with a rut between.[10] The ruts are symbolic of Lady Ludlow's inflexibility. The house is approached through a tunnel of elms and a long flight of steps, emphasising its inaccessibility. Margaret's journey mirrors the fairy tale opening of 'Curious if True' (1860) where Richard Whittingham is similarly guided irresistibly down a lane, bordered with poplars, only to lose his way in an overgrown wood. Both homes bear a resemblance to Sleeping Beauty's Castle, an example of Gaskell's consistent use of fairytales in her fiction.

Throughout her life, Gaskell did indeed linger on the borderland, and her writing provided her with a way to manage her own anxieties, contradictions and inconsistencies. The concept of home, however tenuous and contested, was fundamental to her psychological wellbeing, and close textual analysis reveals the subtle and nuanced way in which she explored its varied meanings.

ENDNOTES

INTRODUCTION

1 The phrase is taken from a comment made by Mrs Ellis Chadwick who states that 'All through her life, she loved to linger on the borderland.' Ellis Chadwick is referring to Gaskell's love of 'strange customs and weird, uncanny stories' but the phrase also seems to aptly encapsulate Gaskell's experience of home and the ways in which home is represented in her fiction. Mrs Ellis H Chadwick, *Mrs Gaskell 'Haunts, Homes and Stories'*, (London: Sir Isaac Pitman and Sons Ltd, 1910), pp 126-127.

2 For an account of Hannah Lumb's life and marriage, see John Chapple, *Elizabeth Gaskell: The Early Years*, (Manchester: Manchester University Press, 1997), pp 92-93.

3 Jenny Uglow, *Elizabeth Gaskell: A Habit of Stories*, (London and New York: Faber and Faber, 1999), p 13.

4 See Winifred Gerin, *Elizabeth Gaskell, A Biography*, (Oxford: The Clarendon Press, 1976), pp 2-6.

5 Gaskell to Eliza Fox, April 26, 1850, John A V Chapple and Arthur Pollard eds, *The Letters of Mrs Gaskell*, (Manchester: Manchester University Press, 1997), p 112.

6 'Libbie Marsh's Three Eras' in Elizabeth Gaskell, Joanne Shattock ed, *The Works of Elizabeth Gaskell: Vol.1: Journalism, Early Fiction and Personal Writing*, (London: Pickering and Chatto, 2005), p 61. Shattock notes that the original prefatory title was 'Life in Manchester', p 47.

7 Gerin, pp 294-295.

8 See for example, James Kay-Shuttleworth, *Four Periods of Public Education as Reviewed in 1832, 1839, 1846, 1862*, intro Norman Morris, (Brighton: The Harvester Press, 1973), 'First Period' pp 3-170, Joseph Adshead, *Distress in Manchester: Evidence (Tabular and Otherwise) of the State of the Labouring Classes in 1840-42*, (London: Henry Hooper, 1842), and *Reports of the Ministry to the Poor in Manchester* 1839–1842.

9 Alexis de Tocqueville, *Journeys to England and Ireland*, Translated by George Lawrence

and K P Mayer, ed J P Mayer, (London: Faber and Faber Ltd, 1958), pp 105-06.

10 De Tocqueville, p 106.

11 John Burnett, *A Social History of Housing 1815–1985*, (London and New York: Methuen, 1986), p 9.

12 Kay-Shuttleworth, p 5.

13 Burnett, p 13.

14 Kay-Shuttleworth, p 13.

15 Gaskell to William Turner, [6 October 1832], John Chapple and Alan Shelston eds, *Further Letters of Mrs Gaskell*, (Manchester: Manchester University Press, 2003), p 21.

16 W. Henry Brown, 'Mrs. Gaskell: A Manchester Influence', *Papers of the Manchester Literary Club*, Vol LVIII, 1932, (Manchester: Sherratt & Hughes, 1932), p 16.

17 'The Diary' in Elizabeth Gaskell, Joanne Shattock, ed, *The Works of Elizabeth Gaskell: Vol.1: Journalism, Early Fiction and Personal Writings*, (London: Pickering and Chatto, 2005), p 7.

18 Gaskell to George Hope, 13 February, John A V Chapple, and Arthur Pollard, eds, *The Letters of Mrs Gaskell*, (Manchester: Manchester University Press, 1997), pp 796-797.

19 Gaskell to George Hope, 13 February, Chapple and Pollard, p 797.

20 Gaskell to ?Anne Robson, [23 December 1841], Chapple and Pollard, p 45.

21   Gaskell to Eliza Fox, [?April 1850], Chapple and Pollard, p 108.

22 Gaskell to ?Catherine Winkworth, undated letter, Chapple and Pollard, p 808.

23 Ruth Watts, *Gender, Power and the Unitarians in England 1769–1860*, (London: Longman, 1998), p 8.

24 Julie Nash, *Servants and Paternalism in the Works of Maria Edgeworth and Elizabeth Gaskell*, (Aldershot and Burlington VT: Ashgate Publishing Company, 2007), p 2.

25 See, for example, Judith Flanders, *The Victorian House: Domestic Life from Childbirth to Deathbed*, (London: Harper Collins, 2003), and Thad Logan, *The Victorian Parlour*, (Cambridge: Cambridge University Press, 2001).

26 James Martineau, 'Great Principles and Small Duties' in *Endeavours after the Christian Life*, Fourth Edition, (London: Longmans, Green, Reader and Dyer, MDCCCLXVII), p 27.

27 Logan, p xii.

28 'Sketches of Remarkable Women' in *The Christian Freeman: A Monthly Unitarian*

Journal devoted to religious, moral, and social progress, Vol XIII, (London: Whitfield Strand, 1869), p 59.

29 See Elizabeth Gaskell, Joanne Shattock ed, *The Works of Elizabeth Gaskell, Volume 1, Journalism, Early Fiction and Personal Writings,* (London: Pickering & Chatto, 2005), pp xiii to xiv for a useful summary.

30 Robert L Selig, *Elizabeth Gaskell: A Reference Guide,* (Boston: G. K. Hall & Co, 1977), p x.

31 David Masson, quoted in Elizabeth Gaskell, Joanne Shattock ed, *The Works of Elizabeth Gaskell: Vol.1: Journalism, Early Fiction and Personal Writings.* (London: Pickering and Chatto, 2005), p ix.

32 Gaskell to Catherine Winkworth, [11 to 14 Oct. 1854], Chapple and Pollard, p 310.

33 Elizabeth Gaskell, Linda H Peterson ed, *The Works of Elizabeth Gaskell: Vol. 8: The Life of Charlotte Brontë,* (London: Pickering and Chatto, 2006), pp viii–xxiv.

34 Rosemarie Bodenheimer, *The Real Life of Mary Ann Evans: George Eliot, Her Letters and Fiction,* (Ithaca and London: Cornell University Press, 1994), pp 5-6.

35 Hilary M Schor, *Scheherazade in the Marketplace: Elizabeth Gaskell and the Victorian Novel,* (New York: Oxford University Press, 1992). Holly E Pike, *Family and Society in the Works of Elizabeth Gaskell,* (New York: Peter Lang Publishing Inc, 1995), Deirdre D'Albertis, *Dissembling Fictions: Elizabeth Gaskell and the Victorian Social Text,* (Basingstoke: Macmillan Press, 1997).

36 Joanne Shattock, 'Elizabeth Gaskell: Journalism and Letters', in Laurel Brake and Marysa Demour eds, *The Lure of Illustration in the Nineteenth Century: Picture and Press,* (Basingstoke: Palgrave Macmillan, 2009), p 119. See also Bodenheimer, 1994, pp 7 and 16, and David Barton and Nigel Hall eds, *Letter Writing as a Social Practice,* (Amsterdam/Philadelphia: John Benjamins Publishing Company, 2000), and Fran Baker, 'Intimate and trusted correspondents: the Gaskells, Greens and Jamisons', *Gaskell Journal,* Vol 24, 2010, p 10.

37 See James How, *Epistolary Spaces: English Letter Writing from the Foundation of the Post Office to Richardson's Clarissa,*(Aldershot: Ashgate Publishing Ltd, 2003), pp 9-12 for a discussion of the right to send letters untampered with through the Post Office.

38 Bodenheimer, 1994, p 8.

39 Gaskell to Elizabeth Gaskell, [19 August 1838], Chapple and Pollard, p 34.

40 Gaskell to Elizabeth Gaskell, [19 August 1838], Chapple and Pollard, p 34.

41 Ellis Chadwick, pp 201-202.

42 See Baker, p 3 for a discussion of the way in which family archives are shaped by decisions on which letters should be included.

43 Gaskell to ?Anne Robson, [23 December 1841], Chapple and Pollard, p 46.

44 Gaskell to George Smith, [?December 1856], Chapple and Pollard, p 426.

45 *Letters and Memorials of Catherine Winkworth, edited by her sister,* Vol 1, (Clifton: E. Austin and Son, Printers, Chronicle Office, 1883), p vii.

46 Winkworth, 1883, Dedication.

47 Angus Easson, *Elizabeth Gaskell,* (London, Boston and Henley: Routledge & Kegan Paul, 1979), p 232.

48 Gaskell to Marianne and Margaret Emily Gaskell, [?1846] Chapple and Pollard, p 48 and Gaskell to Marianne Gaskell, [?August 1860], Chapple and Pollard, p 915.

49 Coral Lansbury, *Elizabeth Gaskell: The Novel of Social Crisis,* (London: Paul Elek, 1975), p 209.

50 Bruce Redford, *The Converse of the Pen: Acts of Intimacy in the Eighteenth-Century Familiar Letter,* (Chicago: University of Chicago Press, 1986), pp 1-2.

51 Pamela Corpron Parker, 'Woman of Letters: Elizabeth Gaskell's Autograph Collection and Victorian Celebrity' in Maureen Daly Goggin and Beth Fowkes Tobin, eds, *Material Women, 1750–1950: Consuming Desires and Collecting Practices,* (Farnham: Ashgate Publishing Ltd, 2009), p 266.

52 Winkworth, 1883, p vii.

53 Corpron Parker, p 276.

54 Gaskell to John Forster, [17 May 1854], Chapple and Pollard, p 289.

55 Gaskell to John Forster, [17 May 1854], Chapple and Pollard, p 289.

56 Gaskell to Catherine Winkworth, [11 to 14 Oct. 1854], Chapple and Pollard, p 307.

57 Gaskell to ?Anne Shaen, [?24 April 1848], Chapple and Pollard, p 57.

58 Elizabeth Gaskell, Deirdre D'Albertis ed, *The Works of Elizabeth Gaskell: Vol. 6: Ruth, (1853),* (London: Pickering and Chatto, 2006), p 214.

59 Summerscale notes the association of coaches with seduction and prostitution: 'The late-eighteenth-century guide to prostitution 'Harris's List of Covent Garden Ladies: Or a Man of Pleasure's Kalendar for the Year' recommended coaches for illicit trysts. [...] By 1838, reported the 'Crim Con Gazette', the London hackney-cab commissioners were so disturbed by the immorality conducted in their vehicles that they proposed to curtail both the pleasure and privacy by banning coach blinds and coach cushions altogether.' Kate Summerscale, *Mrs Robinson's Disgrace: The Private*

Diary of a Victorian Lady, London: Bloomsbury, 2012, pp 86-87.

60 *Ruth*, Vol 6, p 214.

61 *Ruth*, Vol 6, p 215.

62 *Ruth*, Vol 6, p 216.

63 *Ruth*, Vol 6, p 216.

64 Tim Dolin, 'Cranford and the Victorian Collection', *Victorian Studies*, (36, No 2, Winter 1991), p 194.

65 Ellis Chadwick, p 52.

66 *Cranford* in Elizabeth Gaskell, Alan Shelston ed, *The Works of Elizabeth Gaskell: Vol.2 : Novellas and Shorter Fiction 1: The Moorland Cottage, Cranford and Related Writings*, (London: Pickering and Chatto, 2005), p 167.

67 *Cranford*, Vol 2, p 210.

68 *Cranford*, Vol 2, n 45, p 350.

69 Jeanette Eve, 'The Floral and Horticultural in Elizabeth Gaskell's novels', *Gaskell Society Journal*, (Vol 7, 1993), p 9.

70 See Patsy Stoneman, *Elizabeth Gaskell*, (Brighton: The Harvester Press Ltd, 1987), p 89 for the way in which letters are used to comment on Deborah Jenkyns' character.

71 *Cranford*, Vol 2, p 202.

72 *Cranford*, Vol 2, p 203.

73 *Cranford*, Vol 2, p 275.

74 'My Lady Ludlow' in Elizabeth Gaskell, Charlotte Mitchell ed, *The Works of Elizabeth Gaskell: Vol.3: Novellas and Shorter Fiction II: Round the Sofa, and Tales from Household Words (1852-9)*, (London: Pickering and Chatto, 2005), p 146.

75 Charlotte Mitchell explains that 'A spinster or a widow bears arms on a lozenge; a man's arms are displayed on a shield, and a married woman uses her husband's shield. As heiress of the Hanbury family Lady Ludlow has brought her husband's family the right to quarter the arms of her family with theirs (though in fact EG makes a technical error since Lady Ludlow herself would correctly have displayed the Hanbury arms on an inescutcheon of pretence).' 'My Lady Ludlow' Vol 3, p 455.

76 'My Lady Ludlow' Vol 3, p 212.

77 Elizabeth Gaskell, Josie Billington ed, *The Works of Elizabeth Gaskell: Vol. 10: Wives and Daughters (1866)*, (London: Pickering and Chatto, 2005), p 381.

78 *Wives and Daughters*, Vol 10, p 383.

79 *Wives and Daughters,* Vol 10, pp 384-385.

80 *Wives and Daughters,* Vol 10, p 385.

81 *Wives and Daughters,* Vol 10, p 389.

82 *Wives and Daughters,* Vol 10, p 389.

83 Elizabeth Gaskell, Joanne Wilkes ed, *The Works of Elizabeth Gaskell: Vol. 5: Mary Barton: A Tale of Manchester Life,* (London: Pickering and Chatto, 2005), p 38.

84 *Mary Barton,* p 7.

85 See Heather Glen, 'Elizabeth Gaskell's resurrection', *The Times Literary Supplement,* November 8, 2006, for a more detailed examination of this passage.

86 *Mary Barton,* Vol 5, p 38.

87 *Mary Barton,* Vol 5, p 38.

88 *Mary Barton,* Vol 5, p 39.

89 *Mary Barton,* Vol 5, p 39.

90 *Mary Barton,*Vol 5, p 39.

91 *Mary Barton,* Vol 5, p 39.

92 William Gaskell, *The Duties of the Individual to Society: A Sermon on Occasion of the Death of Sir John Potter M.P. Preached at Cross Street Chapel, Manchester, October 31ˢᵗ, 1858,* (London: E T Whitfield, 1858), p 4.

93 Mike Hepworth, 'Privacy, Security and Respectability: The ideal Victorian home', in Tony Chapman and Jenny Hockey eds, *Ideal Homes? Social change and domestic life,* (London and New York: Routledge, 1999), p 29.

CHAPTER ONE

1 Ordnance Survey, Manchester Sheet 44, 1851.

2 Gaskell to Eliza Fox, Monday, May 29, 1849, John A. V. Chapple, and Arthur Pollard eds, *The Letters of Mrs Gaskell,* (Manchester: Manchester University Press, 1997), p 81.

3 Ordnance Survey, Manchester Sheet 45, 1851.

4 Gaskell to Eliza Fox, [?April 1850], Chapple and Pollard, p 108.

5 Barbara Brill, *William Gaskell: 1805–1884, A Portrait,* (Manchester: Manchester Literary and Philosophical Publications, 1984), p 87.

6 Floorplan kindly provided by Bernard Taylor Partnership, Architects.

7 Gaskell to Anne Robson, [?10 May 1865], Chapple and Pollard, pp 758-759.

8 Jenny Uglow, *Elizabeth Gaskell: A Habit of Stories,* (London and New York: Faber

and Faber, 1999), p 260.

9 Elizabeth Haldane, *Mrs Gaskell and Her Friends,* (London: Hodder and Stoughton Ltd, 1931), p 73, and Mrs. Ellis H Chadwick, *Mrs. Gaskell: Haunts, Homes and Stories,* (London: Sir Isaac Pitman and Sons Ltd, 1910), p 253.

10 I am indebted to Janet Allan, Chair of the Manchester Historic Buildings Trust, for these insights which are contained in the deeds of the Plymouth Grove house.

11 Judith Flanders, *The Victorian House: Domestic Life from Childbirth to Deathbed,* (London: Harper Collins, 2003), p 215.

12 Hopkins, p 316.

13 Gaskell to George Smith, [?1 October 1859], Chapple and Pollard, p 577.

14 'My Lady Ludlow' in Elizabeth Gaskell, Charlotte Mitchell ed, *The Works of Elizabeth Gaskell, Volume 3, Novellas and Shorter Fiction II Round the Sofa and Tales from Household Words (1852-9),* (London: Pickering & Chatto, 2005), p 169.

15 'My Lady Ludlow', Vol 3, pp 178-179.

16 Edgar Wright, '*My Lady Ludlow:* Forms of Social Change and Forms of Fiction (1)', *Gaskell Society Journal,* Vol 3, 1989, p 33.

17 Elizabeth Gaskell, Joanne Wilkes ed, *The Works of Elizabeth Gaskell: Vol. 5: Mary Barton (1838) and William Gaskell, 'Two Lectures on the Lancashire Dialect'.,* (London: Pickering and Chatto, 2005), p 115.

18 Deirdre D'Albertis, *Dissembling Fictions: Elizabeth Gaskell and the Victorian Social Text,* (Basingstoke: Macmillan Press Ltd, 1997), p 51.

19 Martin Hewitt, 'District visiting and the constitution of domestic space in the mid-nineteenth century' in Inga Bryden and Janet Floyd eds, *Domestic Space: Reading the nineteenth-century interior,* (Manchester and New York: Manchester University Press, 1999), pp 123-125. See also Anna Clark, 'The politics of seduction in English popular culture 1748–1848', in *The Progress of Romance: The Politics of Popular Fiction,* ed Jean Radford, (London and New York: Routledge and Kegan Paul, 1986), pp 47-70 for a discussion of Gaskell's use of the myth of seduction in *Mary Barton.*

20 Mary H Kuhlman, 'Education through experience in *North and South',* *Gaskell Society Journal,* Vol 10, 1996, p 20, and Michiel Heyns, 'The Steam-Hammer and the Sugar-Tongs: Sexuality and Power in Elizabeth Gaskell's "North and South"', *English Studies in Africa,* 32:2, 1989, p 91.

21 Tim Dolin, 'Cranford and the Victorian Collection', *Victorian Studies,* 36, No 2, Winter 1991, p 198, and see also Barbara Leah Harman, 'In Promiscuous Company:

Female Public Appearance in Elizabeth Gaskell's *North and South*', *Victorian Studies*, 1988, Vol 31, Pt 3, pp 351-374.

22 Alexandra Warwick, 'Victorian Gothic', in Catherine Spooner and Emma McEvoy eds, *The Routledge Companion to Gothic*, (London and New York: Routledge, 2007), p 30.

23 Elizabeth Gaskell, Deirdre D'Albertis ed, *The Works of Elizabeth Gaskell: Vol. 6: Ruth*, (London: Pickering and Chatto, 2005), p 7.

24 Angus Easson, 'Noah's Arks and Birds' Nests: Domestic Space in *Ruth*', in Francesco Marroni and Alan Shelston eds, *Elizabeth Gaskell: Text and Context*, (Pescara: Tracce, 1999), p 97.

25 E Holly Pike, *Family and Society in the Works of Elizabeth Gaskell*, (New York: Peter Lang Publishing Inc, 1995), p 56.

26 Hilary M Schor, *Scheherazade in the Marketplace: Elizabeth Gaskell and the Victorian Novel*, (New York, Oxford: Oxford University Press, 1992), p 54.

27 Rosemarie Bodenheimer, *The Politics of Story in Victorian Social Fiction*, (Ithaca: Cornell University Press, 1988), p 150.

28 Victoria Williams, 'Gaskell as Scheherazade': Fairytale themes in *Cousin Phillis* and *North and South*', *Gaskell Journal*, Vol 24, 2010, pp 106-107.

29 Angus Easson, 'The Sentiment of Feeling: Emotions and Objects in Elizabeth Gaskell (1)', *Gaskell Society Journal*, Vol 4, 1990, p 69.

30   Elizabeth Gaskell, Elisabeth Jay ed, *The Works of Elizabeth Gaskell: Vol. 7: North and South*, (London: Pickering and Chatto, 2005), p 54.

31 Wendy Parkins, *Mobility and Modernity in Women's Novels 1850s–1930s: Women Moving Dangerously*, (Basingstoke: Palgrave MacMillan, 2009), p 25.

32 John Burnett, *A Social History of Housing 1815–1985*, (London and New York: Methuen, 1986), p 13.

33 Burnett, p 108.

34 Burnett, pp 9-10.

35 M.J. Daunton, *House and Home in the Victorian City: Working-Class Housing 1850–1914*, (London: Edward Arnold, 1983), p 13.

36 Inga Bryden and Janet Floyd eds, *Domestic Space: Reading the nineteenth-century interior*, (Manchester & New York: Manchester University Press, 1999), p 12.

37 See for example, Gaskell to William Robson, [c. 20 February 1850], John A. V. Chapple and Arthur Pollard eds, *The Letters of Mrs Gaskell*, (Manchester: Manchester University Press, 1997), p 105, and Gaskell to Marianne Gaskell, Friday [10 September

1852], Chapple and Pollard, p 198.

38 Gaskell to Marianne Gaskell, [4 May 1852], Chapple and Pollard, p 850.

39 See David Roberts, 'The Paterfamilias of the Victorian Governing Classes' in, Anthony S Wohl ed, *The Victorian Family Structure and Stresses*, (London: Croom Helm, 1978), p 60

40 Gaskell to Marianne Gaskell, [?29 April 1856], Chapple and Pollard, p 386 and Gaskell to Charles Eliot Norton, March 9th [1859], Chapple and Pollard, p 537.

41 Gaskell to Eliza Fox, Monday, [?Early February,] 1853, Chapple and Pollard, pp 222-223.

42 See Michael Wheeler, 'Elizabeth Gaskell's Unitarianism', *Gaskell Society Journal*, Vol 6, 1992, p 38 for a discussion of the parabolic episodes in *Ruth*.

43 Mike Hepworth, 'Privacy, Security and Respectability: The ideal Victorian home', in Tony Chapman and Jenny Hockey eds, *Ideal Homes? Social change and domestic life*, (London and New York: Routledge, 1999), p 18.

44 James Martineau, 'The Family in Heaven and Earth' in, *Endeavours after the Christian Life*, Fourth Edition, (London: Longmans, Green, Reader and Dyer, MDCCCLXVII), p 452.

45 *Cassell's Household Guide: being a complete encyclopaedia of domestic and social economy etc.*, (London: 1869), Vol II, p 266-267.

46 Cassell's, p 344.

47 Robert Poole, 'A poor Man I know' – Samuel Bamford and the making of *Mary Barton*', *The Gaskell Journal*, Vol 22, 2008, p 105.

48 Cassell's, p 344.

49 *Letters and Memorials of Catherine Winkworth, edited by her sister*, Vol II, (Clifton: E. Austin and Son, Printers, Chronicle Office, 1886), p 429.

50 *North and South*, Vol 7, p 244.

51 Cassell's, p 344.

52 Cassell's, p 346.

53 Mary Elizabeth Hotz, *Literary Remains: Representations of Death and Burial in Victorian England*, (Albany: State University of New York Press, 2009).

54 Edwin Chadwick, *A Supplementary Report on the Results of a Special Inquiry into the Practice of Interment in Towns*, (London: W. Clowes and Sons, 1843), p 41.

55 Chadwick, p 46.

56 Hotz, p 4.

57 Hotz, p 22.

58 Pat Jalland, *Death in the Victorian Family*, (Oxford: Oxford University Press, 1996).

59 Jalland, pp 49-51.

60 William Gaskell, *The Duties of the Individual to Society: A sermon on Occasion of the Death of Sir John Potter M.P. Preached at Cross Street Chapel, Manchester, October 31st, 1858, with the address at the Interment on the day preceding*, (London: E.T Whitfield, 1858), pp 16 and 18.

61 William Gaskell, '*A Sermon preached in Cross-Street Chapel, Manchester, September 25th 1859, on the occasion of the death of John Ashton Nicholls, Esq., F.R.A.S., with a sketch of his life*, (London: E.T Whitfield, 1859), p 12.

62 Gaskell, 1859, p 16-17.

63 Martineau, pp 453-454.

64 Gaskell to Elizabeth Gaskell, [18 March 1837], Chapple and Pollard, p 9.

65 Uglow, pp 106-7.

66 Gaskell to Elizabeth Gaskell, [18 March 1837], Chapple and Pollard, pp 9-10.

67 Jalland, p 120.

68 James Kay-Shuttleworth, *Four Periods of Public Education as Reviewed in 1832, 1839, 1846, 1862*, intro Norman Morris, (Brighton: The Harvester Press, 1973), 'First Period' pp 3-170, Joseph Adshead, *Distress in Manchester: Evidence (Tabular and Otherwise) of the State of the Labouring Classes in 1840-42*, (London: Henry Hooper, 1842) and *Reports of the Ministry to the Poor in Manchester 1839–1842*, p 123.

69 Jalland, p 124.

70 See Tina Young Choi, 'Writing the Victorian City: Discourses of Risk, Connection, and Inevitability', *Victorian Studies*, Summer 2001: 43,4, p 561-589.

71 Gaskell to Eliza Fox, [?April 1850], Chapple and Pollard, pp 109-10.

72 See Dewi Williams, 'The Death of Willie Gaskell', *The Gaskell Society Journal*, Vol 13, 1999, pp 108-109 for a description of the boarding house and the family who lived there.

73 Gaskell to Fanny Holland, Tuesday [9 March 1847] in which she describes the death of her son Willie from scarlet fever. John Chapple and Alan Shelston eds, *Further Letters of Mrs Gaskell*, (Manchester: Manchester University Press, 2003), p 36.

74 Jalland, p 125.

75   Gaskell to Eliza Fox, Tuesday [27] Aug: 1850, Chapple and Pollard, pp 129-130.

76 Maria Edgeworth to Mary Holland, 27 December 1848, John Rylands, MS 732/52.

77 *Mary Barton*, Vol 5, p 205.

78 Hotz, p 7.

79 Hotz, p 15.

80 Ellis Chadwick, p 438.

81 *Mary Barton*, Vol 5, p 68.

82 *Mary Barton*, Vol 5, p 70.

83 See Arthur Pollard, 'Faith and Family: Fundamental Values in *Mary Barton*', *Gaskell Society Journal*, Vol 3, 1989 p 4 for a discussion of the way in which Harry Carson's death cuts across class boundaries.

84 Emily Jane Morris, ''Ready to hear and to help': Female agency and the reclamation of the fallen woman in Elizabeth Gaskell's 'Lizzie Leigh'., *The Gaskell Journal*, Vol 23, 2009, p 40. Julie Nash also points out that James Leigh has forfeited his right to paternal authority because of his lack of compassion for his disgraced daughter. Julie Nash, *Servants and Paternalism in the Works of Maria Edgeworth and Elizabeth Gaskell*, (Aldershot and Burlington VT: Ashgate Publishing Company, 2007), p 104.

85 Gaskell to Elizabeth Holland, [?Early April 1859], Chapple and Pollard, pp 548-549.

86 Morris, p 44.

87 Deborah Denenholz Morse, 'Stitching Repentance, Sewing Rebellion: Seamstresses and Fallen Women in Elizabeth Gaskell's Fiction', in Vanessa D Dickerson ed, *Keeping the Victorian House: A Collection of Essays*, (New York and London: Garland Publishing Inc, 1995), p 40.

88 'Lizzie Leigh' in Elizabeth Gaskell, Joanne Shattock ed, *The Works of Elizabeth Gaskell: Vol.1: Journalism, Early Fiction and Personal Writings*, (London: Pickering and Chatto, 2005), p 24.

89 'Lizzie Leigh', Vol 1, pp 149-150.

90 'Lizzie Leigh', Vol 1, p 149.

91 *The Book of Common Prayer and Administration of the Sacraments*, (Cambridge: Cambridge University Press), p 152.

92 'Lizzie Leigh', Vol 1, p 150.

93 'Mr Harrison's Confessions' in Elizabeth Gaskell, Alan Shelston ed, *The Works of Elizabeth Gaskell*, Volume 2, <u>Novellas and Shorter Fiction 1, *The Moorland Cottage, Cranford* and Related Writings</u>, (London: Pickering & Chatto, 2005), p 119.

94 Gaskell to Elizabeth Gaskell, [30 March 1838], Chapple and Pollard, pp 12-13.

95 'The Doom of the Griffiths' in Elizabeth Gaskell, Charlotte Mitchell ed, *The*

Works of Elizabeth Gaskell: Vol. 3: Novellas and Shorter Fiction II Round the Sofa and Tales from Household Words (1852 -9), (London: Pickering and Chatto, 2005), p 311.

96 Vanessa D Dickerson,*Victorian Ghosts in the Noontide: Women Writers and the Supernatural,* (Columbia and London: University of Missouri Press, 1996), p 113.

97 Uglow, p 125.

98 Felicia Bonaparte, *The Gypsy-Bachelor of Manchester: The Life of Mrs. Gaskell's Demon,* (Charlottesville and London: University Press of Virginia, 1992), p 225.

99 Jalland, p 67.

100 Hotz, p 65, sees this as reminiscent of 'Christ's acceptance of his ultimate mission in the garden at Gethsemane', reminding Margaret of the need for her to step out of her allocated private sphere into the public realm of work.

101 Jalland, p 68.

102 John A V Chapple, *Elizabeth Gaskell: The Early Years,* (Manchester: Manchester University Press, 1997), p 339.

103 See for example, Chapple and Shelston, p 36 and p 156 .

104 Letter from John Stevenson to Elizabeth Stevenson, (27 Dec [1819]), Papers of John Geoffrey Sharps, File 3, Box 30, John Rylands Library, Manchester.

105 Stevenson, 17th June, 1827, File 3, Box 30.

106 John A V Chapple, *Elizabeth Gaskell: A portrait in letters,* (Manchester: Manchester University Press, 1980), p 4.

107 Stevenson, 30 July [1828], File 3, Box 30.

108 Stevenson, File 3, Box 30.

109 Stevenson, 15 August 1828, file 3, Box 30.

110 Chapple, 1997, p 338.

111 Joseph A Kestner, *Masculinities in Victorian Painting,* (Aldershot: Scolar Press, 1995), p 34.

112 See John R Reed, *Victorian Conventions,* (Ohio University Press: USA, 1975), Chapter Ten for a discussion of The Return Convention in Victorian literature.

113 *Mary Barton*, Vol 5, p 125.

114 *Mary Barton*, Vol 5, p 125.

115 *Mary Barton*, Vol 5, p 161.

116 Kestner, pp 55-56.

117 *Cranford*, Vol 2, p 214.

118 *Cranford*, Vol 2, p 215.

119 William J Hyde, "'Poor Frederick" and "Poor Peter": Elizabeth Gaskell's Fraternal Deviants', *Gaskell Society Journal*, Vol 9, 1995, pp 21-26.

120 *North and South*, Vol 7, pp 225-226.

121 *North and South*, Vol 7, p 236.

122 *North and South*, Vol 7, p 229.

123 *North and South*, Vol 7, p 239 and p 227.

124 *North and South*, Vol 7, p 230.

125 Stevenson, 15 August, 1828, File 3, Box 30.

126 *North and South*, Vol 7, p 44.

127 Jill Matus, *Shock, Memory and the Unconscious in Victorian Fiction*, (Cambridge: Cambridge University Press, 2009), p 71. For further information on the Victorians and dreams, also see Kate Summerscale, *Mrs Robinson's Disgrace: The Private Diary of a Victorian Lady*, (London: Bloomsbury, 2012), p 57 and pp 148-149.

128 See Larry K Uffleman, <u>Elizabeth Gaskell's *North and South*: the Novel in Progress</u>, *Gaskell Society Journal*, Vol 14, 2000, p 8, for a discussion of the epigraphs used as a commentary on Frederick's return home.

129 John Geoffrey Sharps, *Mrs. Gaskell's Observation and Invention: A Study of her Non-biographic Works*, (Fontwell: Linden Press, 1970), p 403.

130 Stevenson, Jan/Feb 1821, File 3, Box 30.

131 Elizabeth Gaskell, Marion Shaw ed, *The Works of Elizabeth Gaskell: Vol. 9: Sylvia's Lovers*, (London: Pickering and Chatto, 2006), p 61.

132 *Sylvia's Lovers*, Vol 9, p 62.

133 *Sylvia's Lovers*, Vol 9, p 62.

134 *Sylvia's Lovers*, Vol 9, p 325.

135 Kestner, Chapter 3, 'The Gallant Knight'.

136 D'Albertis, p 131.

CHAPTER TWO

1 Part of this chapter is adapted, with permission, from my article 'Cross-dressing and interpretations of gender in *Cranford* and 'The Grey Woman', *The Gaskell Journal*, Vol 24, 2010, pp 73-84.

2 John Stevenson to Elizabeth Stevenson, 16 July 1827, Papers of John Geoffrey Sharps, File 3, Box 30, John Rylands Library, Manchester.

3 Gaskell to Marianne Gaskell, [22 November 1852], John A. V. Chapple and Arthur Pollard eds, *The Letters of Mrs Gaskell*, (Manchester: Manchester University Press, 1997), p 213.

4 Gaskell to John Forster, Wednesday night – [17 May 1854]. Chapple and Pollard, p 290. Rosa Bonheur was an animalier (an animal painter and sculptor) who went to the slaughter house at Roule to study animal anatomy. Delia Gaze ed, Maja Mihajlovic and Leanda Shrimpton picture editors, *Dictionary of Women Artists, Vol 1, Introductory Surveys, Artists A–I*, (London and Chicago: Fitzroy Dearborn Publishers, 1977), pp 288-291.

5 Gretchen Van Slyke, 'The Sexual and Textual Politics of Dress: Rosa Bonheur and Her Cross-Dressing Permits', *Nineteenth-Century French Studies*, Vol 26, Nos 3 & 4, Spring-Summer 1998, p 328.

6 Gaskell to Marianne Gaskell, [c. 28 March 1851], Chapple and Pollard, p 147.

7 Gaskell to Eliza Fox, [? April 1850], Chapple and Pollard, p 108.

8 Gaskell to W. W. Story, May 9th [1862], Chapple and Pollard, p 687.

9 Gaskell to Charles Eliot Norton, April 22nd [1862], Chapple and Pollard, p 682.

10 Gaskell to Emily ?Tagart, [? & 30 December 1851], Chapple and Pollard, p 174. See also Jenny Bourne Taylor and Sally Shuttleworth eds, *Embodied Selves: An Anthology of Psychological Texts 1830 – 1890*, (Clarendon Press: Oxford, 1998), Chapter 2, pp 106-110 for an extract from Henry Holland, *On Sleep, and the relations of dreaming and insanity*, illustrating the Victorian interest in dreaming as the revelation of hidden thoughts and feelings.

11 See, for example, Dickens's leading article, 'Sucking Pigs', in *Household Words*, 8 November 1851, pp 145-147.

12 In 1863, 'The Cage at Cranford' was published in *All the Year Round*. The iron cage which is intended to support women's skirts, allowing them to walk more freely, arrives in Cranford as the latest fashion from Paris, but Miss Pole, for whom it is intended as a present, misunderstands its purpose and uses it instead as a cage for her parrot. Far from liberating Miss Pole, the cage eventually is cut up to make 'two good comfortable English calashes'. *Cranford* in Elizabeth Gaskell, Alan Shelston ed, *The Works of Elizabeth Gaskell*, Volume 2, (London: Pickering & Chatto, 2005), p 313.

13 Ute Kauer, 'Narrative cross-dressing in Charlotte Brontë's *The Professor*,' *Brontë Society Transactions*, (26:2, 2001), pp 167-187.

14 Charlotte Brontë, *Villette* (1853), (London, Edinburgh, Paris, Melbourne, Toronto

and New York: Thomas Nelson & Sons Ltd, 1952), p 165.

15 Fanny Trollope also memorably uses cross-dressing to effect the escape of Major Allen, dressed as his wife in Frances Trollope, Tamara S Wagner, ed, *The Barnabys in America; or, Adventures of the Widow Wedded* (1843), (London: Pickering & Chatto, 2011), p 318.

16 Ann Heilmann, '(Un)masking desire: cross-dressing and the crisis of gender in New Woman fiction', *Journal of Victorian Culture*, 5:1, 2000, pp 83-111.

17 Caroline Huber notes the astonishing amount of cross-dressing in *Cranford* and the range of 'puzzling transvestite images.' Caroline P Huber, '"Heroic Pioneers": The Ladies of Cranford', *The Gaskell Society Journal*, Vol 21, 2007, pp 43-44.

18 *Cranford*, Vol 2, p 206.

19 *Cranford*, Vol 2, p 207.

20 *Cranford*, Vol 2, p 207.

21 *Cranford*, Vol 2, p 207.

22 *Cranford*, Vol 2, p 208.

23 John Tosh, *A Man's Place: Masculinity and the Middle Class Home in Victorian England*, (New Haven and London: Yale University Press, 1999), p 97.

24 *Cranford*, Vol 2, p 209.

25 *Cranford*, Vol 2, p 209.

26 David Roberts,'The Paterfamilias of the Victorian Governing classes' in *The Victorian Family: Structure and Stresses*, Anthony S Wohl ed, (London: Croom Helm, 1978), p 72.

27 Terence R Wright, *Elizabeth Gaskell 'We are not angels': Realism, Gender, Values*, (Basingstoke: Macmillan Press Ltd, 1995), p 136.

28 *Cranford*, Vol 2, p 209.

29 *Cranford*, Vol 2, p 209.

30 Wright, p 136.

31 Susan P Casteras, 'Reader, Beware: Images of Victorian Women and Books', *Nineteenth-Century Gender Studies*, Issue 3.1, Spring 2007.

32 *Cranford*, Vol 2, p 210.

33 *Cranford*, Vol 2, p 210.

34 *Cranford*, Vol 2, p 210.

35 *Cranford*, Vol 2, p 210.

36 *King James Bible* Matthew 6, verses 28 -29.

37 N. M. Jacobs, 'Gender and Layered Narrative in "Wuthering Heights" and "The Tenant of Wildfell Hall"', *The Journal of Narrative Technique,* Vol 16, No 3, Fall, 1986, p 207.

38 *Letters and Memorials of Catherine Winkworth, edited by her sister.* Vol 1, (Clifton: E. Austin and Son, Printers, Chronicle Office, 1883), p 127, Rebecca White, "A joke spoken in rather a sad tone': *Cranford*, humour, and Heidi Thomas's television adaptation', *The Gaskell Journal,* Vol 22, 2008, p 155 and Eileen Gillooly, 'Humor as Daughterly Defense in Cranford', *ELH,* Vol 59, No 4, Winter 1992, p 901.

39 *Cranford*, Vol 2, p 210.

40 Gaskell to Charles Dickens, Janry 8. [1850], Chapple and Pollard, p 98. Dickens and Angela Burdett-Coutts founded Urania Cottage, a Home for Fallen Women in 1846 with the aim of preparing each inmate for emigration to Australia, South Africa or Canada where they could start a new life. Gaskell wanted Pasley to be able to emigrate to Australia. The outcome of Pasley's story is not known.

41 Graham Storey, Kathleen Tillotson and Nina Burgis eds, *The letters of Charles Dickens,* Madeline House, Graham Storey, Kathleen Tillotson General Eds, Vol Six 1850–1852, (Oxford: Oxford Clarendon Press, 1988), p 623.

42 Judith Flanders, *The Victorian House: Domestic Life from Childbirth to Deathbed,* (London: Harper Collins, 2003), p xxxiv.

43 'My Lady Ludlow', in Charlotte Mitchell, ed. *The Works of Elizabeth Gaskell: Vol. 3: Novellas and Shorter Fiction II Round the Sofa and Tales from Household Words (1852-9).* London: Pickering and Chatto, 2005. Vol 3, p 238.

44 'My Lady Ludlow', Vol 3, p 241.

45 Gregory Anderson, *Victorian Clerks,* (Manchester: Manchester University Press, 1976), and Barbara Leah Harman, 'In Promiscuous Company', *Victorian Studies,* Vol 31, Pt 3, 1988, pp 355-356.

46 'My Lady Ludlow', Vol 3, p 241.

47 Rose Lovell-Smith, 'Anti-Housewives and Ogres' Housekeepers: The Roles of Bluebeard's Female Helper', *Folklore,* 113.2, October 2002, p 203.

48 'The Grey Woman' in Elizabeth Gaskell, Linda Hughes ed, *The Works of Elizabeth Gaskell, Novellas and Shorter Fiction III, Cousin Phillis and Other Tales from All the Year Round and the Cornhill Magazine 1859 – 64,* Volume 4, (London: Pickering & Chatto, 2006), p 135.

49 'The Grey Woman', Vol 4, p 135.

50 'The Grey Woman', Vol 4, p 136.

51 'The Grey Woman', Vol 4, p 140.

52 'The Grey Woman', Vol 4, p 151. See also my discussion of the rescue compulsion in Chapter 1 of this book.

53 'The Grey Woman', Vol 4, p 157.

54 'The Grey Woman', Vol 4, p 157.

55 Coral Lansbury, *Elizabeth Gaskell: The Novel of Social Crisis,* (London: Paul Elek, 1975), pp 211-212.

56 Heilmann, p 89.

57 Lovell-Smith, pp 203-204.

58 Gaskell to Louis Hachette, [c. 17 March 1855], John Chapple and Alan Shelston, eds, *Further Letters of Mrs Gaskell,* (Manchester: Manchester University Press, 2003), p 128. Gaskell discusses a number of living writers, including Wilkie Collins. 'He takes great pains, and devotes himself to novel-writing, as to a profession. His style is considered very good. I do not much admire his books myself, but many good judges do.'

59 Lyn Pykett, *The sensation novel: from The Woman in White to The Moonstone,* (Plymouth:: Northcote House in association with the British Council, 1994), pp 20-21.

60 Lovell-Smith, p 199.

61 Catherine Craft-Fairchild, 'Cross-Dressing and the Novel: Women Warriors and Domestic Femininity', *Eighteenth-Century Fiction,* Vol 10, Number 2, January 1998, p 178.

62 Craft-Fairchild, p 178.

63 Michel Foucault, *The Will to Knowledge: The History of Sexuality Volume 1,* trans. by Robert Hurley, (London: Penguin Books, 1998), p 3.

64 Foucault, p 46.

65 Kathryn Gleadle, *The Early Feminists: Radical Unitarians and the Emergence of the Women's Rights Movement, 1831-51,* (Basingstoke: Macmillan Press, 1995), p 1. For a comprehensive discussion of the links between Christian manliness and nine-teenth-century society, see Norman Vance, *The sinews of the spirit: The ideal of Christian manliness in Victorian literature and religious thought,* (Cambridge: Cambridge University Press, 1985).

66 Jenny Uglow, *Elizabeth Gaskell: A Habit of Stories,* (London: New York, Faber and

Faber, 1999), p 299 and pp 310-313.

67 Ruth Watts, *Gender, Power and the Unitarians in England 1760–1860*, (London and New York: Longman, 1998), pp 190-193.

68 Uglow, pp 311-312.

69 Gleadle, p 6.

70 Gleadle, pp 48-49.

71 John James Tayler, *Parental and filial duties: An address delivered in the School Room, Lower Mosley-Street, Manchester. On Sunday evening, April 17th, 1853*, (Manchester: John Heywood, 1853), p 5.

72 Mary Leman Grimstone, 'Men and Women', *Tait's Edinburgh Magazine*, 1:2, March 1834, p 102.

73 Gaskell to Eliza Fox, [c. February 1850], Chapple and Pollard, pp 106-107, Gaskell to Lady Kay-Shuttleworth, May 14. [1850], Chapple and Pollard, pp 116-117, and Gaskell to Emily Shaen, Oct. 27th, 1854, Chapple and Pollard, p 318.

74 Gaskell to George Smith, Augt 4 [1859], Chapple and Pollard, p 567.

75 Gaskell to Eliza Fox, Monday, [?Early February] 1853, Chapple and Pollard, pp 222-223.

76 John Seed, 'Theologies of power: Unitarianism and the social relations of religious discourse, 1800–50' in R J Morris, ed, *Class, power and social structure in British nineteenth-century towns*, (Leicester: Leicester University Press, 1986), p 139.

77 Seed, p 139.

78 Ruth Watts, 'Rational Religion and Feminism: the Challenge of Unitarianism in the Nineteenth Century' in Sue Morgan ed, *Women, Religion and Feminism in Britain, 1750–1900*, (Basingstoke: Palgrave Macmillan, 2000), p 41.

79 Gleadle, pp 54-70.

80 George Henry Lewes, 'The Principles of Success in Literature', *Fortnightly Review*, May 15, 1865, p 90.

81 Unattributed, 'Recent Works of Fiction', *Prospective Review*, 34, April 1853, p 223.

82 Gleadle, p 55.

83 Gleadle, p 43.

84 Travers Madge, a Manchester philanthropist and Unitarian Mission Visitor, was the driving force behind both the Sunday School and day schools associated with Cross Street Chapel which were located at Lower Mosely Street in Manchester. He not only recruited Gaskell and the Winkworth sisters as teachers, but also edited the

Sunday School Penny Magazine in which Gaskell's short stories, 'Hand and Heart' (1849) and 'Bessy's Troubles at Home' (1852) appeared.

85 Gleadle, p 93.

86 Tayler, pp 3-4.

87 'Hand and Heart' in Elizabeth Gaskell, Joanne Shattock ed, *The Works of Elizabeth Gaskell: Vol. 1: Journalism, Early Fiction and Personal Writings,* (London: Pickering and Chatto, 2005), p 104.

88 Grimstone, p 101.

89 'Hand and Heart', Vol 1, p 108.

90 John Tosh, Manliness and Masculinities in Nineteenth-Century Britain: essays on gender, family and empire, (London: Longman, 2004), pp 48-49.

91 Tosh p 31.

92 Claudia B Nelson, 'Sex and the Single Boy: Ideals of Manliness and Sexuality in Victorian Literature for Boys', *Victorian Studies,* Vol 32, Number 4, Summer 1989, p 526.

93 Tayler, p 7.

94 'Hand and Heart', p 114.

95 Tosh, p 19.

96 Elizabeth Gaskell, Deirdre D'Albertis ed, *The Works of Elizabeth Gaskell: Vol. 6: Ruth,* (London: Pickering and Chatto, 2005), p 51.

97 *Ruth,* Vol 6, pp 51–52.

98 Carol Christ, 'Victorian Masculinity and the Angel in the House', in Martha Vicinus ed, *A Widening Sphere: Changing Roles of Victorian Women,* (Bloomington & London: Indiana University Press, 1977).

99 Nelson, p 525 and p 530.

100 Gleadle, p 16.

101 Kay Millard, 'The Religion of Elizabeth Gaskell', *The Gaskell Society Journal,* Vol 15, 2001, p 9.

102 James Martineau, 'Great Principles and Small Duties' in *Endeavours after the Christian Life,* Fourth Edition, (London: Longmans, Green, Reader and Dyer, MDCCCLXVII), p 24. See also Gaskell to Elizabeth Holland, [?Early April 1859], Chapple and Pollard, pp 548-549 for Gaskell's views on practical charity.

103 *Ruth,* Vol 6, p 280.

104 *Ruth,* Vol 6, p 90.

105 Gleadle, pp 16-18.

106 Priestley was influenced by the writing of David Hartley whose psychology attempted to provide a justification for the theological Doctrine of Necessity. Priestley argued that people always act from a motive rather than arbitrarily. He viewed this as the direct opposite of the Calvinist theory of predestination with which he had been brought up. 'Calvinism, attributing everything to God's Will, made human efforts to change things impious or futile; Philosophical Necessity urged men to change circumstances so that they themselves might be formed in more perfect ways.' Joseph Priestley, Jack Lindsay, intro, *Autobiography of Joseph Priestley, Memoirs written by Himself. An account of further Discoveries in Air.* (Bath: Adams & Dart, 1970), p 40.

107 William Gaskell, *Unitarian Christians called to bear witness to the truth: A Sermon preached before the supporters of the British and Foreign Unitarian Association, at their Annual Meeting, in Essex-Street Chapel, London, June 11, 1862,* (London: Edward T Whitfield, 1862), pp 6-7.

108 *Ruth*, Vol 6, p 153.

109 Unattributed, *Prospective Review*, p 232.

110 Elizabeth Gaskell, Elisabeth Jay, ed, *The Works of Elizabeth Gaskell: Vol. 7: North and South,* (London: Pickering and Chatto, 2005), p 21.

111 *North and South*, Vol 7, p 316.

112 Jill Matus, *Shock, Memory and the Unconscious in Victorian Fiction,* (Cambridge: Cambridge University Press, 2009), pp 63–64.

113 Tosh, p 32.

114 Gleadle, p 47.

115 'My Lady Ludlow' in Elizabeth Gaskell, Charlotte Mitchell ed, *The Works of Elizabeth Gaskell: Vol. 3: Novellas and Shorter Fiction II 'Round the Sofa' and Tales from 'Household Words' (1852–9),* (London: Pickering and Chatto, 2005), p 153.

116 'My Lady Ludlow', Vol 3, p 159.

117 'My Lady Ludlow', Vol 3, p 162.

CHAPTER THREE

1 Elizabeth Gaskell, Joanne Shattock ed, *The Works of Elizabeth Gaskell: Vol.1: Journalism, Early Fiction and Personal Writings,* (London: Pickering and Chatto, 2005), p 303.

2 Elizabeth Gaskell, Elizabeth Jay ed, *The Works of Elizabeth Gaskell: Vol. 7: North and*

South, (London: Pickering and Chatto, 2005), p 27.

3 *North and South*, Vol 7, p 27.

4 *Cassell's Household Guide: being a complete encyclopaedia of domestic and social economy etc.* (London: 1869), Vol I, index.

5 See for example, 'Lizzie Leigh', Vol.1, p 137, and Judith Flanders, *The Victorian House: Domestic Life from Childbirth to Deathbed*, (London: Harper Collins, 2003), p 77-78.

6 See Mary H Kuhlman, 'Education through experience in <u>North and South</u>', *Gaskell Society Journal*, Vol 10, 1996, pp 14-26 for an alternative assessment of Margaret's skills.

7 See Jane Hamlett, *Material Relations: Domestic Interiors and Middle-Class Families in England, 1850-1910*, (Manchester and New York: Manchester University Press, 2010), pp 86-87 for a discussion of the way in which Victorian handicrafts can be considered as a statement of feminine control of the domestic interior.

8 'Company Manners, Vol 1, p 309.

9 See Francesco Marroni, 'The Shadow of Dante: Elizabeth Gaskell and *'The Divine Comedy''*, *Gaskell Society Journal*, Vol 10, 1996, pp 1-13 for Gaskell's use of Dante in this novel.

10 *North and South*, Vol 7, p 27.

11 *North and South*, Vol 7, p 27.

12 *North and South*, Vol 7, p 32.

13 Coral Lansbury, *Elizabeth Gaskell: The Novel of Social Crisis*, (London: Elek Paul Books Ltd, 1975), p 107. See Jenny Uglow, *Elizabeth Gaskell: A Habit of Stories*, (London: New York, Faber and Faber, 1999) pp 228-231 for a brief account of Froude's life.

14 *North and South*, Vol 7, p 76.

15 Flanders, p 156.

16 *North and South*, Vol 7, p 76.

17 See Terence R Wright, *Elizabeth Gaskell, "We are not angels": realism, gender, values*, (Basingstoke: Macmillan, 1995), p 107 for a discussion of the importance of time in *North and South*.

18 *North and South*, Vol 7, p 63. See Marjorie Garson, *Moral Taste: Aesthetics, Subjectivity, and Social Power in the Nineteenth-Century Novel*, (Buffalo and London: University of Toronto Press, 2007), for a discussion of taste in *North and South*.

19 Helen Smith, *Decorative Painting in the Domestic Interior in England and Wales c1850–1890*, (New York and London: Garland Publishing, 1984), p 228.

20 Nadine Rottau, 'Everyone to his taste' or 'truth to material?': the role of materials in collections of applied arts' in John Potvin and Alla Myzelev eds, *Material Cultures, 1740–1920: The Meanings and Pleasures of Collecting*, (Farnham and Burlington: Ashgate Publishing Ltd, 2009), p 71.

21 Charles L Eastlake, *Hints on Household Taste in Furniture, Upholstery, and Other Details*, (Boston: James R Osgood and Company, 1872), p 11 and Owen Jones, *On the True and the False in the Decorative Arts: Lectures delivered at Marlborough House June 1852*, (London: 1863), pp 17-18.

22 Eastlake, p 116.

23 Jones, p 28.

24 *Cassell's Household Guide: being a complete encyclopaedia of domestic and social economy etc.*, (London: 1869), Vol II, p 200.

25 Catherine E Stowe and Harriet Beecher Stowe, *The American Woman's Home*, (New York: J B Ford: 1869), p 94.

26 Jeanette Eve, 'The Floral and Horticultural in Elizabeth Gaskell's novels', *Gaskell Society Journal*, Vol 7, 1993, p 2.

27 Mrs Loftie, p 76.

28 *North and South*, Vol 7, p 30.

29 Mrs Loftie, p 126.

30 See Lorna Huett, 'Commodity and collectivity: Cranford in the context of Household Words', *The Gaskell Society Journal*, Vol 17, 2003, p 47 for a discussion of the similar use of domestic objects to illustrate contrasting moral and social attitudes.

31 *North and South*, Vol 7, p 74.

32 Valentine Cunningham, *Everywhere Spoken Against: Dissent in the Victorian Novel*, (Oxford: Clarendon Press, 1975), p 133 and p 137.

33 Wendy Craik, 'Lore, Learning and Wisdom: Workers and Education in *Mary Barton* and *North and South*, *The Gaskell Society Journal*, Vol 2, 1988, p 23.

34 Susan P Casteras, 'Reader, Beware: Images of Victorian Women and Books, *Nineteenth-Century Gender Studies*, Issue 3.1, Spring 2007.

35 *North and South*, Vol 7, p 74.

36 Mrs Loftie, p 85.

37 *North and South*, Vol 7, p 74.

38 Mrs. Loftie, p 87.

39 Angus Easson, 'The Sentiment of Feeling: Emotions and Objects in Elizabeth Gaskell (1)', *Gaskell Society Journal*, Vol 4, 1990, p 68.

40 Patricia Ingham, *The Language of Gender and Class: Transformation in the Victorian Novel*, (London & New York: Routledge, 1996), p 58.

41 North and South, Vol 7, p 91.

42 Thad Logan, *The Victorian Parlour*, (Cambridge: Cambridge University Press, 2001), p 29.

43 *Cassell's Household Guide: being a complete encyclopaedia of domestic and social economy etc.*, (London: 1869), Vol I, p 2.

44 *North and South*, Vol 7, pp 106-107.

45 Logan, p 30.

46 See Lindsy Lawrence, 'Gender Play "At our social table": The New Domesticity in the *Cornhill* and Elizabeth Gaskell's *Wives and Daughters*', *The Gaskell Journal*, Vol 22, 2008, pp 22-41 for a discussion of the multi-functionality of the dining room as a metaphor for family literary magazines such as the *Cornhill*.

47 Mrs Loftie, p 3.

48 Easson, p 74.

49 Mrs Loftie, p 74.

50 Tim Dolin, 'Cranford and the Victorian Collection', *Victorian Studies*, 36, No 2, Winter 1991, p 179.

51 Dolin, p 179. Dolin comments: '[*Cranford*] is associated with that variety of Victorian objects produced by middle-class feminine work – needlework, decorative crafts, domestic arrangement – and is most often characterized as a female collection:'.

52 Robert Ellis, Preface to the *Official Descriptive and Illustrated Catalogue: Great Exhibition of the Works of Industry of All Nations,: 1851*, (London: William Clowes and Sons, MDCCLI), p v.

53 *Catalogue, Great Exhibition,* p 763. See Ann B Shteir, '"Fac-Similes of Nature": Victorian Wax Flower Modelling', *Victorian Literature and Culture*, 2007, Vol 35, p 649 for an account of wax flower modelling.

54 *Cassell's Household Guide: being a complete encyclopaedia of domestic and social economy etc.* (London: 1869), Vol III, p 19.

55 Lori Anne Loeb, *Consuming Angels: Advertising and Victorian Women*, (New York: Oxford: Oxford University Press, 1994), p 13. See also Judith Flanders, '*Consuming*

Passions: Leisure and Pleasure in Victorian Britain', (London: Harper Collins, 2006), p 26.

56 *North and South*, Vol 7, pp 149-150.

57 See for example, Ruskin's comments on Holman Hunt's *The Awakening Conscience* in John Ruskin, 'Arrows of the Chase', Vol. I, *Letters on Art*, part III, 'Pre-Raphaelitism, (Orpington: George Allen, 1880).

58 Chris Owen, *The Gaskells' House, 84 Plymouth Grove, Ardwick, Manchester, Period Rooms, Report of research and proposals by Chris Owen with specialist consultant Peter Brears. Information and reference works provided by Janet Allen.* (Unpublished report: Museum Casts 2011), p 22.

59 Hilary M Schor, *Scheherazade in the Marketplace: Elizabeth Gaskell and the Victorian Novel,* (New York: Oxford, Oxford University Press, 1992), p 128.

60 North and South, Vol 7, p 77.

61 *North and South, V*ol 7, p 77.

62 See Jill Matus, *Shock, Memory and the Unconscious in Victorian Fiction,* (Cambridge: Cambridge University Press, 2009), pp 77-78 for a discussion of how Thornton's attraction to Margaret destabilises his emotional responses.

63 Elizabeth Gaskell, Marion Shaw ed, *The Works of Elizabeth Gaskell: Vol. 9: Sylvia's Lovers,* (London: Pickering and Chatto, 2005), p 39.

64 North and South, Vol 7, p 356.

65 *North and South, V*ol 7, p 356.

66 *North and South, V*ol 7, p 356.

67 *North and South, V*ol 7, p 356.

68 Logan, p 113.

69 Philippa Tristram, *Living Space in Fact and Fiction,* (London and New York: Routledge, 1989), p 103.

70 Alexander Boyd and Son, *The English Fireplace: Its Advantages, its Objections and its rivals. Considered with a view to utility and economy,* (London: John Bumpus, 1874).

71 Catherine E Stowe and Harriet Beecher Stowe, *The American Woman's Home,* (New York: J B Ford: 1869).

72 Elizabeth Gaskell, Joanne Wilkes ed, *The Works of Elizabeth Gaskell: Vol. 5: Mary Barton: A Tale of Manchester Life,* (London: Pickering and Chatto, 2005), p 18 and p 21.

73 'The Half-Brothers' in Elizabeth Gaskell, Charlotte Mitchell ed, *The Works of Elizabeth Gaskell: Vol.3: Novellas and Shorter Fiction II: <u>Round the Sofa</u>, and Tales from <u>Household Works</u> (1852-9),* (London: Pickering and Chatto, 2005), p 436.

74 'Company Manners', Vol 1, p 304.

75 Gaskell to Marianne Gaskell, [? January 1853], Chapple and Pollard, p 857.

76 'The Moorland Cottage' in Elizabeth Gaskell, Alan Shelston ed, The Works of Elizabeth Gaskell: Vol. 2: Novellas and Shorter Fiction I, The Moorland Cottage, Cranford and Related Writings. (London: Pickering and Chatto, 2005), p 31.

77 'Martha Preston', Vol 1, p 123.

78 See Felicia Bonaparte, *The Gypsy-Bachelor of Manchester: The Life of Mrs. Gaskell's Demon*, (Charlottesville and London: University Press of Virginia, 1992), pp 150-151 for a further discussion of fire as a metaphor for sexual passion in Gaskell's fiction.

79 Elizabeth Gaskell, Marion Shaw ed, *The Works of Elizabeth Gaskell: Vol. 9: Sylvia's Lovers*, (London: Pickering and Chatto, 2005), p 81.

80 *Sylvia's Lovers*, Vol 9, p 87.

81 *Sylvia's Lovers*, Vol 9, p 281.

82 'Morton Hall', Vol 3, p 38.

83 Elizabeth Gaskell, Josie Billington ed, *The Works of Elizabeth Gaskell: Vol. 10: Wives and Daughters (1866)*, (London: Pickering and Chatto, 2005), p 204.

84 Wives and Daughters, Vol 10, p 203.

85 *Mary Barton*, Vol 5, p 19.

86 Gaskell to Elizabeth Holland, [2 December 1838], Chapple and Pollard, p 39.

87 *Mary Barton*, Vol 5, p 19.

88 See *Official Descriptive and Illustrated Catalogue of the great exhibition:* 1851, (London: William Clowes and Sons, MDCCCLI), Vol 2, p 748 for an exhibitor showing a papier-mâché piano and piano stool, an upholstered easy chair and a variety of tea trays, tea chest and tea caddys.

89 In October 1849, the *Morning Chronicle* announced 'that it was to undertake a survey of the condition of the labouring classes in England and Wales under the general title of "Labour and the Poor". The reports of the survey were published over a period of two years and provided the mid-nineteenth-century Englishman with the most comprehensive view of the working classes that he had ever seen.' Angus Bethune Reach, J Ginswick ed, *Labour and the Poor in England and Wales, 1849–1851: The Letters to the Morning Chronicle from the Correspondents in the Manufacturing and Mining Districts, the Towns of Liverpool and Birmingham, and the Rural Districts, Vol 1: Lancashire, Cheshire, Yorkshire*, (Gainsborough: Frank Cass, 1983), p xi.

90 Bethune Reach, p 21.

91 *Cassell's Household Guide: being a complete encyclopaedia of domestic and social economy etc.,* (London: 1869), Vol III, p 179.

92 Mary Elizabeth Braddon, *Lady Audley's Secret* (1862), ed. David Skilton, (Oxford: Oxford University Press, 1988), p 232.

93 Carolyn Steedman, 'What a rag rug means' in Inga Bryden and Janet Floyd eds, *Domestic Space: Reading the nineteenth-century interior,* (Manchester and New York: Manchester University Press, 1999), p 34.

94 Bethune Reach, p 21.

95 *Mary Barton,* Vol 5, p 99.

96 Mary Elizabeth Hotz, *Literary Remains: Representations of Death and Burial in Victorian England,* (Albany: State University of New York Press, 2009), pp 49-50.

97 Edgar Wright, *Mrs Gaskell: The Basis for Re-assessment,* (London: Oxford University Press, 1965), p 213.

98 'My Lady Ludlow, Vol 3, p 170.

99 'My Lady Ludlow', Vol 3, p 170.

100 'My Lady Ludlow, Vol 3, p 173.

101 Elizabeth Gaskell, Josie Billington ed, *The Works of Elizabeth Gaskell: Vol. 10: Wives and Daughters,* (London: Pickering and Chatto, 2006), p 204.

102 *Wives and Daughters,* Vol 10, p 204.

103 *Wives and Daughters,* Vol 10, p 205.

104 *Wives and Daughters,* Vol 10, p 205.

CHAPTER FOUR

1 See for example, Henry Mayhew, *London Labour and the London Poor,* Vol 1, (London: Griffin, Bohn and Company, 1861), p 43 and George Godwin, *London Shadows: A Glance at the "Homes" of the Thousands,* (London: G Routledge & Col, 1854), p 10.

2 *Census of Great Britain, 1851,* (London: Longman, Brown, Green & Longmans, 1854), p xxxv.

3 M.J. Daunton, *House and Home in the Victorian City: Working-Class Housing 1850–1914,* (London: Edward Arnold, 1983), pp 11-13.

4 William Gaskell, *The Duties of the Individual to Society: A Sermon on the Occasion of the Death of Sir John Potter M.P.,* (London: E T Whitfield, 1858), p 3.

5 Gaskell, 1858, p 4.

6 'An Accursed Race' in Elizabeth Gaskell, Charlotte Mitchell ed, *The Works of*

Elizabeth Gaskell: Vol.3: Novellas and Shorter Fiction II: Round the Sofa, and Tales from Household Works (1852-9), (London: Pickering and Chatto, 2005), pp 296-309.

7 See Louise Henson, 'History, Science and social change: Elizabeth Gaskell's 'evolutionary' narratives', *The Gaskell Society Journal,* Vol 17, 2003, p 19 for a discussion of the debate between monogenists and polygenists which was current at the time of writing 'An Accursed Race'.

8 Julian Wolfreys, *Being English: Narrative Idioms and Performances of National Identity from Coleridge to Trollope,* (Albany: State University of New York Press, 1994), p 83.

9 Wolfreys, p 84.

10 James Kay-Shuttleworth, *Four periods of Public Education as Reviewed in 1832, 1839, 1846, 1862,* (Brighton: The Harvester Press, 1973), p 10.

11 Felicia Bonaparte claims that Gaskell associates the French with her demonic other: Felicia Bonaparte, *The Gypsy-Bachelor of Manchester: The Life of Mrs. Gaskell's Demon,* (Charlottesville and London: University Press of Virginia, 1992), p 70.

12 'An Accursed Race', Vol 3, p 307.

13 'An Accursed Race', Vol 3, p 309. See Wolfreys, p 88 for a discussion of the ambiguity of this epitaph and Mrs Ellis H Chadwick, *Mrs. Gaskell: Haunts, Homes and Stories,* (London: Sir Isaac Pitman and Sons Ltd, 1910), pp 312-313 who notes the importance of the epitaph to Gaskell who quoted it 28 years after leaving Stratford as a schoolgirl, never having revisited the town.

14 Gaskell to unknown correspondent, Tuesday Ap: 14 [?1852], John A. V. Chapple and Arthur Pollard eds , *The Letters of Mrs Gaskell,* (Manchester: Manchester University Press, 1997), p 183.

15 Gaskell to Lady Kay-Shuttleworth, March 4th [1854], Chapple and Pollard, p 268.

16 Gaskell to Mrs Mary Robberds, [?June ?1861], John Chapple and Alan Shelston eds, *Further Letters of Mrs Gaskell,* (Manchester: Manchester University Press, 2003), p 225.

17 Gaskell to Emily Shaen, Oct. 27th, 1854, Chapple and Pollard, p 320.

18 Elizabeth Gaskell, Joanne Wilkes ed, *The Works of Elizabeth Gaskell: Vol. 5: Mary Barton,* (London: Pickering and Chatto, 2005), p 11.

19 Gaskell to Eliza Fox, [?April 1850], Chapple and Pollard, pp 109-110.

20 Heather Glen, 'Elizabeth Gaskell's Resurrection', *The Times Literary Supplement,* November 8 2006.

21 *Mary Barton,* Vol 5, p 13.

22 Jill Matus, *Unstable Bodies: Victorian Representations of Sexuality and Maternity*, (Manchester and New York: Manchester University Press, 1995), p 73.

23 Jill Matus, '*Mary Barton* and *North and South*' in Jill Matus ed, *The Cambridge Companion to Elizabeth Gaskell*, (Cambridge: Cambridge University Press, 2007), p 31.

24 Matus, 1995, p 75.

25 *Mary Barton*, Vol 5, p 109.

26 Deborah Anna Logan, *Fallenness in Victorian Women's Writing: Marry, Stitch, Die or Do Worse*, (Columbia and London: University of Missouri Press, 1998), p 84.

27 *Mary Barton*, Vol 5, p 110.

28 Amanda Anderson, *Tainted Souls and Painted Faces: The Rhetoric of Fallenness in Victorian Culture*, (Ithaca and London: Cornell University Press, 1993), p 118.

29 Patsy Stoneman, 'Gaskell, gender and the family' in Jill Matus ed, *The Cambridge Companion to Elizabeth Gaskell*, (Cambridge: Cambridge University Press, 2007), p 143.

30 *Mary Barton*, Vol 5, p 139.

31 *Mary Barton*, Vol 5, p 139.

32 Matus, 2009, p 117.

33 Deborah Denholz Morse, 'Stitching Repentance, Sewing Rebellion: Seamstresses and Fallen Women in Elizabeth Gaskell's Fiction', in Vanessa D Dickerson ed, *Keeping the Victorian House: A Collection of Essays*, (New York and London: Garland Publishing Inc, 1995), p 47.

34 Matus, 2009, p 5.

35 *Mary Barton*, Vol 5, p 194.

36 Matus, 2009, p 71.

37 *Mary Barton*, Vol 5, p 194.

38 *Mary Barton*, Vol 5, p 194.

39 *Mary Barton*, Vol 5, p 194.

40 *Mary Barton*, Vol 5, p 195.

41 Stoneman, p 79.

42 James Martineau, 'The Family in Heaven and Earth' in *Endeavours after the Christian Life*, Fourth Edition, (London: Longmans, Green, Reader and Dyer, MDCCCLXVII), p 461. Jenny Uglow points out that 'although Elizabeth liked Martineau's ideas, she did not exactly like *him*.' Jenny Uglow, *Elizabeth Gaskell: A Habit of Stories* (London: New York, Faber and Faber, 1999), p 131.

43 *Mary Barton*, Vol 5, p 202.

44 *Mary Barton,* Vol 5, p 323.

45 See Bernard Rosenthal, 'Tituba's Story', *The New England Quarterly,* Vol 71, No 2, June 1998, pp 192-194 for Gaskell's use of sources for this story.

46 Maureen F Moran, '"Light no Smithfield fires": Some Victorian Attitudes to Witchcraft', *Journal of Popular Culture,* Spring 2000, 33, 4, p 123.

47 Bonaparte sees in 'Lois the Witch' a sub-textual account of Gaskell's own life: Bonaparte, pp 109-114.

48 'Lois the Witch' in Elizabeth Gaskell, Linda Hughes ed, *The Works of Elizabeth Gaskell, Novellas and Shorter Fiction III, Cousin Phillis and Other Tales from All the Year Round and the Cornhill Magazine 1859-64,* Volume 4, (London: Pickering & Chatto, 2006), p 5.

49 'Lois the Witch', Vol 4, p 5.

50 'Lois the Witch', Vol 4, p 6.

51 'Lois the Witch', Vol 4, p 6.

52 'Lois the Witch', Vol 4, p 6.

53 'Lois the Witch', Vol 4, p 37.

54 'Lois the Witch', Vol 4, p 7.

55 Bonaparte views the character of Lois's aunt as a version of Gaskell's stepmother: Bonaparte, p 25.

56 'Lois the Witch', Vol 4, p 16.

57 'Lois the Witch', Vol 4, p 16.

58 'Lois the Witch', Vol 4, pp 19-20.

59 'Lois the Witch', Vol 4, p 13.

60 'Lois the Witch', Vol 4, p 11.

61 'Lois the Witch', Vol 4, p 11.

62 'Lois the Witch', Vol 4, p 29.

63 'Lois the Witch', Vol 4, p 27.

64 Alexander Morison, *The Physiognomy of Mental Diseases* (1838), 2nd edn., (London: Longman and Co, 1840), 1, pp 83-85 quoted in Jenny Bourne Taylor and Sally Shuttleworth eds, *Embodied Selves: An Anthology of Psychological Texts 1830–1890,* (Oxford: Clarendon Press, 2003), p 262.

65 Vanessa D Dickerson, *Victorian Ghosts in the Noontide: Women Writers and the Supernatural,* (Columbia and London, University of Missouri Press, 1996), pp 125-128.

66 See Philip Rogers, 'The Education of Cousin Phillis', *Nineteenth-Century Literature*, Vol 50, No 1 (June 1995), pp 27 – 50.

67 'Lois the Witch', Vol 4, p 22.

68 'An Accursed Race', Vol 3, p 297.

69 Wolfreys, p 85.

70 See Rebecca Styler, 'Lois the Witch: A Unitarian Tale', *The Gaskell Society Journal*, Vol 21, 2007, pp 73-85 for a discussion of the Unitarian influence on this short story.

71 Elizabeth Gaskell, Marion Shaw ed, *The Works of Elizabeth Gaskell: Vol. 9: Sylvia's Lovers*, (London: Pickering and Chatto, 2006), p 290.

72 See Shirley Foster, '*Sylvia's Lovers*: Gender Construction and Deconstruction' in Francesco Marroni and Alan Shelston eds, *Elizabeth Gaskell Text and Context*, (Pescara: Tracce, 1999), pp 147-167 for a discussion of the portrayal of masculinity in the novel.

73 See Morse, p 67 n 30 for the way in which Gaskell uses the image of the scarlet cloak to identify Sylvia with the sailor's prostitute, Newcastle Bess.

74 *Sylvia's Lovers*, Vol 9, p 30.

75 *Sylvia's Lovers*, Vol 9, p 259.

76 See Elizabeth Leaver, 'The Sender Both of Sunshine & of Storm: The Christian Dimension in Sylvia's Lovers', in Francesco Marroni and Alan Shelston ed, *Elizabeth Gaskell: Text and Context*, (Pescara: Tracce, 1999), pp 193-196 for a discussion of Gaskell's use of fable and Christian parable in *Sylvia's Lovers*.

77 Jean Etienne Esquirol, *Mental Maladies: A Treatise on Insanity*, trans. E.K. Hunt, (Philadelphia: Lea and Blanchard, 1845), pp 200-201, quoted in Taylor and Shuttleworth, p 256.

78 *Sylvia's Lovers*, Vol 9, p xv.

79 *Sylvia's Lovers*, Vol 9, p 257.

80 *Sylvia's Lovers*, Vol 9, p 266.

81 *Sylvia's Lovers*, Vol 9, p 267.

82 Matus, 2009, p 14.

83 *Sylvia's Lovers*, Vol 9, p 267.

84 Matus, 2009, p 64.

85 *Sylvia's Lovers*, Vol 9, p 267.

86 For a discussion of Gaskell's tolerant attitude towards but scant knowledge of mesmerism, see Matus, 2009, p 207, n 18.

87 *Sylvia's Lovers,* Vol 9, pp 267-268.

88 *Sylvia's Lovers,* Vol 9, p 271.

89 *Sylvia's Lovers,* Vol 9, p 272.

90 James Martineau, 'Great Principles and Small Duties' in *Endeavours after the Christian Life,* Fourth Edition, (London: Longmans, Green, Reader and Dyer, MDCCCLXVII), p 30.

91 Sharps sees Kinraid's disappearance as another version of John Stevenson. John Geoffrey Sharps, *Mrs Gaskell's Observation and Invention: A Study of Her Non-Biographic Works,* (Fontwell: Linden Press, 1970), p 403.

92 *Sylvia's Lovers,* Vol 9, p ix.

93 See for example, Frances Twinn, 'Navigational pitfalls and topographical constraints in Sylvia's Lovers', *Gaskell Society Journal,* Vol 15, 2001.

94 Patsy Stoneman, *Elizabeth Gaskell,* (Brighton: The Harvester Press Ltd, 1987), pp 154-155.

95 Bonaparte, pp 205-206.

96 Esquirol in Taylor and Shuttleworth, pp 258-259.

CHAPTER FIVE

1 Pamela Horn, *The Rise and Fall of the Victorian Servant,* (Dublin: Gill and Macmillan, New York: St Martin's Press, 1975), p 22, and Frank E Huggett, *Life Below Stairs,* (London: John Murray, 1977), p 13.

2 Edward Higgs, *Domestic Servants and Households in Rochdale 1851–1871,* (New York and London: Garland Publishing, 1986), p 1, and Moira Donald, 'Tranquil havens? Critiquing the idea of home as the middle-class sanctuary', in Inga Bryden and Janet Floyd eds, *Domestic Space: Reading the nineteenth-century interior,* (Manchester and New York: Manchester University Press, 1999), p 104.

3 Horn, p 18.

4 See, for example, Jane Hamlett, *Material Relations: Domestic Interiors and Middle-Class families in England, 1850–1910,* (Manchester and New York: Manchester University Press, 2010), pp 56-59, and Higgs, p 53.

5 Isabella Beeton, *Mrs. Beeton's Book of Household Management,* (London: Ward Lock,1863), p 1001.

6 Higgs, p 3.

7 Julie Nash, *Servants and Paternalism in the Works of Maria Edgeworth and Elizabeth*

Gaskell, (Aldershot: Ashgate Publishing Ltd, 2008), p 11.

8 Elizabeth Gaskell, Elisabeth Jay ed, *North and South* (1855), Volume 7, (London: Pickering & Chatto, 2005), p 338.

9 Karen Chase and Michael Levenson, 'On the Parapets of Privacy', in Herbert F Tucker ed, *A Companion to Victorian Literature and Culture,* (Oxford: Blackwell Publishing Ltd, 2004), p 429.

10 Leigh Hunt, *The Old Lady and The Maid-Servant,* (London & Toronto: J. M. Dent & Sons Ltd), 1929, p 22.

11 See Mariana Valverde, 'The Love of Finery: Fashion and The Fallen Woman in Nineteenth-Century Social Discourse', *Victorian Studies,* Vol 32, Pt 2, 1989, p 182 for a detailed discussion of conflicts around class and power triggered by servants' dress.

12 Gaskell to Marianne Gaskell, [?Late March 1859], John A. V. Chapple and Arthur Pollard eds, *The Letters of Mrs Gaskell,* (Manchester: Manchester University Press, 1997), p 546.

13 Liz Stanley ed, *The Diaries of Hannah Cullwick, Victorian Maidservant,* (New Brunswick: Rutgers University Press, 1984), p 32 and John Seed, 'Theologies of power: Unitarianism and the social relations of religious discourse, 1800–50', in R J Morris, ed, *Class, power and social structure in British nineteenth-century towns,* (Leicester: Leicester University Press, 1986), p 137.

14 Robert Kerr, 'On the Problem of Providing Dwellings for the Poor' *RIBA Proceedings,* 1871, *The English Gentleman's House,* 3rd edn., (London: John Murray, 1871), p 68.

15 Judith Flanders, *The Victorian House,* (London: Harper Collins, 2003), p 278.

16 Nash, p 116.

17 Gaskell to Marianne Gaskell, [22 November 1852], Chapple and Pollard, p 212.

18 Elizabeth Langland, *Nobody's Angels: Middle-class Women and Domestic Ideology,* (Ithaca and London: Cornell University Press, 1995), p 14.

19 Nash, p 20. See also Elizabeth Gaskell, Alan Shelston ed *The Works of Elizabeth Gaskell, Novellas and Shorter Fiction 1 The Moorland Cottage, Cranford and Related Writings,* Volume 2, (London: Pickering & Chatto, 2005), pp 221-222 for a description of the multi-tasking shared of necessity between Miss Betty Barker and her maid, and Elizabeth Gaskell, Charlotte Mitchell ed, *The Works of Elizabeth Gaskell, Novellas and Shorter Fiction II, Round the Sofa and Tales from Household Words (1852–9),* Volume 3, (London: Pickering & Chatto, 2005), pp 230-231 for Miss Galindo's preference for a

servant with some infirmity who was incapable of carrying out 'a single duty usually required of a servant', but whose employment nevertheless enabled Miss Galindo to keep up the appearance of social respectability.

20 Sarah Stickney Ellis, *The Daughters of England: their position in society, character & responsibilities,* (London: Fisher, Son, & Co., 1842), p 61.

21 Gaskell to Marianne Gaskell, [?May 1851], Chapple and Pollard, p 154, Gaskell to Marianne Gaskell, [March 1860], Chapple and Pollard, p 603, Gaskell to Marianne Gaskell, [?10 September 1860], Chapple and Pollard, pp 635-636.

22 See also Donald, pp 110-111 for a discussion of the amount of work involved in being the mistress of a middle-class establishment.

23 Ellis, p 204.

24 Ellis, pp 325-326.

25 Mrs Loftie, *The Dining Room,* (London: Macmillan and Co, 1878), p 128.

26 Elizabeth Gaskell, Joanne Wilkes ed, *The Works of Elizabeth Gaskell,* Mary Barton: A Tale of Manchester Life *and* William Gaskell Two Lectures on the Lancashire *Dialect),* Volume 5, (London: Pickering & Chatto, 2005), p 170.

27 Nash, p 98.

28 Jenny Uglow, *Elizabeth Gaskell: A Habit of Stories,* (London: Faber and Faber, 1999), pp 263-264, and Gaskell to ?Holbrook Gaskell, [c.1837], Chapple and Pollard, pp 11-12, Gaskell to Mrs Fielden, May 28th [1860], Chapple and Pollard, p 617 .

29 See Christine Lingard, 'A Dear Good Valuable Friend' in *The Gaskell Society Newsletter,* Autumn 2011, Number 52, pp 20-23 for an account of Hearn's life.

30 See for example, Leonore Davidoff and Catherine Hall, *Family Fortunes: Men and Women of the English middle class 1780–1850,* (London: Hutchinson, 1987), p 21 and Nash, pp 11-29.

31 'French Life' in Elizabeth Gaskell, Joanne Shattock ed, *The Works of Elizabeth Gaskell, Journalism, Early Fiction and Personal Writings,* Volume 1, (London: Pickering & Chatto, 2005), p 362.

32 'French Life', Vol 1, p 362.

33 Gaskell to Marianne Gaskell, Friday [September 1851], Chapple and Pollard, p 162, Gaskell to Marianne Gaskell, [23 October 1851], Chapple and Pollard, p 164, Gaskell to Charles Eliot Norton, Monday, August 27 [1860], pp 633-634.

34 Uglow, p 157.

35 Leonore Davidoff, *Worlds Between: Historical Perspectives on Gender and Class,*

(Cambridge: Policy Press, 1995), p 109.

36 'The Diary', Vol 1, p 11.

37 Jonathan Gathorne-Hardy, *The Rise and Fall of the British Nanny*, (London: Weidenfeld, 1993), p 77.

38 'The Moorland Cottage' in Elizabeth Gaskell, Alan Shelston ed, The Works of Elizabeth Gaskell: Vol. 2: Novellas and Shorter Fiction I, The Moorland Cottage, Cranford and Related Writings, (London: Pickering and Chatto, 2005), p ix and p 5.

39 'The Moorland Cottage', Vol 2, p 5.

40 'The Moorland Cottage', Vol 2, p 7.

41 'The Moorland Cottage', Vol 2, p 7.

42 'The Moorland Cottage', Vol 2, p 7.

43 'The Moorland Cottage', Vol 2, p 10.

44 'The Moorland Cottage', Vol 2, p10.

45 'The Moorland Cottage', Vol 2, p10.

46 'The Moorland Cottage', Vol 2, p 11.

47 'The Moorland Cottage'. Vol 2, p 22.

48 'The Moorland Cottage', Vol 2, p 78.

49 'The Old Nurse's Story' in Elizabeth Gaskell, Charlotte Mitchell ed, *The Works of Elizabeth Gaskell, Novellas and Shorter Fiction II, Round the Sofa, and Tales from Household Words (1852–9)*, Volume 3, (London: Pickering & Chatto, 2005), p 3.

50 'The Old Nurse's Story', Vol 3, p 3.

51 Horn, p 48.

52 Elizabeth Gaskell, Elisabeth Jay ed, *North and South* (1855), Volume 7, (London: Pickering & Chatto, 2005), p 67.

53 Jean Fernandez, *Victorian Servants, Class, and the Politics of Literacy*, (New York and Abingdon: Routledge, 2010), p 81.

54 Fernandez, p 3.

55 Fernandez, pp 81-82.

56 'The Old Nurse's Story', Vol 3, p 4.

57 'The Old Nurse's Story', Vol 3, p 4.

58 'The Old Nurse's Story', Vol 3, p 4.

59 'The Old Nurse's Story', Vol 3, p 4.

60 'The Old Nurse's Story', Vol 3, p 4.

61 'The Old Nurse's Story', Vol 3, p 5. Davidoff points out that 'the majority of girls

moved from parental control, in their parents' home, into service and then into their husband's home – thus experiencing a lifetime of personal subordination in private homes.' (Davidoff, p 21).

62 'The Old Nurse's Story', Vol 3, p 5.

63 'The Old Nurse's Story', Vol 3, p 5.

64 'The Old Nurse's Story', Vol 3, p 6.

65 'The Old Nurse's Story', Vol 3, p 6.

66 'The Old Nurse's Story', Vol 3, p 6.

67 'The Old Nurse's Story', Vol 3, p 6.

68 'The Old Nurse's Story', Vol 3, p 6.

69 Gathorne-Hardy, p 77.

70 'The Old Nurse's Story', Vol 3, p 7.

71 'The Old Nurse's Story', Vol 3, pp 7-8.

72 'The Old Nurse's Story', Vol 3, p 8.

73 'The Old Nurse's Story', Vol 3, p 11.

74 'The Old Nurse's Story', Vol 3, p 11.

75 'The Old Nurse's Story', Vol 3, p 18. For a discussion of Dickens's views on the end of the story, see Annette B Hopkins, 'Dickens and Mrs. Gaskell', *Huntingdon Library Quarterly*, 9, 1946, pp 354-355.

76 Jill Matus, *Shock, Memory and the Unconscious in Victorian Fiction*, (Cambridge: Cambridge University Press, 2009), p 100.

77 Fernandez, p 84.

78 Chase and Levenson, p 428.

79 Huggett, p 65.

80 Gaskell to Charles Eliot Norton, Monday, Decr[7], Chapple and Pollard, p 488.

81 See Avarind Adiga, *The White Tiger*, (London: Atlantic Books, 2008), for a modern interpretation of this theme.

82 Horn, p 9.

83 'Right at Last', Vol 3, p 94.

84 'Right at Last', Vol 3, p 96.

85 'Right at Last', Vol 3, p 97.

86 'Right at Last', Vol 3, p 105.

87 'Right at Last', Vol 3, p xiii and p 105.

88 'The Manchester Marriage', Vol 3, p 109.

206 THE MEANINGS OF HOME IN ELIZABETH GASKELL'S FICTION

89 'The Manchester Marriage', Vol 3, p 109.

90 'The Manchester Marriage', Vol 3, p 117.

91 'The Manchester Marriage', Vol 3, p 121.

92 See for example, Henry Mayhew, *London Labour and the London Poor*, IV, (London: Griffin, Bohn and Company, 1861), pp 234-235.

93 Horn, p 139.

94 'The Manchester Marriage', Vol 3, p 125.

95 'The Manchester Marriage', Vol 3, p 454, n 18.

96 Elizabeth Gaskell, Linda Hughes ed, *The Works of Elizabeth Gaskell, Novellas and Shorter Fiction III, Cousin Phillis and Other Tales from All the Year Round and the Cornhill Magazine 1859-64,* Volume 4, (London: Pickering & Chatto, 2006), p viii.

97 'A Dark Night's Work', Vol 4, p 210.

98 'A Dark Night's Work', Vol 4, p 210.

99 'A Dark Night's Work', Vol 4, p 220.

100 'A Dark Night's Work', Vol 4, p 222.

101 'A Dark Night's Work', Vol 4, p 221.

102 'A Dark Night's Work', Vol 4, pp 221-222.

103 'A Dark Night's Work', Vol 4, p 222.

104 Gaskell to Marianne Gaskell, [?Early October 1848], Chapple and Pollard, p 58 and Gaskell to Marianne and Margaret Emily Gaskell, [1846], Chapple and Pollard, p 826.

105 'A Dark Night's Work', Vol 4, p 256.

106 'A Dark Night's Work', Vol 4, p 260.

107 'A Dark Night's Work', Vol 4, p 273.

108 'A Dark Night's Work', Vol 4, p 300.

109 'A Dark Night's Work', Vol 4, p 311.

CONCLUSION

1 See Lawrence Stone, *Broken Lives: Separation and Divorce in England 1660-1857,* (Oxford: Oxford University Press, 1993), p 26, for example, for a case study based discussion of the difficulty of conducting a clandestine love affair without the collusion of servants.

2 Angus Easson, 'The Sentiment of Feeling: Emotions and Objects in Elizabeth Gaskell (1)', *Gaskell Society Journal*, Vol 4, 1990, p 66.

3 Elizabeth Gaskell, Marion Shaw ed, *The Works of Elizabeth Gaskell: Vol. 9: Sylvia's Lovers*, (London: Pickering and Chatto, 2006), p 11.

4 Elizabeth Gaskell, Linda H Peterson ed, *The Works of Elizabeth Gaskell: Vol. 8: The Life of Charlotte Brontë*, (London: Pickering and Chatto, 2006), p 12.

5 Jenny Uglow, *Elizabeth Gaskell: A Habit of Stories*, (London and New York: Faber and Faber, 1999), p 327.

6 'Half a Life-Time Ago' in Elizabeth Gaskell, Charlotte Mitchell ed, *The Works of Elizabeth Gaskell: Vol. 3: Novellas and Shorter Fiction II Round the Sofa and Tales from Household Words (1852 -9)*, (London: Pickering and Chatto, 2005), p 345.

7 Elizabeth Gaskell, Alan Shelston ed, *The Works of Elizabeth Gaskell: Vol. 2: Novellas and Shorter Fiction I, The Moorland Cottage, Cranford and Related Writings*, (London: Pickering and Chatto, 2005), p ix.

8 Gaskell to Eliza Fox, April 26, 1850, Chapple and Pollard, p 111, Gaskell to Marianne Gaskell, [Early November 1851], Chapple and Pollard, p 170 and Gaskell to Marianne Gaskell, [10 March 1851], Chapple and Pollard p 831.

9 Elizabeth Gaskell, Elisabeth Jay ed, *The Works of Elizabeth Gaskell: Vol. 7: North and South*, (London: Pickering and Chatto, 2005), p 27.

10 'My Lady Ludlow' in Elizabeth Gaskell, Charlotte Mitchell, ed, *The Works of Elizabeth Gaskell: Vol. 3: Novellas and Shorter Fiction II Round the Sofa and Tales from Household Words (1852-9)*, (London: Pickering and Chatto, 2005), p 456.

BIBLIOGRAPHY

PRIMARY SOURCES

Unpublished materials

Edgeworth, Maria to Holland, Mary. 27 December 1848. John Rylands, MS 732/52.

Stevenson, John to Stevenson Elizabeth. Various letters in papers of John Geoffrey Sharps, File 3, Box 30, John Rylands Library, Manchester.

Published primary sources

Gaskell, Elizabeth. *North and South*. Collin, Dorothy ed, with an introduction by Dodsworth, Martin. Harmondsworth: Penguin Books, 1979.

Billington, Josie, ed. *The Works of Elizabeth Gaskell: Vol. 10: Wives and Daughters*. London: Pickering and Chatto, 2006.

D'Albertis, Deirdre, ed. *The Works of Elizabeth Gaskell: Vol. 6: Ruth (1853)*. London: Pickering and Chatto, 2006.

Hughes, Linda, ed. *The Works of Elizabeth Gaskell: Vol. 4: Novellas and Shorter Fiction III Cousin Phillis and Other Tales from All the Year Round and the Cornhill Magazine 1859 – 64*. London: Pickering and Chatto, 2006.

Jay, Elisabeth, ed. *The Works of Elizabeth Gaskell: Vol. 7: North and South*. London: Pickering and Chatto, 2005.

Mitchell, Charlotte, ed. *The Works of Elizabeth Gaskell: Vol. 3: Novellas and Shorter Fiction II Round the Sofa and Tales from Household Words (1852 -9)*. London: Pickering and Chatto, 2005.

Peterson, Linda H, ed. *The Works of Elizabeth Gaskell: Vol. 8: The Life of Charlotte Brontë*. London: Pickering and Chatto, 2006.

Shattock, Joanne, ed. *The Works of Elizabeth Gaskell: Vol.1: Journalism, Early Fiction and Personal Writings*. London: Pickering and Chatto, 2005.

Shaw, Marion, ed. *The Works of Elizabeth Gaskell: Vol. 9: Sylvia's Lovers*. London: Pickering and Chatto, 2006.

Shelston, Alan, ed. *The Works of Elizabeth Gaskell: Vol. 2: Novellas and Shorter Fiction I, The Moorland Cottage, Cranford and Related Writings*. London: Pickering and Chatto, 2005.

Wilkes, Joanne, ed. *The Works of Elizabeth Gaskell: Vol. 5: Mary Barton (1838) and William Gaskell, 'Two Lectures on the Lancashire Dialect'*. London: Pickering and Chatto, 2005.

Gaskell, William. *A Sermon on Occasion of the Death of John Ogle Curtis, late Master of the Lower Mosely Street Schools, Manchester*, preached in Cross Street Chapel, November 29th, 1857. Manchester: Johnson and Rawson, 1857.

- *The Duties of the Individual to Society: A sermon on Occasion of the Death of Sir John Potter M.P. Preached at Cross Street Chapel, Manchester, October 31st, 1858, with the address at the Interment on the day preceding*. London: E.T Whitfield, 1858.

- *A Sermon preached in Cross-Street Chapel, Manchester, September 25th 1859, on the occasion of the death of John Ashton Nicholls, Esq., F.R.A.S., with a sketch of his life*. London: E.T Whitfield, 1859.

- *Unitarian Christians called to bear witness to the truth: A Sermon preached before the supporters of the British and Foreign Unitarian Association, at their Annual Meeting, in Essex-Street Chapel, London, June 11 1862*. London: Edward T. Whitfield, 1862.

Nineteenth-Century Newspapers, Periodicals, reports and maps

Adshead, Joseph. *Distress in Manchester: Evidence (Tabular and Otherwise) of the State of the Labouring Classes in 1840-42*. London: Henry Hooper, 1842.

Census of Great Britain, 1851. London: Longman, Brown, Green & Longmans, 1854.

Chadwick, Edwin. *A Supplementary Report on the Results of a Special Inquiry into the Practice of Interment in Towns*. London: W. Clowes and Sons, 1843.

Dickens, Charles. 'Sucking Pigs'. *Household Words*, 8 November 1851, pp 145-147.

Ellis, Robert. Preface to the *Official Descriptive and Illustrated Catalogue of the Great Exhibition of the Works of Industry of All Nations: 1851*. London: William Clowes and Sons, MDCCCLI.

Green, Henry. *Christian Doctrine as generally held by Unitarians.* John Rylands Library: Jamison Family Archive, Box 4/5.

[Greg. W. R.] Unsigned review of *Mary Barton* in the *Edinburgh Review.* Vol lxxxix (April 1849). 402 – 35.

Grimstone, Mary Leman. 'Men and Women'. *Tait's Edinburgh Magazine,* 1:2 March 1834.

James, Henry. 'The Art of Fiction'. *Longman's Magazine* 4, Sep 1884.

Kerr, Robert. 'On the Problem of Providing Dwellings for the Poor' *RIBA Proceedings,* (1871), *The English Gentleman's House,* 3rd edn. London: John Murray, 1871.

Leeds Mercury, The. November 17, 1849, Issue 6050

Lewes, George Henry. 'The Principles of Success in Literature'. *The Fortnightly Review 1,* 1865, May 15, pp 85-95.

- 'The Principles of Success in Literature'. *The Fortnightly Review 1,*1865, June 1, pp 185 – 196.

Lords' Sessional Papers (1842), Vol XXVII.

Manchester Examiner and Times. Saturday June 14, 1851. Issue 273.

Manchester Times and Gazette. Saturday June 13, 1840. Issue 611.

Manchester Times and Gazette. Friday April 2, 1847. Issue 963.

Manchester Times and Gazette. Saturday April 10th 1847. Issue 66.

Manchester Times. Saturday April 19th, 1851. Issue 257.

Manchester Times. Saturday July 23 1853. Issue 493.

Manchester Times. Saturday January 24, 1857. Issue 775.

Manchester Times. Friday December 24, 1858. Issue 54.

Manchester Times. Saturday May 21, 1864. Issue 337.

Martineau, Harriet. 'Middle-class Education in England'. *Cornhill Magazine,* X. November 1864, pp 549 – 568.

Mayhew, Henry. *London Labour and the London Poor, Vol 1.* London: Griffin, Bohn and Company, 1861.

Official Descriptive and Illustrated Catalogue of the great exhibition: 1851 London: William Clowes and Sons, MDCCCLI, Vol 2.

Ordnance Survey, Manchester Sheet 44, 1851.

Ordnance Survey, Manchester Sheet 45, 1851.

Reach, Angus Bethune. 'Manchester' in *Labour and the Poor in England and Wales, 1849–1851: The Letters to the Morning Chronicle from the Correspondents in the Manufacturing and Mining Districts, the Towns of Liverpool and Birmingham, and the Rural Districts, vol: Lancashire, Cheshire, Yorkshire,* J Ginswick ed. London: Frank Cass, 1983.

Tayler, John James. *Parental and filial duties: An address delivered in the School Room, Lower Mosley-Street, Manchester. On Sunday evening, April 17th, 1853.* Manchester, John Heywood, 1853.

Unattributed. 'Thoughts on Education'. *Monthly Repository and Review of Theology and General Literature,* 3:25. January 1829, pp 44-48.

Unattributed. 'On Female Education and Occupations'. *Monthly Repository,* 7:73 January 1833, pp 489-498.

Unattributed. 'Recent Works of Fiction'. *Prospective Review,* 34. April 1853, pp 222-247.

Unattributed. 'Sketches of Remarkable Women' in *The Christian Freeman: A Monthly Unitarian Journal devoted to religious, moral, and social progress,* Vol XIII. London: Whitfield Strand, 1869.

Nineteenth-Century books

Beeton, Isabella. *Mrs. Beeton's Book of Household Management.* London: Ward Lock, 1863.

Boyd, Alexander and Son. *The English Fireplace: Its Advantages, its Objections and its rivals. Considered with a view to utility and economy.* London: John Bumpus, 1874.

Braddon, Mary Elizabeth. *Lady Audley's Secret.* (1862) Skilton, David ed. Oxford: Oxford University Press, 1988.

Brontë, Charlotte. *The Professor.* (1857). London: Allan Wingate, 1949.

- *Villette.*(1853) London Edinburgh Paris Melbourne Toronto and New York: Thomas Nelson & Sons Ltd, 1952.

Cassell's Household Guide: being a complete encyclopaedia of domestic and social economy etc. London: 1869, Vols I-IV.

Collins, Wilkie. *The Woman in White.* London: Chatto & Windus, 1892.

de Tocqueville, Alexis. *Journeys to England and Ireland,* Translated by George Lawrence and K P Mayer, ed J.P. Mayer. London: Faber and Faber Ltd, 1958.

Eastlake, Charles L. *Hints on Household Taste in Furniture, Upholstery, and Other Details.* Boston: James R Osgood and Company, 1872.

Ellis, Sarah Stickney. *The Daughters of England: their position in society, character & responsibilities.* London: Fisher, Son, & Co, 1842.

Godwin, George. *London Shadows: A Glance at the "Homes" of the Thousands.* London: G. Routledge & Co, 1854.

Hughes, Thomas. *Tom Brown's Schooldays. By an old boy.* London: 1857.

Hunt, Leigh. *The Old Lady and The Maid-Servant.* London & Toronto: J. M. Dent & Sons Ltd, 1929.

Jones, Owen. *On the True and the False in the Decorative Arts: Lectures delivered at Marlborough House June 1852.* London: 1863.

Kay-Shuttleworth, James. *Four Periods of Public Education as Reviewed in 1832, 1839, 1846, 1862,* intro Morris, Norman. Brighton: The Harvester Press, 1973.

Loftie, Mrs. *The Dining-Room.* London: Macmillan and Co, 1878.

Martineau, James. *Endeavours after the Christian Life*, Fourth Edition. London, Longmans, Green, Reader and Dyer, MDCCCLXVII.

Priestley, Joseph. *Lectures on history, and general policy: to which is prefixed, an essay on a course of liberal education for civil and active life and, an additional lecture on the constitution of the United States.* Dublin: Byrne, 1803.

Priestley, Joseph. Lindsay, Jack intro. *Autobiography of Joseph Priestley, Memoirs written by Himself. An account of further Discoveries in Air.* Bath: Adams & Dart, 1970.

Ruskin, John. 'Arrows of the Chase', Vol. I, *Letters on Art,* part III, 'Pre-Raphaelitism. Orpington: George Allen, 1880.

- 'Of Queen's Gardens' in *Sesame and Lilies and Unto This Last*, intro. Meynall, Alice. London: Blackie and Son Ltd, 1907.

Stowe, Catherine E and Stowe, Harriet Beecher. *The American Woman's Home.* New York: J B Ford: 1869.

Trollope, Frances, Wagner Tamara S, ed. *The Barnabys in America; or, Adventures of the Widow Wedded* (1843). London: Pickering & Chatto, 2011.

Wade, Richard. *A Sketch of the Origin and History of the Lower Mosely Street Day and Sunday Schools.* Manchester: Wood, Smith & Shaw, 1898.

Wharton, Edith and Codman, Ogden Jr. *The Decoration of Houses.* New York: Norton, 1897.

Winkworth, S. *Letters and Memorials of Catherine Winkworth, edited by her sister.* Vol 1. Clifton: E. Austin and Son, Printers, Chronicle Office, 1883.

Winkworth, S. *Letters and Memorials of Catherine Winkworth, edited by her sister. Completed by her niece Margaret Shaen.* Vol II. Clifton: E. Austin and Son, Printers, Chronicle Office, 1886.

SECONDARY SOURCES

Adiga, Avarind. *The White Tiger.* London: Atlantic Books, 2008.

Allen, Dennis W. *Sexuality in Victorian Fiction.* Norman and London: University of Oklahoma Press, 1993.

Allott, Miriam. 'Writers and their work' No 124, *Elizabeth Gaskell.* London: Longmans Green & Co, 1960.

Anderson, Amanda. *Tainted Souls and Painted Faces: The Rhetoric of Fallenness in Victorian Culture.* Ithaca and London, Cornell University Press, 1993.

Anderson, Gregory. *Victorian Clerks.* Manchester, Manchester University Press, 1976.

Anderson, Robert. 'Joseph Priestley: Public Intellectual,' *Chemical Heritage Newsmagazine*, 23. Spring 2005, No 1.

Baker, Fran 'Intimate and trusted correspondents: the Gaskells, Greens and Jamisons'. *Gaskell Journal.* Vol 24, 2010. pp 1–17.

Barringer, Tim. *Men at Work: Art and Labour in Victorian Britain.* New Haven & London: Yale University Press, 2005.

Barton, David and Hall, Nigel eds. *Letter Writing as a Social Practice.* Amsterdam/ Philadelphia, John Benjamins Publishing Company, 2000.

Beaujot, Ariel. '"The Beauty of her Hands": The Glove and the Making of the Middle-Class Body', in Daly Goggin, Maureen and Fowkes Tobin, Beth eds. *Material Women, 1750–1950: Consuming Desires and Collecting Practices* Farnham: Ashgate Publishing Ltd, 2009. pp 167–183.

Beer, John. 'Elizabeth Gaskell's Legacy from Romanticism'. *The Gaskell*

Journal. Vol 20, 2008. pp 42-55.

Beer, John. *Romanticism, Revolution and Language: The Fate of the word from Samuel Johnson to George Eliot.* Cambridge: Cambridge University Press, 2009.

Billington, Josie. 'Faithful Realism: Ruskin and Gaskell'. *The Gaskell Society Journal.* Vol 13,1999.

Blair, Emily. '"The Wrong Side of the Tapestry"; Elizabeth Gaskell's *Wives and Daughters'. Victorian Literature and Culture.* Vol 33, 2005. pp 585–597.

Bodenheimer, Rosemarie. 'Private Grief and Public Acts' in Timko, Michael, Kaplan, Fred and Guiliano, Edward eds. *Dickens Studies Annual.* Volume 9. New York: AMS Press, 1981.

- *The Politics of Story in Victorian Social Fiction.* Ithaca: Cornell University Press, 1988.

- *The Real Life of Mary Ann Evans: George Eliot, Her Letters and Fiction.* Ithaca and London: Cornell University Press, 1994.

Bolam, C. G., Goring, Jeremy, Short, H. L., Thomas, Roger. *The English Presbyterians: From Elizabethan Puritanism to Modern Unitarianism.* London: George Allen & Unwin Ltd, 1968.

Bonaparte, Felicia. *The Gypsy-Bachelor of Manchester: The Life of Mrs. Gaskell's Demon.* Charlottesville and London: University Press of Virginia, 1992.

Book of Common Prayer and Administration of the Sacraments and other Rites and Ceremonies of the Church according to the Use of the Church of England.

Bourne Taylor, Jenny and Shuttleworth, Sally eds. *Embodied Selves: An Anthology of Psychological Texts 1830–1890.* Clarendon Press: Oxford, 1998.

Brake, Laurel and Demour, Marysa eds. *The Lure of Illustration in the Nineteenth Century: Picture and Press.* Basingstoke: Palgrave Macmillan, 2009.

Brantlinger, Patrick, and Thesing, William B, eds. *A Companion to the Victorian Novel.* Oxford: Blackwell Publishing Ltd, 2005.

Brill, Barbara. *William Gaskell: 1805–1884: A Portrait.* Manchester: Manchester Literary and Philosophical Publications, 1984.

Brown, W. Henry. 'Mrs. Gaskell: A Manchester Influence'. *Papers of the Manchester Literary Club.* Vol LVIII, 1932. Manchester: Sherratt & Hughes, 1932.

Bryden, Inga and Floyd, Janet eds. *Domestic Space: Reading the nineteenth-century interior*. Manchester and New York: Manchester University Press, 1999.

Bullough, Vern LeRoy and Bullough, Bonnie. *Cross Dressing, Sex, and Gender*. Philadelphia: University of Pennsylvania Press, 1993.

Burnett, John. *A Social History of Housing 1815–1985*. London and New York: Methuen, 1986.

Caine, Barbara. *Victorian Feminists*. Oxford: Oxford University Press, 1993.

Casteras, Susan P. 'Reader, Beware: Images of Victorian Women and Books. *Nineteenth-Century Gender Studies*. Issue 3.1, Spring 2007.

Chapman, Tony and Hockey, Jenny eds. *Ideal Homes? Social change and domestic life*. London and New York: Routledge, 1999.

Chapple, John A. V. and Wilson, Anita eds. *Private Voices: The Diaries of Elizabeth Gaskell and Sophia Holland*. Keele: Keele University Press, 1996.

Chapple, John A.V. *Elizabeth Gaskell: The Early Years*. Manchester: Manchester University Press, 1997.

Chapple, John A. V. and Pollard, Arthur eds. *The Letters of Mrs Gaskell*. Manchester: Manchester University Press, 1997.

Chapple, John A V. *Elizabeth Gaskell: A Portrait in Letters*. Manchester, Manchester University Press, 1980.

- Review in *The Gaskell Society Journal*. Volume 7, 1993. pp 82–84.

Chapple, John and Shelston, Alan eds. *Further Letters of Mrs Gaskell*. Manchester: Manchester University Press, 2003.

Chapple, John 'Elizabeth Gaskell and Roman Catholicism'. *The Gaskell Society Journal*. Vol 20, 2006. pp 14–27.

Chase, Karen and Levenson, Michael. 'On the Parapets of Privacy' in Tucker, Herbert F ed. *A Companion to Victorian Literature and Culture*. Oxford: Blackwell Publishing Ltd, 2004.

Choi, Tina Young. 'Writing the Victorian City: Discourses of Risk, Connection, and Inevitability'. *Victorian Studies*. Summer 2001: 43,4. pp 561–589.

Christ, Carol. 'Victorian Masculinity and the Angel in the House' in Vicinus, Martha ed. *A Widening Sphere: Changing Roles of Victorian Women*. Bloomington & London: Indiana University Press, 1977.

Clark, Anna. 'The politics of seduction in English popular culture 1748–1848', in Radford, Jean ed. *The Progress of Romance: The Politics of Popular*

Fiction. London and New York: Routledge and Kegan Paul, 1986.

Colby, Robin B. *"Some Appointed Work To Do" Women and Vocation in the Fiction of Elizabeth Gaskell*. Westport, Connecticut: London: Greenwood Press, 1995.

Colby, Robin. 'Elizabeth Gaskell: A Model of Motherhood'. *The Gaskell Society Journal*. Vol 11, 1997. pp 55-67.

Colby, Vineta. *Yesterday's Woman: Domestic Realism in the English Novel*. Princeton: Princeton University Press, 1974.

Corpron Parker, Pamela. 'Woman of Letters: Elizabeth Gaskell's Autograph Collection and Victorian Celebrity' in Daly Goggin, Maureen and Fowkes Tobin, Beth eds. *Material Women, 1750–1950: Consuming Desires and Collecting Practices*. Farnham: Ashgate Publishing Ltd, 2009, pp 265–278.

Craft-Fairchild, Catherine. 'Cross-Dressing and the Novel: Women Warriors and Domestic Femininity'. *Eighteenth-Century Fiction*. Vol 10, Number 2, January 1998. pp 171–202.

Craik, Wendy. 'Lore, Learning and Wisdom: Workers and Education in *Mary Barton* and *North and South*'. *The Gaskell Society Journal*. Vol 2, 1988, pp 13 - 33.

Cunningham, Valentine. *Everywhere Spoken Against: Dissent in the Victorian Novel*. Oxford: Clarendon Press, 1975.

D'Albertis, Deirdre. *Dissembling Fictions: Elizabeth Gaskell and the Victorian Social Text*. Basingstoke: Macmillan, 1997.

Daunton, M.J. *House and Home in the Victorian City: Working-Class Housing 1850–1914*. London: Edward Arnold, 1983.

Davidoff, Leonore and Hall, Catherine. *Family Fortunes: Men and Women of the English middle class 1780–1850*. London: Hutchinson, 1987.

Davidoff, Leonore. *Worlds Between: Historical Perspectives on Gender and Class*. Cambridge: Policy Press, 1995.

Debrabant, Mary. 'Birds, Bees and Darwinian Survival Strategies in *Wives and Daughters*'. *The Gaskell Society Journal*. Vol 16, 2002. pp 14-29.

Dentith, Simon. *Society and Cultural Forms in Nineteenth-Century England*. Basingstoke: Macmillan Press Ltd, 1998.

Dickerson, Vanessa D ed. *Keeping the Victorian House: A Collection of Essays*. New York and London: Garland Publishing Inc, 1995.

- *Victorian Ghosts in the Noontide: Women Writers and the Supernatural.* Columbia and London, University of Missouri Press, 1996.

Dolin, Tim. 'Cranford and the Victorian Collection'. *Victorian Studies.* Vol 36, No 2, Winter 1991. pp 179–206.

Donald, Moira. 'Tranquil Havens? Critiquing the idea of home as the middle-class sanctuary' in Bryden, Inga and Floyd, Janet eds. *Domestic Space: Reading the nineteenth-century interior.* Manchester and New York: Manchester University Press, 1999.

Duberman, Martin B, Vicinus, Martha and Chauncey, George eds. *Hidden from history: reclaiming the gay and lesbian past.* New York: New American Library, 1989.

Duthie, Enid L. *The Themes of Elizabeth Gaskell.* London and Basingstoke: The Macmillan Press Ltd, 1980.

Easson, Angus. *Elizabeth Gaskell.* London, Boston and Henley: Routledge & Kegan Paul, 1979.

- 'The Sentiment of Feeling: Emotions and Objects in Elizabeth Gaskell (1)'. *Gaskell Society Journal.* Vol 4, 1990. pp 64-78.

- ed. *Elizabeth Gaskell, The Critical Heritage.* London and New York: Routledge, 1991.

- 'Noah's Arks and Birds' Nests: Domestic Space in *Ruth*' in Marroni, Francesco and Shelston, Alan eds. *Elizabeth Gaskell: Text and Context.* Pescara: Tracce, 1999.

Ellis Chadwick, Mrs H. *Mrs. Gaskell: Haunts, Homes and Stories.* London: Sir Isaac Pitman and Sons Ltd, 1910.

Esquirol, Jean Etienne. *Mental Maladies: A Treatise on Insanity.* Hunt, E.K trans. Philadelphia: Lea and Blanchard, 1845, pp 200–1, in Bourne Taylor, Jenny and Shuttleworth, Sally eds. *Embodied Selves: An Anthology of Psychological Texts 1830 – 1890.* Oxford: Clarendon Press, 2003.

Eve, Jeanette. 'The Floral and Horticultural in Elizabeth Gaskell's novels'. *Gaskell Society Journal.* Vol 7, 1993. pp 1–15.

Fernandez, Jean. *Victorian Servants, Class, and the Politics of Literacy.* New York and Abingdon: Routledge, 2010.

Flanders, Judith. *The Victorian House: Domestic Life from Childbirth to Deathbed.* London: Harper Collins, 2003.

- *Consuming Passions: Leisure and Pleasure in Victorian Britain.* London: Harper Collins, 2006.

Foster, Shirley. *'Sylvia's Lovers:* Gender Construction and Deconstruction' in Marroni, Francesco and Shelston, Alan eds. *Elizabeth Gaskell Text and Context.* Pescara: Tracce, 1999. pp 147 – 167.

- 'Violence and Disorder in Elizabeth Gaskell's Short Stories'. *The Gaskell Society Journal.* Vol 10, 2005.

Foucault, Michel. *The Will to Knowledge: The History of Sexuality Volume 1,* trans. by Hurley, Robert. London: Penguin Books, 1998.

Fraser, Hilary. 'The Victorian Novel and Religion' in Brantlinger, Patrick and Thesing, William B eds. *A Companion to the Victorian Novel.* Oxford: Blackwell Publishing Ltd, 2005.

Freud, Sigmund. *Studies on Hysteria.* London: 1985.

Fryckstedt, Monica C. *Elizabeth Gaskell's Mary Barton and Ruth: a challenge to Christian England.* Stockholm: Almqvist, 1982.

Ganz, Margaret. *Elizabeth Gaskell: The Artist in Conflict.* New York: Twayne Publishers Inc, 1969.

Garson, Marjorie. *Moral Taste: Aesthetics, Subjectivity, and Social Power in the Nineteenth-Century Novel.* Buffalo and London: University of Toronto Press, 2007.

Gathorne-Hardy, Jonathan. *The Rise and Fall of the British Nanny.* London: Weidenfeld, 1993.

Gaze, Delia ed. Mihajlovic, Maja and Shrimpton, Leanda picture editors. *Dictionary of Women Artists, Vol 1, Introductory Surveys, Artists A–I.* London and Chicago: Fitzroy Dearborn Publishers, 1977.

Gerin, Winifred. *Elizabeth Gaskell, A Biography.* Oxford: The Clarendon Press, 1976.

Gillooly, Eileen. 'Humor as Daughterly Defense in Cranford'. *ELH,* Vol 59, No 4.Winter 1992. pp 883–910.

Gilmour, Robin. *The Idea of the Gentleman in the Victorian Novel.* London: Allen & Unwin, 1981.

Gleadle, Kathryn. *The Early Feminists: Radical Unitarians and the Emergence of the Women's Rights Movement, 1831-51.* Basingstoke: Macmillan Press, 1995.

Glen, Heather. *Elizabeth Gaskell's resurrection,* article in the *Times Literary*

Supplement, November 8, 2006 (www.timesonline.co.uk).

Goggin, Maureen Daly and Fowkes, Tobin Beth, eds. *Material Women, 1750–1950: Consuming Desires and Collecting Practice*. Farnham: Ashgate Publishing Ltd, 2009.

Guest, Harriet. 'The Deep Romance of Manchester: Gaskell's *Mary Barton*' in Snell, K D M ed. *The Regional Novel in Britain and Ireland 1800–1990*. Cambridge, Cambridge University Press, 1998.

Haldane, Elizabeth. *Mrs Gaskell and Her Friends*. London: Hodder and Stoughton Ltd, 1931.

Hallenbeck, S. 'How To Be a Gentleman Without Really Trying: Gilbert Markham in *The Tenant of Wildfell Hall*'. *Nineteenth-Century Gender Studies*. Issue 1, Winter 2005.

Hamlett, Jane. *Material Relations: Domestic Interiors and Middle-Class Families in England, 1850-1910*. Manchester and New York: Manchester University Press, 2010.

Harman, Barbara Leah. 'In Promiscuous Company'. *Victorian Studies*. Vol 31, Pt 3, 1988. pp 351–374.

Heilmann, Ann. '(Un)masking desire: cross-dressing and the crisis of gender in New Woman fiction'. *Journal of Victorian Culture*. 5:1, 2000. pp 83-111.

Henson, Louise. 'History, Science and social change: Elizabeth Gaskell's 'evolutionary' narratives'. *The Gaskell Society Journal*. Vol 17, 2003. pp 12–33.

Hepworth, Mike. 'Privacy, Security and Respectability: The ideal Victorian home' in Chapman, Tony and Hockey, Jenny eds. *Ideal Homes? Social change and domestic life*. London and New York: Routledge, 1999. pp 17-30.

Hewitt, Martin. 'District visiting and the constitution of domestic space in the mid-nineteenth century' in Bryden, Inga and Floyd, Janet eds. *Domestic Space: Reading the nineteenth-century interior*. Manchester and New York: Manchester University Press, 1999. pp 121-141.

Heyns, Michiel. 'The Steam-Hammer and the Sugar-Tongs: Sexuality and Power in Elizabeth Gaskell's *North and South*'. *English Studies in Africa*. 32:2, 1989. pp 79-94.

Higgs, Edward. *Domestic Servants and Households in Rochdale 1851-1871*. New York and London: Garland Publishing, 1986.

Holme, Thea. *The Carlyles at Home*. London: Oxford University Press, 1965.

Holmes, Rachel. *Scanty particulars: the life of Dr James Barry.* London: Penguin, 2003.

Holt, Raymond V. *The Unitarian Contribution to Social Progress in England.* London: George Allen & Unwin Ltd, 1938.

Hopkins, Annette B. 'Dickens and Mrs. Gaskell'. *Huntingdon Library Quarterly,* 9, 1946. pp 354-5.

- *Elizabeth Gaskell: Her Life and Work.* London: John Lehmann, 1952.

Horn, Pamela. *The Rise and Fall of the Victorian Servant.* Dublin: Gill and Macmillan. New York: St Martin's Press, 1975.

Hotz, Mary Elizabeth. *Literary Remains: Representations of Death and Burial in Victorian England.* Albany: State University of New York Press, 2009.

How, James. *Epistolary Spaces: English Letter Writing from the Foundation of the Post Office to Richardson's Clarissa.* Aldershot: Ashgate Publishing Ltd, 2003.

Huber, Caroline P. '"Heroic Pioneers": The Ladies of *Cranford*'. *The Gaskell Society Journal.* Vol 21, 2007. pp 38-49.

Huett, Lorna. 'Commodity and collectivity: *Cranford* in the context of *Household Words*'. *The Gaskell Society Journal.* Vol 17, 2003. pp 34-49.

Huggett, Frank E. *Life Below Stairs.* London: John Murray, 1977.

Hughes, Linda K. 'Gaskell the Worker'. *The Gaskell Society Journal.* Vol 20, 2006. pp 28-46.

Hyde, William J. '"Poor Frederick" and "Poor Peter": Elizabeth Gaskell's Fraternal Deviants'. *Gaskell Society Journal.* Vol 9, 1995. pp 21-26.

Ingelbien, Raphael. 'Elizabeth Gaskell's 'The Poor Clare' and the Irish Famine'. *Irish University Review.* Vol 40, Number 2, Autumn/Winter 2010. pp 1-19.

Ingham, Patricia. *The Language of Gender and Class: Transformation in the Victorian Novel.* London & New York: Routledge, 1996.

Jacobs, N. M. 'Gender and Layered Narrative in *Wuthering Heights* and *The Tenant of Wildfell Hall*'. *The Journal of Narrative Technique.* Vol 16, No 3, Fall, 1986. pp 204-219.

Jalland, Pat. *Death in the Victorian Family.* Oxford: Oxford University Press, 1996.

Kauer, Ute. 'Narrative cross-dressing in Charlotte Brontë's *The Professor*'.

Brontë Society Transactions. 26:2, 2001. pp 167-187.

Kestner, Joseph A. *Masculinities in Victorian Painting.* Aldershot: Scolar Press, 1995.

Kissel, Susan. *In Common Cause: The "Conservative" Frances Trollope and the "Radical" Frances Wright.* Bowling Green: Bowling Green State University Popular Press, 1993.

Kuhlman, Mary H. 'Education through experience in *North and South*'. *Gaskell Society Journal.* Vol 10, 1996. pp 14-26.

Lambourne, Lionel. *Victorian Painting.* London: Phaidon Press Inc, 2004.

Langland, Elizabeth. *Nobody's Angels: Middle-class Women and Domestic Ideology.* Ithaca and London: Cornell University Press, 1995.

Lansbury, Coral. *Elizabeth Gaskell: The Novel of Social Crisis.* London: Paul Elek Ltd, 1975.

Laquer, Thomas. *Making Sex: Body and Gender from the Greeks to Freud.* Cambridge MA and London: Harvard University Press, 1990.

Lawrence, Lindsy. 'Gender Play "At our social table": The New Domesticity in the *Cornhill* and Elizabeth Gaskell's *Wives and Daughters*'. *The Gaskell Journal.* Vol 22, 2008. pp 22-41.

Leaver, Elizabeth. 'The Sender Both of Sunshine & of Storm: The Christian Dimension in *Sylvia's Lovers*' in Marroni, Francesco and Shelston, Alan eds. *Elizabeth Gaskell: Text and Context.* Pescara: Tracce, 1999. pp 169-198.

Lewis, P M. 'Mummy, Matron and the Maids: Feminine Presence and Absence in Male Institutions, 1934-63' in Roper, Michael and Tosh, John eds. *Manful Assertions: Masculinities in Britain since 1800.* London and New York: Routledge, 1991.

Lingard, Christine. 'A Dear Good Valuable Friend' in *The Gaskell Society Newsletter.* Autumn 2011. Number 52. pp 20-23.

Loeb, Lori Anne. *Consuming Angels: Advertising and Victorian Women.* New York: Oxford: Oxford University Press, 1994.

Logan, Deborah Anna. *Fallenness in Victorian Women's Writing: Marry, Stitch, Die or Do Worse.* Columbia and London: University of Missouri Press, 1998.

Logan, Thad. *The Victorian Parlour.* Cambridge: Cambridge University Press, 2001.

Lovell, Terry. *Consuming Fiction.* London: Verso, 1987.

Lovell-Smith, Rose. 'Anti-Housewives and Ogres' Housekeepers: The Roles of Bluebeard's Female Helper'. *Folklore*. 113.2, October 2002.

Luria, Sarah. 'The architecture of manners: Henry James, Edith Wharton and The Mount' in Bryden, Inga and Floyd, Janet eds. *Domestic Space: Reading the nineteenth-century interior.* Manchester and New York: Manchester University Press, 1999.

Lyall, Edna. 'Mrs. Gaskell' in *Women Novelists of Queen Victoria's Reign. A Book of Appreciations by Mrs. Oliphant et al.* London: Hurst and Blackett, 1987.

Marroni, Francesco. 'The Shadow of Dante: Elizabeth Gaskell and *The Divine Comedy'. Gaskell Society Journal.* Vol 10,1996. pp 1-13.

Marroni, Francesco and Shelston, Alan eds. *Elizabeth Gaskell: Text and Context.* Pescara: Tracce, 1999.

Martin, Carol A. 'Elizabeth Gaskell's Contributions to the Works of William Howitt'. *Nineteenth-Century Fiction.* 40:1, June 1985. pp 94-100.

Matus, Jill. *Unstable Bodies: Victorian Representations of Sexuality and Maternity.* Manchester and New York: Manchester University Press, 1995.

- '*Mary Barton* and *North and South*' in Matus, Jill ed. *The Cambridge Companion to Elizabeth Gaskell.* Cambridge: Cambridge University Press, 2007.

- *The Cambridge Companion to Elizabeth Gaskell.* Cambridge: Cambridge University Press, 2007.

- *Shock, Memory and the Unconscious in Victorian Fiction.* Cambridge: Cambridge University Press, 2009.

Mellor, Anne K. 'Were Women Writers "Romantics?". *Modern Language Quarterly.* 62:4, December 2001. pp 393-405.

Millard, Kay. 'The Religion of Elizabeth Gaskell'. *The Gaskell Society Journal.* Vol 15, 2001.

Moran, Maureen F. 'Light no Smithfield fires: Some Victorian Attitudes to Witchcraft' . *Journal of Popular Culture.* Spring 2000, 33,4. pp 123-151.

Morse, Deborah Denholz. 'Stitching Repentance, Sewing Rebellion: Seamstresses and Fallen Women in Elizabeth Gaskell's Fiction' in Dickerson, Vanessa D ed. *Keeping the Victorian House: A Collection of Essays.* New York and London: Garland Publishing Inc, 1995.

Morison, Alexander. *The Physiognomy of Mental Diseases* (1838), 2nd edn. London: Longman and Co, 1840, in Bourne Taylor, Jenny and Shuttleworth, Sally eds. *Embodied Selves: An Anthology of Psychological Texts 1830-1890.* pp 83 – 85. Oxford: Clarendon Press, 2003.

Morris, Emily Jane. 'Ready to hear and to help: Female agency and the reclamation of the fallen woman in Elizabeth Gaskell's 'Lizzie Leigh'' . *The Gaskell Journal.* Number 23, 2009, pp 40-53.

Morris, R J, ed. *Class, power and social structure in British nineteenth-century towns.* Leicester: Leicester University Press, 1986.

Nash, Julie. *Servants and Paternalism in the Works of Maria Edgeworth and Elizabeth Gaskell.* Aldershot and Burlington VT: Ashgate Publishing Company, 2007.

Nelson, Claudia B. 'Sex and the Single Boy: Ideals of Manliness and Sexuality in Victorian Literature for Boys'. *Victorian Studies.* Vol 32, Number 4, Summer 1989. pp 525-550.

- 'Growing Up: Childhood' in Tucker, Herbert F ed. *A Companion to Victorian Literature and Culture.* Oxford: Blackwell Publishing Ltd, 2004.

Ohno, Tatsuhiro. 'Statistical Analysis of the Structure of *North and South* in the Quest for Standard Interpretation'. *The Gaskell Journal.* Vol 22, 2008. pp 116-144

Owen, Chris. *The Gaskells' House, 84 Plymouth Grove, Ardwick, Manchester, Period Rooms. Report of research and proposals by Chris Owen with specialist consultant Peter Brears. Information and reference works provided by Janet Allen.* Unpublished report: Museum Casts 2011.

Parkins, Wendy. *Mobility and Modernity in Women's Novels 1850s-1930s: Women Moving Dangerously.* Basingstoke: Palgrave MacMillan, 2009.

Pettitt, Claire. 'Cousin Holman's Dresser: Science, Social Change, and the Pathologized Female in Gaskell's "Cousin Phillis"'. *Nineteenth-Century Literature.* Vol 52, No 4, March 1998. pp 471-489.

Picker, John M. 'The Soundproof Study: Victorian Professionals, Work Space, and Urban Noise'. *Victorian Studies.* Spring 1999/2000: 42, 3. pp 427-453.

Pike, E. Holly. *Family and Society in the Works of Elizabeth Gaskell.* New York: Peter Lang, 1995.

Pollard, Arthur. 'Faith and Family: Fundamental Values in *Mary Barton*'. *Gaskell Society Journal.* Vol 3, 1989. pp 1-5.

Poole, Robert. '"A poor Man I know" – Samuel Bamford and the making of

Mary Barton'. *Gaskell Society Journal.* Vol 20, 2008. pp 96-115.

Poovey, Mary. *Uneven Developments: The Ideological Work of Gender in Mid-Victorian England.* London: Virago Press, 1989.

- 'Disraeli, Gaskell and the Condition of England' in Richetti, John ed. *The Columbia History of the British Novel.* New York: Columbia University Press, 1994.

Potvin, John and Myzelev, Alla eds. *Material Cultures, 1740-1920: The Meanings and Pleasures of Collecting.* Farnham and Burlington: Ashgate Publishing Ltd, 2009.

Pykett, Lyn. *The sensation novel: from The Woman in White to The Moonstone.* Plymouth: Northcote House in association with the British Council, 1994.

Radford, Jean ed. *The Progress of Romance: The Politics of Popular Fiction.* London and New York: Routledge and Kegan Paul, 1986.

Recchio, Thomas E. 'A Monstrous Reading of *Mary Barton*: Fiction as Communitas'. *College Literature,* Oct 1996, 23, 3. pp 2-22.

Redford, Bruce. *The Converse of the Pen: Acts of Intimacy in the Eighteenth-Century Familiar Letter.* Chicago: University of Chicago Press, 1986.

Reed, John R. *Victorian Conventions. Reports of the Ministry to the Poor in Manchester 1839-1842.* Ohio University Press: USA, 1975.

Roberts, David. 'The Paterfamilias of the Victorian Governing Classes' in Wohl, Anthony S ed. *The Victorian Family Structure and Stresses.* London: Croom Helm, 1978.

Rogers, Philip. 'The Education of Cousin Phillis'. *Nineteenth-Century Literature.* Vol 50, No 1, June 1995. pp 27-50.

Roper, Michael and Tosh, John eds. *Manful Assertions: Masculinities in Britain since 1800.* London and New York: Routledge, 1991.

Rosenthal, Bernard. 'Tituba's Story'. *The New England Quarterly.* Vol 71, No 2, June 1998. pp 190-203.

Rottau, Nadine. '"Everyone to his taste" or "truth to material?": the role of materials in collections of applied arts' in Potvin, John and Myzelev, Alla eds. *Material Cultures, 1740 – 1920: The Meanings and Pleasures of Collecting.* Farnham and Burlington: Ashgate Publishing Ltd, 2009. pp 71 - 85.

Sanders, Andrew. 'Varieties of Religious Experience in *Sylvia's Lovers*'. *Gaskell Society Journal.* Vol 6, 1992. pp 15 – 24.

Schor, Hilary M. *Scheherazade in the Marketplace: Elizabeth Gaskell and the Victorian Novel*. New York: Oxford, Oxford University Press, 1992.

Seed, John. 'Theologies of power: Unitarianism and the social relations of religious discourse, 1800-50' in Morris, R J ed, *Class, power and social structure in British nineteenth-century towns*. Leicester: Leicester University Press, 1986. pp 108-156.

Selig, Robert L. *Elizabeth Gaskell: A Reference Guide*. Boston: G. K. Hall & Co, 1977.

Sharps John Geoffrey. *Mrs Gaskell's Observation and Invention: A Study of Her Non-Biographic Works*. Fontwell: Linden Press, 1970.

Shattock, Joanne ed. *Dickens and other Victorians: Essays in Honour of Philip Collins*. Basingstoke: Macmillan Press, 1988.

- 'Elizabeth Gaskell: Journalism and Letters' in Brake, Laurel and Demour, Marysa eds. *The Lure of Illustration in the Nineteenth Century: Picture and Press*. Basingstoke: Palgrave Macmillan, 2009.

Shelston, Alan. 'The Moorland Cottage: Elizabeth Gaskell and Myles Burket Foster'. *The Gaskell Society Journal*. Vol 2, 1988. pp 41-58.

- 'Elizabeth Gaskell and the Sense of the New' in Marroni, Francesco and Shelston, Alan eds. *Elizabeth Gaskell: Text and Context*. Pescara: Tracce, 1999.

- 'Education in the Life and Work of Elizabeth Gaskell'. *The Gaskell Journal*. Vol 22, 2008. pp 56-71.

Shteir, Ann B. '"Fac-Similes of Nature": Victorian Wax Flower Modelling'. *Victorian Literature and Culture*. 2007: 35. pp 649-661.

Smith, Helen. *Decorative Painting in the Domestic Interior in England and Wales c1850-1890*. New York and London: Garland Publishing, 1984.

Snell, K D M, ed. *The Regional Novel in Britain and Ireland 1800–1990*. Cambridge: Cambridge University Press, 1998.

Spooner, Catherine and McEvoy, Emma eds. *The Routledge Companion to Gothic*. London and New York: Routledge, 2007.

Stanley, Liz ed. *The Diaries of Hannah Cullwick, Victorian Maidservant*. New Brunswick: Rutgers University Press, 1984.

Steedman, Carolyn. 'What a rag rug means' in Bryden, Inga and Floyd, Janet eds. *Domestic Space: Reading the nineteenth-century interior*. Manchester and New York: Manchester University Press, 1999.

Stone, Lawrence. *Broken Lives: Separation and Divorce in England 1660–1857.* Oxford: Oxford University Press, 1993.

Stoneman, Patsy. *Elizabeth Gaskell.* Brighton: The Harvester Press Ltd, 1987.

- 'Gaskell, gender and the family' in Matus, Jill ed. *The Cambridge Companion to Elizabeth Gaskell.* Cambridge: Cambridge University Press, 2007.

Storey, Graham, Tillotson, Kathleen and Burgis, Nina eds. *The letters of Charles Dickens.* House, Madeline, Storey, Graham, Tillotson Kathleen, General Eds. Vol Six 1850 – 1852. Oxford: Oxford Clarendon Press, 1988.

Styler, Rebecca. 'Lois the Witch: A Unitarian Tale'. *The Gaskell Society Journal.* Vol 21, 2007. pp 73-85.

The Book of Common Prayer and Administration of the Sacraments and other Rites and Ceremonies of the Church according to the Use of the Church of England.

The Holy Bible. King James Authorized Version.

Tholfsen, Trygve R ed. *Sir James Kay-Shuttleworth on Popular Education.* New York and London: Teachers College Press, 1974.

Tosh, John. *A Man's Place: Masculinity and the Middle Class Home in Victorian England.* New Haven and London: Yale University Press, 1999.

- *Manliness and Masculinities in Nineteenth-Century Britain: essays on gender, family and empire.* London: Longman, 2004.

Tristram, Philippa. *Living Space in Fact and Fiction.* London and New York: Routledge, 1989.

Tucker, Herbert F ed. *A Companion to Victorian Literature and Culture.* Oxford: Blackwell Publishing Ltd, 2004.

Twinn, Frances. 'Navigational pitfalls and topographical constraints in *Sylvia's Lovers*'. *Gaskell Society Journal.* Vol 15, 2001. pp 38 – 52.

Uffleman, Larry K. 'Elizabeth Gaskell's *North and South*: the Novel in Progress'. *Gaskell Society Journal.* Vol 14, 2000. pp 1 – 14.

Uglow, Jenny. *Elizabeth Gaskell: A Habit of Stories.* London: New York, Faber and Faber, 1999.

Valverde, Mariana. 'The Love of Finery: Fashion and The Fallen Woman in Nineteenth-Century Social Discourse'. *Victorian Studies.* Vol 32, Pt 2, 1989. pp 169 – 188.

Vance, Norman. *The sinews of the spirit: The ideal of Christian manliness in Victorian literature and religious thought.* Cambridge: Cambridge University Press, 1985.

Van Slyke, Gretchen. 'The Sexual and Textual Politics of Dress: Rosa Bonheur and Her Cross-Dressing Permits'. *Nineteenth Century French Studies.* Vol 26, Nos 3 & 4, Spring-Summer 1998. pp 321-335.

Vicinus, Martha ed. *A Widening Sphere: Changing Roles of Victorian Women.* Bloomington & London: Indiana University Press, 1977.

Vrettos, Athena. 'Victorian Psychology' in Brantlinger, Patrick and Thesing, William B eds. *A Companion to the Victorian Novel.* Oxford: Blackwell Publishing Ltd, 2005.

Warwick, Alexandra. 'Victorian Gothic' in Spooner, Catherine and McEvoy, Emma eds. *The Routledge Companion to Gothic.* London and New York: Routledge, 2007.

Watts, Ruth. *Gender, Power and the Unitarians in England 1760–1860.* London and New York: Longman, 1998.

- 'Rational Religion and Feminism: the Challenge of Unitarianism in the Nineteenth Century' in Sue Morgan ed, *Women, Religion and Feminism in Britain, 1750–1900.* Basingstoke: Palgrave Macmillan, 2000. pp 39-52.

Webb, R.K . 'The Gaskells as Unitarians' in Shattock Joanne ed. *Dickens and other Victorians: Essays in Honour of Philip Collins.* Basingstoke: Macmillan Press, 1988.

Weyant, Nancy S. *Elizabeth Gaskell: An Annotated Bibliography of English Language Sources 1976 – 1991.* Metuchen, N.J. and London: Scarecrow, 1994.

Weyant, Nancy S. *Elizabeth Gaskell: An Annotated Bibliography of English Language Sources 1992–2001.* Lanham, Maryland, Toronto, Oxford: The Scarecrow Press, 2004.

Wheeler, Michael. 'Two Tales of Manchester Life'. *The Gaskell Society Journal.* Vol 3, 1989. pp 6-28.

- 'Elizabeth Gaskell's Unitarianism'. *Gaskell Society Journal.* Vol 6, 1992. pp 25-41.

White, Rebecca. '"*A joke spoken in rather a sad tone*": *Cranford*, humour, and Heidi Thomas's television adaptation'. *The Gaskell Journal. V*ol 22, 2008. pp 145-160.

Wigmore-Beddoes, Dennis G. *Yesterday's Radicals: A Study of the Affinity between Unitarianism and Broad Church Anglicanism in the Nineteenth Century.* Cambridge and London: James Clarke & Co., 1971.

Williams, Dewi. 'The Death of Willie Gaskell'. *The Gaskell Society Journal.* Vol 13, 1999. pp 108-109.

Williams, Victoria. 'Gaskell as Scheherazade: Fairytale themes in 'Cousin Phillis' and *North and South*'. *Gaskell Journal.* Vol 24, 2010. pp 100-114.

Wohl, Anthony S ed. *The Victorian Family Structure and Stresses.* London: Croom Helm, 1978.

Wolfreys, Julian. *Being English: Narrative Idioms and Performances of National Identity from Coleridge to Trollope.* Albany: State University of New York Press, 1994.

Wright, Edgar. *Mrs Gaskell: The Basis for Re-assessment.* London: Oxford University Press, 1965.

- '*My Lady Ludlow*: Forms of Social Change and Forms of Fiction (1)'. *Gaskell Society Journal.* Vol 3, 1989. pp 29-41.

Wright, Terence. *Elizabeth Gaskell "We are not angels": Realism, Gender, Values.* Basingstoke: Macmillan Press Ltd, 1995.

Wrigley, Mark. 'Untitled: The Housing of Gender' in Colomina, Beatriz ed. *Sexuality and Space.* New York: Princeton Architectural Press, 1992.

INDEX

234 THE MEANINGS OF HOME IN ELIZABETH GASKELL'S FICTION

Victorian Secrets

Victorian Secrets is an independent publisher dedicated to producing high-quality books from and about the nineteenth century, including critical editions of neglected novels.

FICTION

All Sorts and Conditions of Men by Walter Besant

The Angel of the Revolution by George Chetwynd Griffith

The Autobiography of Christopher Kirkland by Eliza Lynn Linton

The Beth Book by Sarah Grand

The Blood of the Vampire by Florence Marryat

The Dead Man's Message by Florence Marryat

Demos by George Gissing

East of Suez by Alice Perrin

Henry Dunbar by Mary Elizabeth Braddon

Her Father's Name by Florence Marryat

The Light that Failed by Rudyard Kipling

A Mummer's Wife by George Moore

Not Wisely, but Too Well by Rhoda Broughton

Robert Elsmere by Mrs Humphry Ward

Thyrza by George Gissing

Twilight Stories by Rhoda Broughton

Vice Versâ by F. Anstey

Weeds by Jerome K. Jerome

Weird Stories by Charlotte Riddell

Workers in the Dawn by George Gissing

For more information on any of our titles, please visit:

www.victoriansecrets.co.uk

Victorian Secrets

Dorothea's Daughter and Other Nineteenth-Century Postscripts

by Barbara Hardy

Dorothea's Daughter is a stunning new collection of short stories based on novels by Jane Austen, Charlotte Brontë, Charles Dickens, George Eliot, and Thomas Hardy. They are postscripts, rather than sequels, entering into dialogues with the original narratives by developing suggestions in the text. The authors' conclusions are respected, with no changes made to the plot; instead, Barbara Hardy draws out loose threads in the original fabric to weave new material, imagining moments in the characters' future lives.

BARBARA HARDY
Dorothea's Daughter
and other nineteenth-century postscripts

"These stories are subtle, thoughtful, knowledgeable, civilized and incisive" John Carey, *George Eliot Review*

"a highly successful collection, and a highly enjoyable one" Amy L. Montz, *Neo-Victorian Studies*

The stories are:

- Twilight in Mansfield Parsonage (*Mansfield Park* by Jane Austen)
- Mrs Knightley's Invitation (*Emma* by Jane Austen)
- Adèle Varens (*Jane Eyre* by Charlotte Brontë)
- Lucy Snowe and Paulina Bretton: the Conversation of Women (*Villette* by Charlotte Brontë)
- Edith Dombey and Son (*Dombey and Son* by Charles Dickens)
- Harriet Beadle's Message (*Little Dorrit* by Charles Dickens)
- Lucy Deane (*The Mill on the Floss* by George Eliot)
- Dorothea's Daughter (*Middlemarch* by George Eliot)
- 'Liza-Lu Durbeyfield (*Tess of the D'Urbervilles* by Thomas Hardy)

For more information, please visit:

www.victoriansecrets.co.uk

28344629R00136

Printed in Great Britain
by Amazon